THE POWER
OF WOMEN

THE POWER
OF WOMEN

GUY BELLAMY

SIMON & SCHUSTER
A VIACOM COMPANY

First published in Great Britain by Simon & Schuster Ltd, 1997
A Viacom Company

Simon & Schuster Ltd
West Garden Place
Kendal Street
London W2 2AQ

Simon & Schuster of Australia Pty Ltd
Sydney

A CIP catalogue record for this book is available
from the British Library

ISBN 0-684-820846

Typeset in Goudy Modern 15/16pt
Palimpsest Book Production Limited, Polmont, Stirlingshire
Printed and bound in Great Britain by
Butler & Tanner, Frome & London

For Melanie Wallace
and Susan Brown

Part One

She was the sort of woman who, if accidentally locked in alone in the National Gallery, would start rearranging the pictures.

Anon

Men were made for war. Without it they wandered greyly about, getting under the feet of women, who were trying to organise the really important things of life.

Alice Thomas Ellis
The Sin Eater

I

One of the first things that Janice Dawson had been told by her future husband during the tender opening days of their relationship, when confidences were offered and dreams diffidently defined, was that he was going to be a millionaire. The information was vouchsafed with the confidence of youth and Janice received it with a similar innocence. But in the fifteen years that had slipped by since, he had done nothing to alter his permanent condition of extreme poverty, and now he was out of work.

Bowing to the demands of her Electrolux hoover in the sitting room of their small semi-detached house, Janice had no time to brood on vanquished hopes and blasted dreams, but she allowed herself a wave of anger at the way things were, at the way things had turned out. It was a source of perpetual irritation to her that a woman's standard of living too often depended on the talent and energy of her husband, and that if he was short of either, the wife was short of very much more.

The iniquity of it rankled, but she seemed powerless to change what was almost a law of nature.

In trying to shift the economic balance, she took on job after job and brought to all of them a doggedness and tenacity that was almost simple-minded. A more complex intelligence would have weighed the odds and quit, but Janice Dawson plunged on, disregarding difficulties and failing to recognise the obstructions that life dropped in her track.

She gave talks on four lovingly studied subjects to schools and colleges, clubs and institutes, hospitals and lunches and old people's homes. And when she had finished talking, people gave her money. For somebody as naturally talkative as Janice, it was a bit like an alcoholic getting a job as a wine-taster, but Janice knew that you had to play to your strengths. Her other little occupations included working part-time in a charity shop, writing a women's column in the local free newspaper, helping to run a nursery school two mornings a week and making cakes to order for the discerning glutton.

Bursting with ideas, she was a woman who found silence impossible to deal with, finding it both offensive and wasteful. Confronted by an aural vacuum, she poured out a volley of words — discursive, anecdotal, admonitory — which often owed nothing to the conversation that had gone before. After chatting to Janice, many listeners were left draped over the ropes like a boxer who has been cruelly mismatched by an unscrupulous manager. Some went home and took a couple of Veganin tablets, but those who really knew her took the tablets first.

She moved the sofa and hoovered up fluff, bits of paper and other unrecognisable pieces of dross which always managed to hide there. She worked quickly and efficiently as if a supervisor with a stop-watch was inspecting her efforts.

Janice Dawson was thirty-eight and a formidable barrel of energy. A face that had once been designated pretty was still attractive, although it carried more weight and bore more lines these days. Her slim figure had gone too: she was a careless eater. The dark hair that had once fallen in curls to her shoulders was shorter now. 'Neat and businesslike' was how she described it.

Janice felt sometimes that she had slipped from youth into the role of middle-aged matron without that period of fun which was supposed to be part of your early thirties, but then she thought that she had missed a lot of other things, too: dinner at the Ritz, Concorde to New York, holidays in the Aegean.

She switched off the hoover and unplugged it. Her husband had disappeared and so he was probably in the bath, the kitchen floor needed cleaning and some clothes needed washing, she had two cakes to make before she could think about dinner, and the dog was in the throes of some sexual endeavour with a cushion.

Janice Dawson kicked the dog and went out to find bucket and sponge for the kitchen floor. She had no time for self-pity.

*   *   *

As Sam Dawson lay in the bath contemplating the wreckage of his life he wondered whether, if he fell asleep, he would slip peacefully below the surface putting everybody, including himself, out of their misery, or whether he would awake noisily, snorting and gulping, and making a mess on the bathroom floor that would further add to his wife's permanent sense of dissatisfaction. Lying on his back with a dripping foot on each tap, he was reminded that the racing driver Damon Hill had said that this was exactly what it was like in a modern Grand Prix racing car. Uncomfortable or not, Damon Hill made a million pounds from this cramped, prostrate position. Sam Dawson couldn't make ten pounds standing up.

He lay there trying to remember whether he had washed his feet. Often, he knew, he had unthinkingly washed them twice. Bathing was such a mindless activity that his restless thoughts wandered elsewhere, analysing failures, considering possibilities, dreaming of triumphs that time would eventually deny him. And then he found himself washing his feet again.

Vertical and chastened, he felt debilitated by the muggy heat his bath had produced. The crumpled figure that he spied in the full-length mirror did not look forty, Sam Dawson's age. He looked fifty. On a bad day in a poor light he could pass for sixty. He was tall and thin and his deportment was not good. His round face was tired, particularly round the eyes where bags and wrinkles had gathered which only cosmetic surgery could eradicate. One horizontal worry line traversed his forehead, but it was his hair that really convinced him that his best days were in the distant past. Grey around the ears, it was receding from the front so that his forehead seemed to grow each week. This was a particular source of pain to Sam, being too blatant to disguise.

He leaned over the blue sink and opened the window. A vista of green fields and green hills rolled in waves to a distant motorway. For a moment he stood there, absorbing this pastoral prospect; the horizon was probably eight miles away and he couldn't see a single building.

When he had been unexpectedly dumped here he had tried to summon up some feeling of enthusiasm for the bucolic life. The English countryside lingered in the imagination, even if you lived in Mile End or Rotherhithe, and he had come here from a place where most of the earth's surface was covered with cement or Tarmac. But now in the steamy heat of his bathroom he gazed out of the tiny window and could dismantle the myth of the countryside's endless pleasures, and meticulously list other aspects of the experience: the herds of cows that not only blocked the road as you came round a bend on two wheels, but also contrived to shit on your door as they swayed past your stalled motor; the leisurely way that tomorrow meant next week, and next week meant next month; the tiny but strangely alarming creatures who had decided to share your house with you, along with the spiders that you could throw a saddle over. And the smells! The new chemical fertilizers that covered a field and filled your nostrils when you opened a window, the fragrant aroma of bovine excreta, the pungent, nose-grabbing odours that emerged from the dinky industrial buildings that appeared mysteriously to combat unemployment. With more pigs than pubs, more sheep than shops, the bosky environs of Somerset had swiftly palled.

Money had brought the Dawson family west – or rather, the lack of it. When it became necessary to sell their house to appease the bank, Janice, who took a much more romantic view of green fields and distant hills, suggested that they could buy a similar house for less money if they shifted one hundred miles west, pointing out, at the same time, that as Sam had been made redundant they were no longer tied to the expensive acres whose only boast was that they were within commuting distance of London.

In this, as in so much else, she was right, but Sam Dawson did not see why this poverty-driven trek should end here. He could already envisage the cardboard box in Penzance, with the baked beans, the paraffin lamp and the coins tossed generously towards him by boisterous Cornish holidaymakers. Poverty could become a habit. The westward drift could continue. Were there tramps in the Scilly Isles? Could you doss in the Azores?

He abandoned his rueful examination of the landscape and picked up a towel. The financial worries which brutally truncated his sleep no longer seemed to deserve a moment's thought. His condition was the norm. The country was in debt. The planet was skint. The value of money diminished hourly and the delightful truth which illustrated this most clearly was that in twenty fraught years, the Mars Bar had held its value infinitely better than the gold bar.

His mind was full of facts like that, none of them useful or likely to earn him money. Every time you step forward you use fifty-four muscles. In each ejaculation there is potentially enough sperm to produce the population of the United States. On average, the Queen receives four turds every week in the post. Sam Dawson knew more than he needed to know, but none of it helped in his present predicament. At night he prayed that he would never wake up – then found, perversely, that he couldn't get to sleep.

He put on a blue shirt, grey slacks, an old pair of suede shoes that looked like Cornish pasties, and went downstairs. This house, a standard semi-detached with three bedrooms, had come cheap but with plummeting house prices was already worth less than they had paid for it.

In the kitchen Janice Dawson was hitting a steak with something before putting it in the grill.

'Hallo, my little bundle of dynamite,' he said. 'Been buying cheap meat?'

'We buy cheap everything these days, Sam. Have you done your jobs?'

Sam Dawson sat down. 'Jobs?' he asked.

Janice poured chips into a chip pan. 'It's up there,' she said, nodding towards a pad on the wall where shopping lists, telephone numbers, aides-mémoire and other memoranda were all held together by the metallic hug of one oversize bulldog clip. Sam Dawson looked at the imprisoned instructions. He had never been lazy but he was lazy now. He had lost his impetus along with his job, and adjusted seamlessly to the unhurried lifestyle that seemed appropriate to their new setting.

He read:

1. Cut the lawn
2. Trim hedge
3. Mend deckchair
4. Clean French windows
5. Take Footprint to vet
6. Organise bonfire
7. Ring school re J.
8. Car tax
9. Pay newsagent bill (overdue)
10. Remove spider (utility room).

'Even when I worked for money I didn't get that much done in a day,' he said.

'Perhaps that's why they made you redundant, darling,' said his wife, who never stopped moving.

'How could I take Footprint to the vet? You had the car. What's the matter with him anyway?'

'He's limping.'

'And Jake? What did I have to ring the school about?'

'Mainly to see whether he's still there.'

Sam Dawson, smelling food, got up and laid the table in the kitchen. There were still a few little jobs that he could handle.

'I think if he'd disappeared the school would prob, ably have rung us,' he said mildly. Schools, he imagined, became quite neurotic when they mislaid pupils.

Jake, the problem son at a problem age, fifteen, had taken to disappearing in the night in search of what adventures they never found out. Janice Dawson, secretly disappointed at the result her years of organised motherhood had produced, saw one last chance to turn her only child into something useful: boarding school. And so, at the moment when their financial problems were increasing, they dug into Sam's newly arrived redundancy money to send him to an expensive boarding school not many miles from where they now lived. Janice Dawson spent her rare free moments imagining that her son, in his lonely war on boredom, had decamped from his new surroundings, and was stealing, raping and pillaging his way across the West Country.

'I don't know who worries me most,' she said, placing two plates of steak and chips on the table. 'Him or you.'

Sam Dawson, seeing the conversational journey that he was being invited to embark on, got up and went to see whether there was a bottle anywhere that held the remnants of red wine. He had once had a small wine cellar, then he had a wine rack in the kitchen; now he had, or might have, a half-empty bottle somewhere with a rubber top through which you could extract the air. He found it hiding behind the bread bin and pulled out the top.

'Tell me about the spider in the utility room,' he said, pouring wine. 'Friendly chap, is he?'

'I think it's got a nidus behind the washing machine. You'll have to move it to look.'

Sam drank some wine. Cutting the steak required more strength than he thought a steak should demand. He had once eaten only fillet.

'What's a nidus, my little encyclopedia? It's not just the quantity of your words these days, it's the quality.'

'It's a nest, dear. Please get rid of it.'

'Rely on me.'

'That's what I used to do,' Janice said sadly.

2

Come to sunny Somerset, that forgotten county that you're always hurrying through to visit somewhere else. Where once men lived in caves at the dawn of history, there are now Palladian mansions set in deer parks, water mills and cider mills, and Abbeys that are a thousand years old. For this is a place that is steeped in history and legend.

Arthur and his wife, Queen Guinevere, are buried, or are believed to be buried, in the grounds of Glastonbury Abbey, the earliest Christian sanctuary in the British Isles, King Alfred let the cakes burn as he dozed in a peasant's cottage in Somerset after a surprise attack by the Danes at Chippenham, St Patrick got to Somerset before you, and St Dunstan was born there.

Today it might be known for its cider, its cheese and its sheepskin coats; for the largest village, the smallest city, the oldest road; but withies are still grown for basket-weaving, peat still extracted for agricultural use. The remains of Arthur's Abbey, destroyed by fire in 1148, rebuilt, and then demolished again during Reformation riots in the sixteenth century, is a tourist attraction, as is the nearby Tor which towers above the moors or Levels, the reclaimed wetlands that are at the heart of the county. On top of the Tor you can shelter in the remains of a fourteenth-century church where the last Abbot of Glastonbury was hanged in 1539. The history, like all history, is stained with blood.

Sam Dawson, who had a studious bent, had assimilated this information and much more. He had read about apple orchards and thatching, cheese dairies and vineyards, and felt that he was already an expert on a part of the country that he had rarely seen until recently. But he was still surprised one morning when Tim Bonner paused before driving off on one of their regular rounds of golf to impart another piece of news.

'Did you know,' he said, fixing Sam with a puzzled frown, 'that Jesus came to Somerset when He was a boy?'

'No, I seem to have missed that one, Tim,' he said. 'Where did you get it from?'

'The Tourist Office.'

'Inventive minds labour in their vaults,' said Sam Dawson admiringly. 'On the other hand, it could be true. His childhood isn't exactly well documented.'

He watched as his opponent addressed the ball. Tim Bonner was thirty-five, and although this made him only five years younger than Sam, there seemed to be at least a decade between them. In contrast to Sam's lanky frame and greying, receding hair, Tim had a short, compact, muscular body, a full head of blond hair and a fresh, good-looking face. Tim called him 'old man' but Sam suspected that this was not the matey sobriquet that might be used among friends, but a more sinister allusion to the gap between their ages. They had met in a pub and quickly discovered that they had two things in common: they were both out of work and they both enjoyed a round of golf. He was the only friend that Sam had made.

Tim Bonner placed a ball on his tee and peered pessimistically up the fairway. 'I expect He used the Channel Tunnel,' he said.

Sam watched as his opponent prepared to swing. His drives were ugly to watch but strangely effective. His arms were rigid and his whole body turned with the swing but the ball invariably rolled to a stop in a much more favourable position than the balls dispatched by Sam's graceful action.

'Tim, do you know what anachronism means?' he asked.

'Fear of spiders?'

'Telephones in Shakespeare plays. That sort of thing.'

'Got you. Perhaps He used a fishing boat then. Up the Severn, landfall at Bristol, and down the A37. How long is this hole?'

'Just over two hundred yards.'

'On the green in one then?'

'Show me.'

The ball soared high at bullet-like speed and then dropped slowly like a parachutist into the centre of the green. Sam Dawson followed its journey resentfully and then placed his own ball on the tee. He threw some blades of grass into the air, a gesture that revealed nothing that was of use to him, but made him feel more professional, more proficient. He looked down the fairway towards the green. It seemed to have moved farther away since Tim Bonner drove.

'How's the new job going?' he asked.

Tim Bonner's current occupation was selling water purifiers to householders who were supposed to fit them to their taps. 'The firm and I have come to an agreement,' he said.

'They told you to sod off, and you agreed?'

'Something like that. Everybody's buying bottled water, aren't they?'

'What did Beverley say?'

'She managed to conceal her enthusiasm at the news.'

'You'd think that after six jobs in two years she'd admire your versatility. What's your next idea?'

'It hasn't arrived yet.'

Sam Dawson bent over the ball, took a final look at the distant target, and swung.

'Nice action, old man,' said Tim Bonner. 'Pity about the ball.'

In the clubhouse afterwards, victory was celebrated and defeat assuaged by halves of lukewarm shandy. Pints of lager were an occasional extravagance now, and the stake money attached to these games had shrunk.

'Just a fiver, was it?' asked Tim Bonner.

Sam Dawson sipped his shandy and shrugged. The quality of his day had not been improved by his opponent's combative performance.

'You evince a perceptible reluctance to come across with the boodle,' Tim suggested.

'Probably on account of I don't have any,' said Sam Dawson. 'I'll pay you next time.'

'What happened to money, anyway? People used to carry it around and spend it. There must be the same amount in existence, or more than there used to be, but nobody has any.'

'The banks have got it all.'

Sam Dawson, who had expected on his arrival in the West Country to find himself surrounded by demented yokels in funny hats, promiscuous milkmaids and squinting sheep-shaggers with arms of steel, had been surprised by the company he found himself keeping. His neighbours were sophisticated and astute. They had more money than he had. (Everybody had more money than he had.) Some had made it in huge quantities and moved to the more salubrious surroundings of fields and hills to enjoy their loot; others, who still retained a tenuous link with the commercial demands of the working world, had found that exciting technological developments like e-mail and the fax meant that they could pursue a career and earn a living 200 miles from the dreary offices

where they were once compelled to sit. This transfer
to soft landscapes and verdant horizons seemed to have
affected them, physically and mentally: their walk had
an unusual energy and their face a ready smile.

Sam Dawson realised soon after he arrived here that
he did not fit this template, and for a while he wondered
why. He did not possess the surplus energy, he could not
flash the mandatory smile, and throwing 'good mornings' to complete strangers made him uneasy, fearful
that his uninvited friendliness would be misconstrued.
When he arrived at the explanation for his feeling of
being misplaced, the brutal truth cut deep. He was
supposed to have arrived here with money! This was
not a place to bring your furniture and your overdraft
to: work was hard to find. You came here to enjoy the
money you had already made.

He sipped his shandy and wondered with a terrible
feeling of apprehension what the future held. Tim
Bonner, in a bright yellow sweater and brown slacks,
was gazing thoughtfully through the window. Sun
slanted down on a flat landscape that carried the eye
to a horizon of hills several miles away.

'This Jesus thing,' he said. 'We could make money
out of it.'

'What?' said Sam.

'Follow the footsteps of Christ. We could call it the
Jesus Trail. Pilgrims would fly in from all over the
world in search of a sacred experience – and I'd be
there, selling route maps, booklets, tracts, refreshments,
souvenirs.'

'Souvenirs? Like the espadrilles that Jesus wore on the walk, do you mean?'

'And His headgear. What do you suppose He wore?'

'On his head? A Sony Walkman, I expect, or the usual back-to-front baseball cap.'

'We could mark out the places where He stopped to eat.'

'The Coke stalls, the burger bars.'

'We could sell maps of the route He took from Bristol.'

'Perhaps He landed at Poole. Perhaps He came up from Weymouth.'

'Sam, your poverty is no longer a mystery to me.'

'You mean I'm honest?'

'I create, you demolish.'

'I've heard some pretty nutty ideas in my time, but this one could get nominated for an Oscar.'

Tim Bonner smiled. 'You're wrong, old man. I think there's some mileage here. The religious mind is very susceptible.'

Sam Dawson finished his drink and stood up. 'They'll have to be bloody susceptible if you're going to flog them Christ's espadrilles. Same time next week?'

'Be there or be square.'

Sam Dawson marched between fields of violent yellow rape clutching a sweat-dampened list. It was over 90 degrees again and merely to think had him leaking water from every pore. Years ago the newspapers carried huge headlines saying PHEW! WHAT A SCORCHER!

and a big 82° alongside. Now it was over 90 degrees every day and nobody seemed to notice. Ice shelves were disintegrating, glaciers dissolving into the sea. Global climatic changes were altering the maps, but nobody cared.

He mopped the sweat from his brow with the rolled-up sleeve of his shirt and looked at the list. It said: *lawn, hedge, deckchair, windows, vet, bonfire, phone school, car tax, newsagent, spider.* If heatstroke didn't get him — or some other trivial setback like gangrene or leprosy — he reckoned that he should be able to delete a few list items before dinner. The car would have been a help but Janice had driven off in it to her part-time job in the charity shop. Sam Dawson had always heard that charity began at home but this had proved not to be the case, so while he had no money, his wife had driven off to help people who had no money.

He went into the newsagent which was also a small, village-sized supermarket. He realised, as he stared at the stacked fodder, that he had dreamed recently that he worked here for £5 a week.

His dreams were becoming more vivid, and no longer involved dreary trips back to his schooldays or early years as a wage-earner. In last night's stirring fantasy he had sequestered some pulchritudinous tart in the spare bedroom but when she courteously unzipped his trousers, sawdust poured forth and covered the floor in one pyramid-shaped pile. What did it mean? Morose with lust, he ordered a can of orange. In the dream he had settled for a hemlock spritzer.

Back in the street and the heat he drank the orange and dropped the can in a bin. Then he deleted newsagent from his list and set off for home, trying to brace himself for the pleasure of mowing the lawn in a heatwave.

Tim Bonner, he decided, must be going through the same gear changes as he was. He was younger, but in a similar domestic situation – one child, even if the mother wasn't actually his wife. Above all, he was jobless and faced the same agonies of inadequacy and insecurity, although somehow he disguised it better. At the golf club he managed to create the impression that he was a bright young man who had made his pile and quit.

Sam Dawson wished that he could convey an impression that would improve the world's opinion of him. Recently he had floated the idea of growing a beard. His wife's reaction could not have been more scathing if he had mooted a spot of bigamy. 'Always a bad sign when a middle-aged man grows a beard,' said Janice. 'Next thing you know, he's snorting cocaine or seducing the au pair.' Sam abandoned the beard idea and beat his brains endlessly in the search for some other image-improving change.

He was neither surprised nor disappointed to discover that the lawn mower was out of fuel; such irritations were the norm now, and he took them without a murmur. He found the can and set off on another half-mile trek through the heat for some litres of four-star.

What had once been a green patchwork-quilt country-side was now starting to look a little brown. He walked past cider-apple orchards and strawberry fields and half-expected, as he always did on these journeys, to come across some quaint idea from the past, like the side-by-side toilet or the penny-farthing bike. He had already found a man living in a nearby cottage without electricity who had his portable television wired up to the battery on his tractor. His impression that he had moved into another world was helped immeasurably by the exotic place names: down the road there was a village called *Ryme Intrinseca*.

Back home, in the customary role of sweating factotum, he attacked the jobs before him in a sort of thoughtless frenzy. The lawn was cut and the hedge trimmed in half an hour. He mended the deckchair and gathered up the material for a bonfire while trying to gauge the weight that he must be losing. His shirt was soaked, his knees stuck to his trousers. Finally, in a desperate effort to justify his presence here, he cleaned the windows.

What he really wanted was a proper job, but he was beginning to believe that he was too old to start again.

Tim Bonner had come to Somerset five years earlier by way of Kalamata, a mysterious route for a journey that had begun in the Weald of Kent. He was thirty then, bright, handsome, and unswervingly unsuccessful in almost everything that he attempted. What it was that spiralled his career ever downwards, what missing granule or present flaw, he could never identify or isolate. Careers barely launched took an immediate earthbound trajectory; plans that he had assembled in moods of dangerous optimism crumbled and decomposed before he could set them in motion.

He took a holiday (he took a lot of holidays at that time, usually between jobs and sometimes instead of them), and sitting on a rock in Greece like the bronze mermaid in Copenhagen Harbour, was Beverley Callard, a sun-tanned and smiling enchantress who had the aura of a mythological figure whose business it was to lure sailors to their grave. Tim Bonner, comprehensively lured, shinned up the rock with an athleticism that she found irresistible. It took two hours and the urgent need for privacy to bring them both down.

But Beverley wasn't some flibbertigibbet that you could run into too easily on holidays like this. She was twenty-seven then, a tall, slim, shapely brunette with eyebrows made sexy by being thicker than usual, cool blue eyes and a brain like razor blades. Most impressive of all, she had her own business, and most convenient of all, she was on holiday here alone.

Tim Bonner had been propositioned by a bewildering variety of girls, not all of them hideous, but Beverley Callard stood apart from the rest of them for several compelling reasons. She didn't wait for sex to float to the top of the agenda, she instigated it. She was never short of money and insisted on paying her full fifty per cent, whatever the occasion. And she didn't want to marry him.

She didn't want to marry him in Greece, and she

didn't want to marry him when they flew back to Britain together. Tim Bonner was ambivalent about this reluctance — relieved and yet secretly hurt. In the event it was irrelevant because they were now as thoroughly hitched up as any couple who had emerged blinking from a church or register office. They had a house — an old barn, converted and extended — with two acres of land. They had a cat called Humbug. And most eloquently of all, they had a blonde three-year-old daughter called Chloë.

The house belonged to Beverley's parents, who had moved on retirement to the sunnier hills of Spain. This left Beverley, and now Tim, with a large and rather grand house and no mortgage. In these somewhat unreal surroundings it was occasionally possible for him to believe that he was a success, as if this house with its four double bedrooms and farmhouse kitchen was the product of his triumphant labours, the fruit of his own efforts. But it was an illusion that could not survive in Beverley's company, where he increasingly felt guilty about his own shortcomings. She never mentioned the house or where it had come from, but she returned too often for his comfort to the subject of money and his continuing failure to produce any.

He came back from the golf course to find Chloë sitting on the floor in the kitchen singing 'God save our ferocious Queen' which rather ruled out the eruption of carnal fervour for which he had planned.

'I thought the small person was going to playgroup?' he said.

Beverley, in short denim pants, was arranging recently picked flowers in a vase. She gazed at him sympathetically. 'It's Sunday,' she said. 'Which is why I'm not at work, if you think about it. I suppose if you haven't got a job, one day is very like another?'

'They do tend to run into each other,' Tim agreed, smoothly ignoring the dissatisfaction that he sensed hovering in the air. 'It's gracious, not ferocious,' he told his daughter. 'God save our *gracious* Queen.'

Chloë looked up, anxious to learn. 'What does gracious mean?'

'Damned if I know. I think it means she waves to people.'

He walked out of the kitchen, through the dining room and the hall, to the lounge at the far end of the house. Barn-conversion homes were always like this, with the rooms laid out in a row. The lounge had an inglenook fireplace across one end, and the floor itself was on two levels, with an iron bannister and steps. He picked up the remote and turned on Teletext to see what had happened in the world while he had been improving his golf.

PAUPER'S FUNERAL FOR HEADLESS TORSO, he read.

And: PRIEST REVEALS SHE IS A LESBIAN.

The day's news became ever more bizarre, and no longer seemed to have the urgency and relevance which had once made him a compulsive newspaper reader. The insatiable desire to know what was going on had been cooled by a flood of trivia. Headless torsos, lesbian priests. He didn't really need to know.

He switched it off as Beverley came in. She put Mahler on the CD. This was not a good sign. It was a quite different situation, and a much nicer atmosphere, when she opted for Jack Jones or Julio.

'I've had an idea,' she said, stretching her bare brown legs across the length of the sofa.

'Tremendous,' Tim said. 'I used to have those.'

'I'm going to start a club.'

Tim Bonner was visibly bemused by this news. He had expected something a lot less ambitious – a new choice of flowers for the hanging basket, a lick of paint in the kitchen, perhaps a trip to the coast.

'A club?' he said. 'What sort of club?'

'A club for women,' said Beverley. 'You and the boys have your drinks and your golf, and what have the women got? Work. Work at home and work at work. Well, I'm going to change all that. I'm going to form a luncheon club for women only, where we can get plastered on sherry or wine and discuss the men in our lives and what we can do about them.'

Tim Bonner recoiled at the prospect of this. He didn't like the sound of it at all. He imagined cloistered harridans rearranging his life over sherry, scheming bitches or witches cackling over his weaknesses and imperfections, and churlish matrons sniffily analysing his faults and discussing how best they could be remedied – and all in his absence.

'It's a wonderful idea, darling,' he said.

'Why don't you like it?' she asked.

'I was never one for splitting the human race into

compartments. Black and white, this religion and that religion, men and women. We're all people, aren't we?'

'Some of us are people,' Beverley said, 'and then there is this sub-division which is known generically as men.'

'And they're inferior, are they, this sub-division?'

'In many ways they are. In many ways they're not. But I'm afraid that in several of the important human qualities, inferior *is* the word.'

Beverley shrugged casually as she said this, as if she was reluctantly resigned to one of life's sadder truths, but Tim's reaction was more animated. Occasionally, in bursts of political interest, she would use phrases like 'environmental footprint', or 'wetland eco-systems', but she had not previously ventured into the sociological and sexual quagmire that she was breezily undertaking here.

'You'll create divisions where none exists,' he told her. 'The sex war is over.'

Beverley looked at him and laughed. 'I must say, Tim, that I don't see why a few women meeting for a weekly chat should fill you with such dread. Half a dozen women in a room can't do much damage, can they?'

'They can if they call it a coven. It can be quite frightening. Why don't you come and play golf with me?'

'You know that I've always tried to avoid witless activities like that.'

'Yes, well, we have to give our brains a rest some time.'

27

'Yours, my love, is on permanent vacation.'

Tim Bonner stood up, disinclined to continue this. He could see where the conversation, with its painful darts and hurtful arrows, was heading, and had no wish to follow the path. Joblessness would be next, and then pennilessness, listlessness and hopelessness.

'I think I'll cut the grass,' he said.

3

What worried Tim Bonner was this: he wouldn't be able to provide for his daughter. When she needed her own computer he would be pushing a crocodile of trolleys across a supermarket car park. By the time that she wanted an eighteen-gear mountain bike he would be dribbling in the plastic knife and fork ward. It was already a relief when her pleas and requests did not require the production of money, and these were the ones that he hurried to satisfy.

She liked to be taken to the play area at the recreation ground and Tim liked to take her. While she rocketed fearlessly down the slide or amused herself on the swings, he could sit down in perfect peace and enjoy a cigarette in the sun. Children tried to include their parents in their games, but the swings and the slide and the climbing frame with its chains and hoops were all too small for Tim, so Chloë had to entertain herself and leave her father in peace.

It was a good place to think. The interruptions and

distractions at home that seemed to prevent more than three consecutive minutes of constructive thought were left behind and he relaxed on the only seat and gazed at the Mendip Hills.

There was always now a vague feeling of uneasiness that a lack of regular income produced, the sense of financial horrors in store plus a lurking inner conviction of failure. His daughter on the slide was happily unaware of these concerns. Money brought all the things that she needed, but she did not yet know where money came from, and did not imagine that it could run out. When you're a child being happy didn't require an effort, and this one, with the energy of a rugby player and the appetite of a monkey-eating eagle, had no room in her young life for doubts.

She came over to him now, distracted from her oscillations on the swing by a more serious matter. She was wearing what looked like denim overalls.

'Daddy, where's Prince?'

Prince was a popular mongrel, a favourite among the children, who had been killed on the road a few days earlier.

'He's gone,' said Tim.

'I know, but where?'

Jesus, thought Tim Bonner. What do three-year-olds know? What were they supposed to know? Having no answers he replied conventionally.

'He's in heaven with God.'

Chloë considered this with an expression that registered total bewilderment.

'What does God want a dead dog for?'

What are my long-term prospects if I'm out of my depth with a three-year-old? he wondered. She wrong-footed him every time. Her thoughts were always ahead of his. Perhaps, deprived of the daily stimulation of work, the brain atrophied and in the end was no match for a three-year-old.

She went back to the slide and descended head first on her stomach. There were only so many ways that you could come down a slide but she was trying them all in strict rotation.

He returned to his thoughts, his dismal forebodings, his blood-chilling picture of the future that beckoned. The previous evening he had worked his way through the appointments section of a Sunday newspaper, hoping to find how people obtained jobs in an age of unemploy-ment. The pages were a mystery to him. People didn't receive salaries any more; they received 'packages'. These involved bonuses and benefits and cars and share options. It sounded good, but when they listed the job requirements that earned these 'packages' he found that he didn't understand any of them. Could he lead, challenge and develop a team within a people-orientated culture which devolved responsibility? Could he develop and implement a sales strategy that would stretch corporate objectives? Was he a charismatic leader and an ideas generator who could challenge the status quo? Above all, could he achieve Pan-European revenue targets?

Beverley had watched him wrestling with these

mysteries and said: 'You're not that sort of person.'

He put the paper down, depressed at the picture it had given him. 'What sort of person aren't I?'

'Company man. Suit, tie. Train to the office every morning. It's not your bag, Timothy.'

'Well, that's a relief. I thought I was about to get sucked into something.'

'On the other hand, how much money have you earned this year?'

'Net or gross?'

'Either would do.'

'Nothing.'

'Well, trying to sell water purifiers was a stupid idea. There's a recession on. People haven't got the money for gimmicks like that.'

'That's what I discovered. I wish you'd told me earlier. So what sort of person am I then?'

Beverley Callard smiled to herself as she considered this. She was stretched out on the sofa with her bare feet draped over one end. Chloë was in bed, the housework was done. It was, for her, a rare moment of relaxation. The television in the corner had been left on from an earlier children's programme but the sound had been turned down, leaving only a mercifully silent tour of Tom Jones's tonsils and Shirley Bassey's armpits.

'You're the sort of person who needs a push. You don't seem to have your own motor any more.'

'Push, baby, push.'

'Yes,' said Beverley. 'I may have to.'

Sitting on his seat in the recreation ground and

admiring his daughter's energy, he could only wonder at the shortage of his own because he had once had a lot of it. He concluded that he had been knocked back by life. After a boxer has been floored a certain number of times, he doesn't get up. He has figured out what is going to happen to him if he does.

Tim Bonner's rebuffs had been on a cosmic scale. The ideas trundled along and for several years he acted on them, turning idle thoughts into commercial enterprises with energy and even enthusiasm. But the world was waiting to repudiate and repel. The initial idea, which became central to all his later ones, was that he should remain self-employed. Nobody became a millionaire unless they were self-employed, and a millionaire was something he earnestly wanted to be.

So he had pursued a succession of entrepreneurial ventures, any one of which, he told himself at one time or another, could have sent him off in his own yacht to the Bahamas. He had begun with cut-price wine after reading an article about booming wine sales in Britain. One day the tyres on his car were slashed and a note left on his windscreen telling him that his wine was too cheap. He replaced the tyres and carried on selling the wine, but a week later his tyres were slashed again and every window in the car was broken. The police advised him to sleep in his car, but as they refused to allow him to carry a gun this did not seem to him like a proposal with a built-in happy ending. He obtained the British franchise in a toy bear, made in Taiwan. It revolved on a small wooden stool and sang *Hava Nagila* with a strange accent. But children wanted toys that year that carried guns or some more modern sci-fi device that vaporised enemies. He started a free magazine that was devoted entirely to advertisements for homes, having calculated that if he could guarantee a circulation of 100,000 the money paid to him by estate agents would give him a profit of about £5,000 a week. It was hardly launched when the public, responding to a signal he hadn't seen, stopped buying houses. In a desperate attempt to boost the revenue, he invited people who were trying to sell their homes to advertise privately and avoid the estate agents' commission. The estate agents reacted promptly to this with a professional hauteur that was deeply painful: they withdrew all their advertising. He was left with a year's let on an unwanted office and an unpaid printer's bill. In the long crawl back to solvency he decided that there were only three things that people really needed and would spend their money on: sex, clothes and food; and then, in a further bout of pessimism and retrenchment, he decided that in a recession they would probably economise drastically on the first two. The answer was clear. A glance at a list of the richest men in Britain revealed that the top three were involved in one way or another with filling the nation's stomachs.

Feeling a little as if he had been given an insight denied to others, Tim Bonner embarked upon a bureaucratic labyrinth which would eventually allow him to sell food in what had once been an office. The rules were harsh, the conditions strict. Hygiene inspectors gathered with strange instruments and xeroxed regulations. The bank manager, who had never seen a customer this versatile, listened to the new plans in awe. Was he dealing with a man of protean talents, or somebody not playing with a full deck? Either way, the bank went with it. That month's instructions were to lend.

When the moment arrived to decide what sort of food he was actually going to sell, Tim Bonner was in a bit of a quandary. His culinary talents did not extend far beyond the boil-in-a-bag kipper, and the kitchen had never been his favourite environment. Clearly there was going to be no haunch of venison flamed with porter here. The acreage decreed that this was not even going to be a place where people sat down to eat; they would take it away and eat it somewhere else. The saving on cutlery, crockery and washing up would be a pleasing factor in the financial balancing act, as would the absence of waiters. By the time that he opened, the menu leaned heavily towards sausages and burgers — hamburgers, cheeseburgers, tomato and onion burgers — all with chips and the optional follow up of Häagen-Dazs chocolate chip ice cream.

He could still remember his first customers because he had referred to them ever since as Oliver and Joan. The youth, a surly teenager in a disgustingly filthy T-shirt, said: 'Oliver lager.'

'What?'

'He said he'll have a lager,' said the person with him, who Tim Bonner decided eventually was a girl.

'We don't serve alcohol,' he told her.

'They don't serve alcohol,' the girl said. 'Joan fault. I told you it weren't a wine bar.'

When Tim Bonner decided that people *had* to buy food he had been correct. His mistake was in believing that they had to buy *his* food. The whole world could avoid the slightest pang of hunger without stepping through his door, a truth which grew in his mind as the weeks passed. He opened earlier and closed later, living on hamburgers himself. He finally reached what appeared to be the satisfactory position on his financial graph when he opened at seven in the morning and closed at midnight. He knew then that for the amount of money that he had set himself to earn he would have to be open for at least twenty-eight hours every day.

'What I really wanted,' he told Sam Dawson, 'was to be a millionaire.'

'I once had that fanciful notion myself,' Sam admitted. 'Of course, it didn't seem fanciful then.'

'It's the only thing to be, otherwise you lead a cramped and restricted life.'

'Tell me about it,' Sam said, thinking about his cramped and restricted life. 'Let's get some body-abusing ale down us.'

They were at the golf club where a succession of erratic drives had increased Sam's debt to ten pounds. He had resolved now to reduce this by winning occasionally rather than paying.

'My brother's loaded and he's an idiot,' said Tim Bonner when he had bought them pints of bitter.

'I didn't know you had a brother,' said Sam, drinking an inch or two quite quickly.

'It's a fact I like to overlook,' said Tim. 'He sells second-hand cars and he's made a bundle. He says to me, "If you're so clever, why aren't you rich?" And I say to him, "If you're so rich, why aren't you clever?" He's got – listen to this – he's got two sons called Maurice and Austen. It was only when he had a daughter and called her Mercedes that I realised the prat was naming them after cars.'

'It must be galling for you. Moronic *and* rich. It sort of takes the shine off things.'

'Things don't have much of a shine on them at the moment, but luckily Beverley's taken over responsibility for the family's fiscal fortunes, so I'm sure things are going to improve.'

He sat at the bar with his pint, wearing the sort of relaxed expression that Sam Dawson couldn't quite manage these days. He looked as if he had been absolved of all responsibility and his life from now on could be devoted exclusively to the pursuit of pleasure.

He explained: 'I opened the washing machine in search of a pair of truant socks and found instead forty-nine carefully numbered ping pong balls.'

'I'm not sure I'm with this conversation,' said Sam.

'Oh, the technology is breathtaking in its simplicity. You spin the drum but leave the door ajar and sooner or later thirty balls jump out and roll across the kitchen.

After that, you simply crawl round the floor trying to retrieve them from the back of the fridge, make a note of their numbers and then hurry off to your National Lottery retailer clutching a used fiver.'

'I don't think that's how George Soros made his billions,' said Sam.

'Well, a man preoccupied with highly-leveraged multi-billion dollar investments wouldn't have the time to go out and buy forty-nine ping pong balls which are sometimes not easy to find.'

'Nor do I see the lottery as something to pin your hopes on. Bit like anorexic woofies chasing round a track after a toy rabbit they'll never catch. What's it called? Greyhound racing. What happened to the Jesus Trail? I thought you were going to fill Somerset with credulous tourists?'

'Beverley thinks I'd get arrested for pretending that Jesus was here.'

'It's no more than the Pope does.'

'She thinks he should be arrested as well. Is it your round, or can't I count?'

Sam Dawson bought two pints of bitter and wondered how he could justify the extravagance. He was only able to play golf because it was free, Tim having joined the club months before in a moment of misplaced optimism. Every purchase filled Sam with foreboding these days, particularly the non-essential ones. He put the meagre change in his pocket and resolved to see how long he could go without spending another coin.

'Anyway,' he said, 'the theory that Jesus was here

isn't something that you'd be pretending. It's published in the tourist leaflets.'

'Yes, but nothing conclusive.'

'Well, there's nothing conclusive in that department or we'd all be Christians. Go for it, Timothy. It's better than crawling round the floor looking for ping pong balls.'

'I've reappraised that part of the plan. We pick bits of paper out of a jug now.'

At a prep school in the Mendips Janice Dawson was giving one of her talks. She had four talks and some people had heard them all. She was always hoping to enlarge her repertoire so that she could go round again to those people who had heard all she had to say, but you had to know quite a lot about a subject to talk for an hour and Janice was too busy to learn anything new.

Her subject today was the Second World War — not as it was fought and suffered by men in uniform, but as it was endured by the people left at home in Britain. It was not a subject of great interest to children, but it was one that teachers thought children should be made to listen to, and she had delivered it at many schools. To get their attention she brought with her a suitcase of artefacts that she had collected over the years: ration books, gas masks, identity cards, dried eggs, posters saying *Waste the food and help the Hun*, articles of clothing that children wore then and an audio tape containing air-raid sirens, bombings, gunfire, and fragments of speeches by Winston Churchill. She introduced the children to the word 'evacuees' and was, as usual, surprised to discover how many children today would welcome such a disruption of their lives, a new home, a new family. The saddest thing these children had seen was the death of Bambi's mother, and the Second World War didn't compare to that. The Blitz sounded like an adventure. She dressed one of the girls in the clothes that she would have worn during the war, and just prevented one of the boys from putting on the gas mask which by now contained crumbling asbestos.

'They took it very well,' said the headmistress afterwards. 'Of course, it's all a bit remote for them. Even their grandparents would have been too young to fight.'

'I presume that won't stop them learning about the Boer Wars later on,' said Janice Dawson, replacing her collection in the suitcase. 'You can't give kids too much history. They've got to understand where they've come from, and if you wonder what's going to happen tomorrow it's always helpful to know what happened yesterday.'

The headmistress, a bouncy spinster in her mid-forties, reeled back at this. Janice Dawson's reputation came ahead of her and a further free lecture, just for members of the staff, loomed as a real possibility.

'I'll get your cheque,' she said nervously.

But Janice Dawson, generously recompensed for a trying hour, had no time to hang around. One job was followed by another, and she had to leave this ancient village school which resembled a reformatory and was built in local Ham stone, and head for a more modern village hall twenty miles away where she helped to run a playgroup of youngsters whose loud voices and weak bladders made her head spin. But she was above all a teacher and a guide, and she was never happier than when she was imparting information, no matter how old her audience. Putting knowledge into young heads gave her enormous satisfaction. Knowledge was all that she had to share.

The star of this troupe of moppets was Chloë Bonner, who actually used words like 'embarrass' and 'humiliate', although it wasn't always clear that she knew what they meant. Although three years old, she seemed occasionally to be about ten.

Janice Dawson, finding a receptive audience, spent some time with her and was running through the alphabet cards – each letter adorned by a wild animal whose initial it was – when Beverley Callard arrived to collect her daughter.

The surname disparity worried Janice, particularly as she did not feel able to deliver one of her homilies on the subject, but as the paid help she stood up politely and greeted Chloë's mother.

'Bright girl,' she said.

'They can be bright at three and dumb at six,' said Beverley. 'That's what I read, anyway. Listen, I want to talk to you.'

'Here I am,' said Janice Dawson.

'I'm going to start a sort of club. For women. A luncheon club, perhaps, where we can meet and discuss things, like men and their shortcomings.'

'It sounds subversive, Beverley.'

'It will be. What do you think?'

Janice Dawson barely knew Beverley Callard. She had only met Tim Bonner once, when he picked up her husband for a round of golf. But she liked what she was hearing now.

'It sounds good to me,' she said. 'How do I join?'

'All you do is bring yourself and your opinions along. I'm thinking it should be fortnightly, on Fridays.'

'That's fine with me. Who'll be there?'

Beverley Callard counted on her fingers. 'Monica Titchmarsh is a retired headmistress who serves on the County Council. Vera Selwood writes poetry. She may be a lesbian — I've never found out. Gemma Swan runs a secretarial agency and is on her third husband. She's pretty vitriolic on the subject and should be good fun. There's a lady from Gurney Slade whose claim to fame is that she climbs mountains or swims the Channel or something. I heard her on the radio once. And one from Wookey who acts occasionally on television. Her husband's a retired shipbroker who made his pile in Hong Kong so she doesn't have to act very much. That's about as far as I've got. I'm still working on it. I don't think we want more than about eight anyway or the thing will break up into lots of small conversations instead of one big one.'

'It sounds very interesting,' said Janice.

'Stimulating is what it's going to be,' said Beverley. 'I'm tired of sitting around while Tim plays golf with your husband.'

'Beverley,' said Janice, 'you've got an ally.'

4

When Sam Dawson beat Tim Bonner at golf he regarded it as an upward turn in the descending flightpath of his luck. The bad stuff had exhausted itself and it was time for something nice to happen to him.

They sat outside afterwards at a wooden table on the terrace in search of a cooling breeze and drank iced lemonade.

'I've something to tell you,' said Tim proudly.

'I have something of great importance to discuss with you,' said Sam Dawson. 'You can bat first.'

'"And did those feet",' said Tim.

'And did those feet?' Sam repeated.

Tim Bonner leaned forward enthusiastically in his chair. 'What do those words mean to you?'

'They ring a bell,' Sam admitted. 'It's a hymn.'

'It certainly is,' said Tim. 'A very famous hymn.'

'"And did those feet in ancient time walk upon England's mountains green"?'

'That's it,' said Tim. 'I'm very impressed. Now, what does it refer to? Whose feet? Millions of people sing it every week, but they have no idea what they're singing about.'

'Okay,' said Sam. 'Whose feet?'

'Jesus's feet in Somerset.'

'Pull the other one.'

'No,' said Tim. 'I'm telling you. It's William Blake's *Glastonbury Hymn* although it's better known now as *Jerusalem*. Listen:

> And did those feet in ancient time
> Walk upon England's mountains green?
> And was the Holy Lamb of God
> On England's pleasant pastures seen?
>
> And did the Countenance Divine
> Shine forth upon our clouded hills?
> And was Jerusalem builded here
> Among those dark Satanic mills?'

'Dark Satanic mills?' echoed Sam. 'That's Lancashire, isn't it?'

Tim put down his lemonade. 'I'll tell you it all again, Sam. Clearly you're too excited to concentrate. Joseph of Arimathea was a wealthy merchant in the lead-mining business. He came to Somerset to buy Mendip lead and he brought Jesus with him because Jesus was his nephew. Joseph of Arimathea was the uncle of

Jesus. They stayed at Priddy, between Cheddar and Wells. And that's why Blake wrote the hymn. That's what the hymn's *about*, for God's sake.'

'William Blake was scribbling this stuff in the nineteenth century,' said Sam. 'It's not what they call contemporaneous. He was hardly there with his camcorder, was he?'

Tim Bonner sipped his lemonade and laughed. 'He was two hundred years nearer the event than you are, old man. William Blake is my witness. I reckon my little project is up and running again.'

'Where are these mountains green, anyway? It doesn't sound like Somerset, which is strangely deficient in the mountain department.'

'Poetic licence, isn't it? Along with bows of burning gold and chariots of fire. You have to over-egg it a bit if you're a poet.'

'Oh, Blake could do that all right,' said Sam. 'There are only two words he missed out in his extremely famous hymn. One's Jesus, and the other is Somerset.'

'But he called it *Glastonbury Hymn*. It wasn't Blake who called it *Jerusalem*. There's no doubt what he was talking about, no doubt at all.'

Sam Dawson held up both hands, impressed by this research. 'I give in. I don't want to knock it — you might give me a job. But I thought you weren't going to do it? I thought Beverley had killed it off?'

'She has,' said Tim, looking glum. 'It would be hard enough to do anyway, without her sitting on the sidelines making destructive remarks. But I'm interested in it.'

'So what are you going to do?'

'I'm reading everything I can, including the Bible. Perhaps I'll accumulate enough evidence to win her over. Apparently, when Joseph came back after the Crucifixion he brought the Holy Grail with him. That's what I'd like to get my hands on. Some bugger must have it.'

'If you plan to mingle with the devout I think you'd better watch your language, Timothy.'

'In the Middle Ages, Glastonbury was a major centre of pilgrimage. Well, I'm going to see that it is again.'

'Roll up! Roll up! Get your Jesus memorabilia here!'

'If *you* plan to mingle with the devout as one of my minions, you can drop the idiom of the street-trader. Piety by the boatload is what we're looking for here, along with one of those blank facial expressions that suggests that you've never had your leg over in your life.'

Sam Dawson arranged his features to project an image of chastity and devotion.

'My God, you look as if you've taken up child abuse!'

'I'm getting warm then?' said Sam. 'I'm on the right track.'

The golf club at this time of the day was the haunt of a succession of sun-tanned drinkers, few of whom thought it necessary to get out a golf club. They stood inside at the bar with their gins and their whiskies discussing, Sam imagined from the other side of the window, the heatwave's effect on food prices (milk was going up because there was no grass for the cows), the recession's effect on property prices and inflation's effect on the prospect of a cut in interest rates. They looked universally serious and seldom laughed. Perhaps if you were successful there was small room for jokes, and these people had to be successful or how could they be drinking whisky in a golf club in the middle of a midweek morning? Unless, he sometimes conjectured, they were all villains. Sitting outside with his lemonade he thought that some of them looked shifty enough, but then he had to ask himself whether such thoughts weren't the product of envy.

Tim said: 'What was it that you wanted to discuss? Now that we've breathed new life into the Jesus Trail.'

'I'm worried about your common law.'

'My what?'

'Well, she's not your wife, is she? You seem to have stopped short of that commitment.'

'Beverley? She doesn't want to get married. Her opinion of men isn't too high, and I don't think I've done a lot lately to raise it. Why? What has she done?'

'Something very sinister, Tim. She's formed a club — for women. Worse than that, she's invited my wife to join it. Well, that's like dangling prawns in front of a cat. Can you imagine what will happen when they all get together? We'll be scuppered.'

Tim Bonner looked vaguely uneasy at this. He had forgotten Beverley's declared intention of mobilising a matronly army, but it came back to him now, accompanied by the misgivings he had felt when the subject was first raised.

'I tried to talk her out of it,' he admitted.

'And a piss-poor job you made of it, apparently. She's *recruiting* people, and one of them's my wife. When that lot get together I think we can safely assume that the happiness and comfort of men won't be the first item on their agenda. Or the twenty-first.'

Tim Bonner finished his lemonade and stared unhappily at the empty glass. 'You don't think they might discuss womanly activities like slimming and dressmaking?' he asked hopefully.

'No, I don't. That's not what they talk about. Did you see what Anna Ford, the television lady, said the other day? Let me quote her to you. "Women talking among themselves wonder what men are for". That's where our lot will be pitching it. The fact that neither of us has a job doesn't help. We're not even breadwinners. My wife is a very formidable lady on her own. With a gaggle of troops behind her she'll be bloody invincible. The Alamo with bells on is how I see it. I suggest we buy some white flags.'

'This is a pessimistic scenario, Sam.'

'Neither Janice nor Beverley are women who waste time. They're not going to sit round a table getting tipsy on wine. They're not like men. When they sit down and talk, something positive comes out of it. I'm petrified, frankly.'

This admission produced an expression of deep despondency on Tim Bonner's face.

'I felt a pang of alarm myself when she brought it up, but it hasn't been mentioned since and I thought she'd forgotten it.'

'Women never forget,' said Sam. 'It's one of our problems.'

'Men always do. That's one of theirs.'

Sam Dawson had always expected to do well. He had the brains for it, he had the ambition. He hadn't left school with the most impressive results in the class, but nor had many of today's younger millionaires who soon found themselves squatting on huge and expanding empires that satisfied some public need which they alone had identified. Sam Dawson felt equipped for success, and then fumbled around for something that he could apply himself to.

Looking back, it was hard for him to see where he had gone wrong. His first job, which he had viewed as a temporary money earner while he discovered his true vocation, had him working long hours as an assistant manager in a department store where he consoled himself with the idea that he was absorbing valuable secrets of the retail trade which he could later deploy on his own behalf. It was a job that had been astonishingly easy to get, but surprisingly difficult to escape from. Contemplating a future that was beginning to frighten him, he could see that the only place the assistant managership led to was the managership itself, a post which had reduced successive incumbents to suicidal gloom. He resigned one morning in a mixture of panic and despair, and took a short holiday in France where he spent much of his time patrolling the Atlantic beach and trying to think of the idea that would liberate him from the role of employee. What was the public need that he alone could fulfil?

He studied the histories of the newly-rich. A motor-bike messenger started a courier service that he sold for £50 million. A man who started a milk round in 1948 now owned a dairy group worth £49 million. A sales rep for a textile firm produced home furnishings, working in his garage, and was now worth £86 million. Barrow boys got rich opening pharmacies; market stalls were transformed into discount stores. All these people, from unpromising beginnings, had identified a public need.

But no idea arrived for Sam, and within a week of returning to Britain he had met Janice Bowdery, a bouncing ebullient creature who pushed his thoughts in other directions. He quite forgot the grip he was trying to exert on his future, and was preoccupied instead with the fact that he wanted to marry this girl but had no job.

Janice had a job. She hurtled round town in a little red van that belonged to a property firm that seemed intent on covering the planet with cheap apartments. Janice's job was to meet prospective purchasers on site and reveal to them as persuasively as possible the hidden glories of life in a flat. It was here that she honed her talent for the continuous narrative that barely allowed the listener to intervene. She mastered the politicians' trick of taking breath in the middle of a sentence so that she could jump from one to another, leaving no gap for interruption. Potential buyers wilted before her onslaught; sales flourished.

'I think we should get married,' said Sam Dawson one evening over a vegetarian moussaka that he had ordered by mistake.

'Married?' said Janice, opening her eyes very wide. 'Why?'

'In the first place it will give me the stability and cohesion that I need. In the second place, I want to.'

'That's not the most elegant proposal I've ever heard,' said Janice. 'Not that I've heard any yet. What's in it for me, Sam? As I understand it, you're out of work and lack all sense of direction. You don't want me for my commission, do you?'

Sam brushed this aside with a laugh. The truth was that he found Janice physically attractive and socially pleasant. She was twenty-three then and had not put on the weight. But he also had the idea, which he had heard or read somewhere, that marriage made a man concentrate on the important things and avoid life's sidetracks and trivialities. All the millionaires whose histories he had so assiduously studied, were married. It was, come to think of it, about the only thing they had in common. But — brushing it aside with a laugh — he nevertheless managed to ask: 'Is the commission good?'

'Very good,' said Janice. 'It's the only reason I do it. Really I fancy something more stimulating. I've got ten O-levels, you know!'

She had black shoulder-length hair then, with a fringe at the front. She reminded him of a film star he had fancied in his youth. The two women had the same bright eyes and sensual mouth.

'It's my intention to get a job,' he told her earnestly. 'But my real ambition is to be a millionaire.'

'Now you're talking,' Janice said. 'Any ideas about how you're going to achieve this miracle?'

'What I need,' said Sam, 'is an idea. I've been spending a lot of time looking for one.'

Janice, glimpsing the problem, laughed sharply in a way that unsettled him. He was confiding his secret dreams and expected a more sensitive reception.

'I wish I had time to look for an idea,' she said. 'I want to be rich as well.'

'What happened?'

'Like everybody else, I'm too busy earning a living to make any money. No, what you need, Sam, isn't an idea. It's a job.'

'I'll tell you what I'll do,' said Sam. 'I'll get a job and then I'll ask you to marry me.'

'Don't leave it too long,' said Janice. 'I might get snapped up.'

But nobody had ever proposed to her before and she was strangely moved. Sam, despite his earnest and hopeless quest for wealth, was good company. She also thought that marriage would provide her with an opportunity to change lines. She was tired of extolling kitchens and praising bathrooms while fending off searching questions about the shared lifts and the absent gardens.

The following week with perceptible reluctance Sam answered an advertisement for a shop manager. His initial job as assistant manager in a department store had been a mistake and his work experience thus far qualified him for a very limited number of positions, none of them well-paid. He was offered the job immediately and he took it.

He sold his flat. He bought a house. He got married.

Between a beautifully thatched barn that housed a cider mill, and a museum of rural life that mustily celebrated the virtues of the wooded hills and lowland moors which surrounded them, Beverley Callard had a shop. It was called *Beverley's*, and, reflecting the interests of her father, sold almost anything that contained gold or silver: photograph frames, cigarette cases, antiques, pocket watches, war medals and militaria, silver plate, candlesticks and tea sets, claret jugs, inkstands, clocks and barometers, china-headed dolls and toys. The tiny shop was a jumble of such things, bought mostly in the winter and sold profitably to tourists in the summer. Each year, despite dire predictions, the business produced sufficient profit to keep going and even pay the wages of Beverley's part-time assistant, Melissa, a single mother whose occasional presence allowed Beverley to take time off with her daughter.

But today she was alone, sitting at the back of the shop with a list of telephone numbers in front of her. Through the window at the front she could see the shuffling holidaymakers who, impressed by the unusual heat, had renounced the customary fortnight on a Spanish costa and settled instead for two weeks at home. They wandered into the shop through force of habit and bought things that they would never normally want. But abroad they collected odd souvenirs and so they did it here.

On her lap Beverley Callard had a magazine that, attracted by a come-on line on its glossy cover, she had bought on her way to the shop. The come-on line said: MEN HAVE MORE FUN — OFFICIAL. She flipped through the pages now, ignoring the dietary tips and the fashion advice and the more exotic features on things like balloon safaris, and found the article that she was looking for. It said that while half the men of fifty were happier now than when they were young, women of the same age were permanently harassed and worried. While the men took it easy, women worked harder than their mothers did at the same age. Married men were also the healthiest group, followed by single women, single men and then, at the bottom of the league table, married women.

She put the magazine down feeling both vindicated and angry, and consulted the telephone numbers in front of her.

'Is that Monica Titchmarsh?' she asked when her first call was answered immediately.

'Speaking,' said a very brisk voice.

'It's Beverley Callard. I spoke to you the other day about forming a women's lunch club.'

'You did indeed. How nice to hear from someone who isn't about to involve me in some ghastly planning tangle. Is the lunch club going ahead?'

'Yes, we have seven people which seems to me to be a comfortable number, and we plan to start on Friday. Would that suit you?'

'Let me look at my diary, dear. What time on Friday?'

'One o'clock.'

There was a short pause while Monica Titchmarsh looked at her crowded itinerary. There were meetings to attend without hope of resolution, bureaucrats to bully, voters to pacify, letters to read and possibly answer.

'I can make it,' she pronounced. 'At the hotel you mentioned?'

'That's it,' said Beverley.

'I look forward to it,' said Monica Titchmarsh.

Beverley rang off and re-dialled. A man who was

clearly drunk picked up the phone, dropped it, picked it up again and said: 'Is that Moira?'

'No,' said Beverley. 'It's Beverley Callard. Can I talk to Gemma Swan?'

'At the agency,' the man said. 'Little woman's working.'

Beverley Callard hung up without answering and looked for Gemma Swan's work number on her list. If that was her husband, Gemma Swan sounded like promising material.

The inaugural meeting of the lunch club was held on a sweltering Friday in the back room of a small hotel. A white-clothed table, laid for seven, stood in the centre of the room, and on a smaller table to one side there were several bottles of wine, some of them in ice buckets. The hotel's idea of ventilation was a dazzling collection of gold ceiling fans which sent the same musty smell back to you like a tennis volley. It seemed an unlikely place for a revolution.

The guests, summoned by phone and driven here by a mixture of curiosity and boredom, stood around with glasses of chilled wine while Beverley Callard introduced them to each other, and then took their seats at the table where Beverley sat at the head. The three on her right were Janice Dawson, Vera Selwood, the poet and putative lesbian, and Gemma Swan, the much-married owner of a secretarial agency. On her left were Monica Titchmarsh, the retired headmistress and County Councillor, Davina Smith-Proctor, a single

woman in her thirties who evidently climbed mountains, and Laura Morton, an actress they all recognised
now from some half-remembered soap.

'We were going to call ourselves the Somerset Ladies'
Afternoon Guild, until Janice Dawson pointed out the
acronym,' Beverley told them. 'So now we'll be just
The Lunch Club. It has a nice irony.'

'What's ironic about that?' asked Davina Smith-
Proctor. 'Irony's not my game.'

'T.L.C.,' Beverley explained. 'Tender loving care,
which is not an idea we expect to hear much about
in here.'

Beverley was wearing blue jeans and a blue denim
shirt but the others, uncertain what to expect, had
dressed more carefully. Laura Morton, with her theatrical background, was wearing a leather wrap-around
mini-skirt, and a leather jacket with shoulder pads
and leopard skin cuffs, stiletto-heeled ankle-strapped
shoes and three gilt chains round her neck. The
whole proclaimed a sexual availability which was
wholly inappropriate to the present company and its
objectives.

'What do we expect to hear about in here?' she
asked sweetly.

'I think it's fair to say that the inadequacy of the
male sex was a motivating force in the formation of
this club,' Beverley told them. 'Janice Dawson and I
are attached to a brace of loafers, what the Americans
call "fiscal underachievers", who on top of everything
else seem to have a chemical dependency problem.'

'Drugs?' said Monica Titchmarsh, looking astonished.

'Alcohol,' said Janice Dawson. 'Their social milieu is confined to louche watering holes with names like the Red Lion or King's Head. Or the golf club.'

'Oh, if we're going to bash the men, count me in,' said Laura Morton. 'My old man's done bugger all for twenty years apart from make a couple of million.'

The others stared at her to see whether some more irony was lurking here, but it was immediately clear that there was not. Laura Morton's discontent with her husband was genuine and belligerently intact, untouched by the consolation of her bank statements.

Vera Selwood smoothed the greying hair at her temples with a languid hand and gave them a seraphic smile. 'I've written poems on the subject,' she said.

'On what subject?' asked Gemma Swan.

'On the inadequacy of men, and do we really need them. Published in quite good magazines.' She turned to Janice Dawson on her left. 'Are you the lady who writes the column in the local rag? If you are, you work too hard, judging from all the jobs you write about. Do you find time to sleep?'

'I am and I do,' said Janice Dawson. 'I have to be honest, work suits me. My problem is that it doesn't seem to suit my husband.'

She was going to elaborate on this at considerable length now that the stage was hers, but a waiter came into the room to take their orders. The ignored menus were quickly handed round and, in the cases of Monica Titchmarsh and Vera Selwood, spectacles produced. When some conventional and unadventurous meals had been ordered, Beverley determined to find out about her guests. There seemed to be four married women and three spinsters, including herself, although she had ceased to regard herself as such.

'Let's see,' she said. 'How many of us have children? Gemma?'

Gemma Swan, a tall, lean woman in her thirties with short brown hair that barely covered her ears, put all her energy into running a secretarial agency in Taunton, having discovered that devoting similar energy and application to her marriages was scantily rewarded. Her first husband was a serial adulterer, her second a wife batterer, and the third, the present incumbent, was either impotent or intoxicated, often simultaneously.

She told the table: 'I have a daughter of ten called Saskia by my second husband. Conceived in Tenerife and delivered in a taxi.'

'Really?' said Janice Dawson, thrown somewhat by the explicit nature of the reply.

'Oh yes. Sex was such a rare event that we can pinpoint the precise venue of her conception with unusual accuracy.'

'How sad,' said Vera Selwood. She had a pale elderly face that reflected pain and intelligence in equal measure. She had placed a packet of small cigars on the table and looked as if she would like to light one now rather than play with the tough slice of beef in front of her. Years ago, unknown to those round the table and to most of the world's population, she had published a slim novel about Sapphic love, written entirely from the imagination and described in one of the Sunday newspapers as 'glacial and pellucid'. She still carried the cutting in her handbag, uncertain what the critic was trying to tell her.

'I have cats,' she said. 'You choose to have cats. Children kind of arrive.'

'Not in my experience, I'm glad to say,' said Davina Smith-Proctor, who had a handsome face that wouldn't have looked out of place on a man's shoulders. She had big brown reassuring eyes that had gazed fear-lessly down precipitous escarpments from snow-covered peaks. She had the hands of a Sumo wrestler and the beginnings of a moustache. 'Children? Who needs them!'

Beverley looked round the table, wondering whether this disparate group, with its various axes to grind, might not be the dispassionate, objective symposium that she had envisaged.

'Monica?' she asked hopefully. 'I expect you have grandchildren?'

Monica Titchmarsh, now in her sixties, had a shock of grey hair that evidently received little attention from herself or anybody else. She looked as if she had long since exhausted her patience with the world and could only get satisfaction now from finding fault with it. Problems seemed to follow her around. They followed her from the school where she had once taught to the

Council chamber where she now sat in judgment on municipal questions that always failed to unite the warring factions who had been chosen by an apathetic electorate to try to run the county. And they followed her home. Her husband Gerry had been robbed, mugged and badly beaten up during a business trip to Bristol six months ago and hadn't uttered a word since – a reticence that she initially welcomed but which was now beginning to irritate her.

'I have a son in Saudi,' she said, 'whom I seldom see, and two grandchildren I have never seen. That's how it is these days, I'm afraid. A hundred years ago they'd have lived within a mile of me. Today the world is their playground.'

Janice Dawson felt impelled to offer words of comfort at this Diaspora in the Titchmarsh clan, but before she could start, the actress Laura Morton, who had been paying more attention to the wine than some of the others, said: 'I've got two kids and never see either of them, thank God.'

'Where are they?' asked Beverley.

'One's in a squat in Notting Hill, I believe, and the other's traipsing round India, no doubt indulging his taste for pernicious narcotic substances. The entrancing child becomes the obnoxious adult is what you have to remember. Anyway, sod kids. I thought we were here to sort out the men?'

'We are. We are,' Beverley said with an apologetic smile. 'I just thought it would be useful to know a little about each other.'

63

'You don't want to know too much about me,' said Monica Titchmarsh. 'It'll depress you. It depresses me. I've got a husband who hasn't spoken a word for six months.'

'For six months?' said Janice Dawson incredulously. Silence on this scale was impossible for her to comprehend. The little she had said in the last half hour was hard enough for her to understand. 'What's the matter with him?'

'He got beaten up in Bristol. The doctor calls it post traumatic stress disorder, but I think he's holding his breath like an angry baby.'

'Get him drunk,' said Gemma Swan. 'He'll talk.'

'Discuss sport,' said Laura Morton. 'He'll have something to say.'

'Welcome the peace,' said Davina Smith-Proctor. 'A silent man is a rare commodity.'

These offerings seemed to Beverley to carry the right degree of impatience with the opposite sex and a proper lack of sympathy. She was encouraged to suggest: 'My own opinion is that men need our help, being fairly helpless themselves. Luckily they're highly suggestible creatures. Wind them up and point them in the right direction and they'll go lumbering off to try to do the job, but it would never occur to them to attempt it in the first place. That, I think, is where we come in. We're looking for ideas here.'

'Ideas?' said Gemma Swan.

Beverley finished her meal — some less than satisfactory lamb chops — and pushed her plate away. 'The question we should be asking is: are you satisfied with your husband? And if not: how can we change him?'

'*Change* him?' said Monica Titchmarsh.

'She doesn't mean exchange him for another man,' Janice Dawson explained hastily. 'She means change the man that he is.'

'And we can do that, can we?' asked Laura Morton.

'That's why we're here,' said Beverley, reaching for the wine. 'It's the female gnat that draws the blood.'

5

The mail that arrived for Sam Dawson in Somerset lacked the bulk and the urgency of the post that he had once received. The world was now ignoring him. The mail linked to work had stopped; the flurry of credit-card bills that hit him like a blow in the groin every month had ceased because he no longer used the cards; and people today preferred the instant response of the telephone to the arduous duty of writing a letter. When the postman did find something to slip through his door, it was usually junk mail that was going to everybody — colourful leaflets designed to change their thoughts about how they cleaned their carpets or insured their lives.

On this morning two items brought the postman to the door. One, he could tell at a glance, was a reminder that the car insurance was due for renewal. The other looked more interesting, being addressed to him personally in unfamiliar handwriting and posted in Somerset. He took it into the kitchen where Janice was scrambling eggs.

'Post?' she said.

'Something,' he answered, putting it on the table.

'I thought we might drop in on Jake this morning,' she said. 'If he's still there. It's their sports morning.'

'A gap in your schedule?' he asked.

'Only this morning. I'm in the shop later.'

He sat at the table and waited for food. His wife's energy seemed to make *him* tired, as if he was the person who was expending it. He poured them both a cup of tea and picked up the paper. The heatwave was going to continue and a ban on hosepipes was sweeping across the land.

'How can a country surrounded by water and rained on excessively be short of water, when a huge, hot country like Spain never is?' he asked.

But Janice had more important matters to attend to. 'How many rashers do you want?' she asked. Even off-duty she bustled.

She had been brisk when they got married in a register office in South London, and it had taken a month or two for him to adjust to her pace. He was the branch manager then of a stationers, part of a national chain, and his acquired briskness was a useful asset. It helped him to assert himself, or appear to assert himself; an illusion of authority came with the briskness.

At first, fascinated by the novelty of marriage, the job held some attraction, and what he had seen as an inauspicious start to his career in the department store no longer felt like a mistake. But boredom crept up on him, and then a sense of failure that he had never found the big money-making idea, and now with a family to feed he couldn't take the risks and never would, and finally a deep and hopeless feeling of desperation. Jake had arrived by then and Janice, who had always had two or three little jobs even if she didn't have one proper one, gave up work entirely and devoted herself to rearing their son. His salary cheque was devoured each month before the next one was due, and so he dutifully feigned enthusiasm for a job that depressed him.

Being made redundant was a mixed blessing. On one hand, the release from servitude; on the other, a financial horror story. Janice's idea of moving west and living cheaper, although basically sound, hadn't quite turned out as they had hoped. They had to slash the price of their house before they could sell it, but found that similar reductions were hard to find in Somerset, where people put a price on their home and then sat there, sometimes for years, until it was met. At one house they had gone to see, the lady told them: 'You're the first people we've had looking round in two years!'

'Have you thought of reducing the price?' Sam asked.

'Oh, we wouldn't want to do that,' the woman laughed, as if Sam was making crazy suggestions to humour her.

And so by the time that they were established in

Somerset in their semi-detached home, they had less money than they expected, and bills that they hadn't expected, like Jake's school fees.

They found him later that morning sitting on the edge of a cricket field watching a match. He was a tall, gangling fifteen-year-old, with the big eyes of a dreamer. His hair, like all the boys of that age, was parted in the middle and fell untidily over both ears. Sam Dawson sought in vain to find something of himself in this boy, but nor could he see what had been inherited from his businesslike mother. It was as if he had been planted, cuckoo-like, in the nest.

'Darling,' said Janice, bending to kiss him. She was obviously relieved that he was still here.

He stood up reluctantly and seemed embarrassed.

'What are you two doing here?' he asked.

'We dropped in to see you,' said Sam. 'You're not in the team then?'

'Wrong accent,' said Jake. 'Cricket is a gentlemen's game.'

It hadn't occurred to Sam that his son had any accent at all, but he could see now that it might be a bit nearer the street than some of the rich men's sons who would be at this school whose grounds covered twenty deep green acres.

'It didn't seem to handicap Ian Botham,' he said, but knew anyway that Jake wasn't in the team because he wasn't good enough. 'Why are you watching?' he asked.

'I'm waiting for someone,' Jake said, indicating a distant fielder with his thumb.

'Do you need anything?' asked Janice. 'Do you need money?'

Jake smiled. 'Money's always welcome, Mum.'

She opened her bag and gave him two ten-pound notes. 'How's school?' she asked.

'School's school,' said Jake. 'Nothing lasts for ever.'

'He's not happy,' she said in the car as they drove back. 'He's not settling in there at all.'

'At least he doesn't run away,' said Sam. 'He must like it enough to stay.'

'Early days,' said Janice. 'There's a look behind his eyes that I don't like.'

She was driving today, an arrangement that kept Sam strenuously alert, as she was dropping him off at home before going to the charity shop. Cautious at corners, she perked up on straight roads and pushed through gaps that would have Sam braking. Her driving worried him when he was a passenger and sometimes when he wasn't. He was not convinced that she gave it her full attention, having plenty of other things to occupy her mind. Most women are not bad drivers, he always said, but most bad drivers are women. But the last two bumps in the car — minor collisions, no harm done — had occurred when Sam was at the wheel, and his views on women drivers had been heard less frequently lately.

'How well do you know Beverley Callard?' she asked

as Sam counted the inches between his speeding elbow and a parked car.

'Hardly at all,' he said.

'I thought it would be nice if we had dinner with the pair of them.'

'Dinner?' said Sam. 'With Tim?'

'And Beverley.'

'You don't even like Tim. You think he's a lazy, useless individual who drinks too much. I think those were your words.'

'But I like Beverley, now that I know her. Dinner with the four of us would be interesting.'

'Would this be on neutral territory?'

'Oh, I think so. We can hardly invite ourselves round to their place, and if I've got to cook it will take the pleasure out of the evening.'

'Okay, I'll float the idea.'

'Don't float it, Sam. Fix it.'

She braked, as it seemed to him, with unnecessary sharpness. They had reached their home, and he was dismissed with his instructions. He wandered into the house feeling lost. Sometimes afternoons were difficult to fill. Once, seeing himself as a basket case, he went to watch them make baskets at the willow craft centre. Another afternoon, only vaguely remembered now, was spent at the cider farm and museum. But Footprint was pleased to see him and jumped up when he opened the door. Perhaps he should feed them both.

The dog food that Janice bought now arrived in trays rather than tins and he found one and peeled off the top. He was assailed by a pungent aroma that temporarily quelled his own appetite, but when he scooped it on to Footprint's plastic plate the dog threw himself at it as if he had seen no food for days. Footprint was a six-year-old Springer spaniel whose hobby was eating.

For himself, Sam cleaned some radishes and found a piece of cheese. This evening, with any luck, Janice would produce a decent meal. He took his snack to the kitchen table, sat down and noticed immediately the letter he had forgotten to open that morning. The handwritten address on the envelope was the work of a girl, presumably a secretary, with the i's dotted by bubbles, but the letter was in the businesslike print of a word processor.

Dear Mr Dawson, he read. *It has come to my attention that you have recently taken early retirement after a distinguished career in retailing, and I am wondering if you can be prevailed upon to offer us some assistance here.*

Sam paused at this. Early retirement at forty? A distinguished career in retailing? Here was a man who was trying to make a friend. He read on with mounting scepticism.

We are a growing chain of supermarkets, concentrated in the West Country, and currently have two new stores nearing completion. Even in an age of unemployment it is not easy to procure the competent staff that we need to run these outlets, and so I wonder whether you might be interested in a return to full employment? If so, I would be delighted if you would give me a ring so that we could meet and discuss the matter further.

The signature, emblazoned across one half of the sheet, was *Sheridan Barrett*.

Sam Dawson dropped this letter like hot coals. He didn't even enjoy entering a supermarket as a customer, and to be marooned there all day in its chilly impersonal aisles seemed to him to have much in common with a spell in Dartmoor.

But as he ate his radishes he picked up the letter and read it again. Who was Sheridan Barrett, and how had he heard of Sam? What was a supermarket doing, offering work to unknown strangers when a small advertisement in the local paper would produce a queue of suitable applicants a mile long? He considered these questions with a faint sense of unease. There were people out there who knew all about him, people that he didn't know existed. There was something intrusive about Mr Sheridan Barrett's letter that disturbed him. This wasn't the tranquil rural anonymity that he had supposed.

He dropped the letter on the table for a second time and picked up the last of the cheese. Then he wandered into the sitting room where Footprint had already established a considerable presence in front of the empty fireplace. He turned on the television and was delighted to find that it was cricket.

'"And did those feet"?' murmured Tim Bonner, lying

flat on his back on a sunbed on his lawn. He was wearing red swimming trunks and a blue baseball cap to keep the sun off his face.

Alongside him on another sunbed, Beverley lay reading in a pink bikini. Chloë was at a friend's house, Melissa was in the shop, and Beverley was enjoying a rare moment of relaxation, one that she would prefer without interruptions.

'You're the worse for drink,' she said, not lifting her eyes from the page.

'No, I'm the better for it,' Tim corrected her. 'I've tumbled to your little game. You're trying to convert me from lager lout to Aga lout, aren't you?'

'Some hopes. I'm just trying to retrieve you for the human race — if they want you.'

Tim Bonner pulled the cap further over his face. 'The human race and I have always got on rather well. I've met several of them and they seem okay.'

Beverley ignored this so that she created the peace in which she could read. It was a novel called *Flaubert's Carrot*, or so it seemed to Tim from his prostrate position. He watched resentfully as she read it.

'Why don't we get married?' he asked, as if this was an electrifying idea that had not occurred to him before.

Beverley lowered her book. 'Why on earth would we want to do that?'

'For Chloë?' Tim suggested. 'Anyway, it's what people do.'

'Not any more, it isn't. You know I've never wanted to.'

'What about the cavity-wall insulation salesman from Chipping Ongar?'

'I was younger then,' said Beverley, recalling with a distant frown a teenage moment of weakness.

'You're thirty-two, kid. The sarcophagus beckons.'

'What would I marry you for? Your overdraft?'

'Ouch,' said Tim, reflecting that all conversations with Beverley led to this. She could be discussing anything from the Corn Laws to faith healing but always managed to find her way back to the absorbing topic of his almost empty bank account. He looked at her long, brown legs stretched out on the sunbed and asked: 'I suppose a quick jump would be out of the question?'

Her response to this, or lack of it, betrayed his lack of judgment and he settled again into a comfortable position which might with luck produce sleep. The natural concupiscence of the human race was not a subject that seemed to concern Beverley much now. He sometimes thought that with the production of Chloë she felt that her duties in that direction had been satisfactorily discharged. A more disturbing hypothesis had recently offered itself to him: she was the victim of an ongoing post-natal depression that with some women could last for years. The birth transformed them into an entirely different person. Lately he had begun to think that this was what had happened to Beverley and he'd wondered — quite erroneously, he now knew

– whether marriage, with its solidity and security, would cheer her up.

He slept. The dream, always vivid when he slept in the sun, involved hordes of strangely-clad pilgrims falling out of coaches, clutching rosaries and cameras and in some cases palm branches and unlit candles, all demanding to be shown the route of the Jesus Trail. 'Do you take American Express?' asked a devout but grouchy old man with a white beard, who had flown in from Wellington or Sydney. 'This is the culmination of my life, sir.'

He awoke in a sweat, alarmed at what he had started, and was relieved beyond measure to discover that he had started nothing. Beverley still read her book, the sun had continued its descent, and the world was a little older. When Beverley clamped the book shut and went off for a shower, he stood up himself in case he fell into another sleep which would produce, a few hours later, a restless sleepless night. In the two stable blocks which would house seven horses if they had them, Humbug the cat was in artful pursuit of something, judging by her prowling gait, but she lost interest in this when she saw Tim and followed him indoors for food that would arrive with less effort on her part. Tim zapped the television on and waited for Beverley to vacate the shower. He was reminded by a trailer that the weekly ritual of losing on the National Lottery was only an hour away.

And an hour later the two of them sat in front of the set with a ticket whose numbers had been selected by the cat who had been confronted by a gentle avalanche of forty-nine numbered ping pong balls. Sustained by an irrational optimism, they nevertheless exuded a cheerful cynicism as they stared at the screen.

'Do you realise that once you've bought your ticket you've got more chance of dying before they make the draw than of winning the jackpot?' Beverley said. 'You've got five times more chance of being struck by lightning, more chance of drowning in your bath.'

'Odd things can happen, whatever the odds,' said Tim. 'Aeschylus died when an eagle dropped a tortoise on his bald head, mistaking it for a stone. What sort of odds would he have got from bookmakers on that?'

At that stage, before the first ball had dropped from the drum, he found that optimism was possible.

'I don't think he spent a lot of time in betting shops,' Beverley said. 'He was too busy writing dramas.'

'I'm ahead of you. We're about to speculate on the bulging nature of his bank account. All those drachmas stashed away in capital bonds, all those royalties working for him in offshore accounts.'

'Ssh,' said Beverley, engrossed now by the screen on which the chosen forty-nine balls were being dropped into the drum.

'Why have some numbers only come out once or twice and others nine or ten times? What happened to the law of averages? Has it been repealed?'

'Ssh,' said Beverley. The balls were rolling out now, too fast to check, and she wrote them on the same sheet of paper that she produced every Saturday evening.

When the bonus ball had appeared, she picked up her ticket and compared numbers.

'Amazing,' she said.

'We're obscenely rich?'

'Not exactly. What's amazing is that we didn't get a single number. Not one.'

'Kill the cat,' Tim suggested. But every week the disappointment came as a slight surprise, something that he had to overcome.

'Thirty numbers Humbug chose and not one came out,' Beverley said, re-checking her ticket. 'Shall we put it down to Tim Bonner's bad luck?'

'Don't knock it. If I didn't have it, I wouldn't have any luck at all.'

'We'll have to scrap the five-course dinner and the champagne, and settle for something more modest.'

'I'm glad you mentioned dinner. What did you have in mind?'

'We have to fetch Chloë. On the way back we'll get some fish and chips.'

Confined to the King's Head by a rainstorm that had thoughtlessly clashed with their golf, Sam Dawson and Tim Bonner could see no future beyond the next pint and had soon had several. It was a small and tidy pub which today they shared with two cirrhotic whisky users who were struggling over a crossword.

'I have an announcement to make,' said Tim.

'Receiving you loud and clear,' said Sam.

'I've dropped all idea of the Jesus Trail. I expect

you're relieved to hear it. It was a ridiculous idea. Beverley was quite right.'

Sam was surprised. 'I'm sorry to hear that,' he said. 'I was beginning to believe that it might have potential.'

'I had a dream about it. More a nightmare really, except that it was in the afternoon. Hordes of crazy religious people swamping me with questions. Nutcases from all over the world making impossible demands. The size of the thing was frightening. I was so relieved when I woke up that I hadn't actually started it that I promised myself I never would. All I need now is a new, more manageable idea.'

'What a shame,' said Sam. 'But at least you can stop reading the Bible.'

'I'll miss that. It's got some good yarns in it.'

'Yarns?' said Sam.

'Have you heard about this bloke Job? Blimey, we think *we've* got problems.'

'I think it rhymes with robe. What happened to him?'

'Well,' said Tim, as if he was in possession of hot gossip that was not available to everybody, 'God allowed Satan to test him, to see if he'd still love God when things went wrong. Up till then he'd had everything. To be frank, life had been a bit of a doddle for old Job. Well, Satan really got stuck in. He nicked his oxen, killed his servants, burned his sheep, carried away his camels and then blew his house down, which killed his sons.'

'What did Job say to that?'

'He said "The Lord giveth and the Lord hath taken away".'

'He sounds like a member of the Liberal Party.'

'So God encouraged Satan – apparently they were on speaking terms – to have another go. This time Satan didn't fanny about. He smote Job with boils and scabs from head to foot. His hair fell out, his balls fell off. And God said: "Do you still love me?"'

Tim picked up a new pint and drank a third of it without taking the mug from his lips.

'Well,' he said, when he had wiped his mouth, 'the bald, bollockless bastard, who by this time is covered with boils and other hideous excrescences which greatly diminish his prospects of a leg-over in the foreseeable future even if he was still in possession of his testicles which he isn't, is well pissed-off by now. "With friends like You, God," he says, "I've got to re-think my alliances."'

'Are you sure you've got this right?'

'Not entirely, no. What is this bitter?'

'It's not bitter, it's cider. Enjoy the local brew. If you were in Russia you'd drink vodka. Well, cider's what you drink in Somerset.'

'It's a bit strong. Anyway, if you think you're down on your luck, remember Job.'

Sam Dawson drank some more cider himself. The afternoon stretched before him offering nothing and so there seemed no reason not to.

'I'm glad you're not going to get too wrapped up in

that book, Timothy,' he said. 'Nothing on this earth is more dangerous than a simple mind in the grip of a religion. Zealots, fanatics, guns and bombs. Religion's a bloody virus if you ask me.'

Tim found something to resent here. 'Are you saying I've got a simple mind, old man?' he asked. But before he could receive a reply he'd had another idea, and he lifted himself from his stool at the bar and stumbled as if on prosthetic legs in the direction of the toilet. When he returned, his mind had moved on.

'What do you think they talked about?' he asked.

'Who?'

'The Lunch Club, or whatever they call themselves.'

'I haven't been told. I'd like to have been a fly on the wall.'

'I'd sooner watch Shakespeare in Japanese. Is there going to be a second meeting?'

'I'm afraid there is.'

Tim stared into his cider, considering this possibility. He was obsessed with the idea now that Beverley was suffering from post-natal depression and had been for some time. It was an affliction, he had read, with many more victims than had been realised. And the victims behaved strangely, irrationally and sometimes went crazy. The idea of gathering together half a dozen women who were complete strangers and inviting them to discuss the problems they had with the other sex just because he played golf once a week with Sam Dawson, could fall into any of these categories, or even all three. He finished his drink and pushed his empty mug towards the elderly licensee who was trying to help his other customers with their crossword.

'Why do you always seem to expel more fluid than you drink?' he asked.

Sam Dawson finished his drink — it was Tim's turn to pay. 'Not top of my list of problems, Tim,' he said. 'Poverty, yes. Encroaching baldness, yes. Joblessness, certainly. The mysteries of the bladder? Not on the agenda.'

'Encroaching baldness?' said Tim, encouraged. 'You *are* getting a bit thin on top, aren't you?' He ran a hand through his own blond mop, to reassure himself. 'At least you'll be able to swim faster. Chrome domes bullet through the water.'

'I don't swim,' said Sam, taking his new pint. 'But women will be impressed at my high testosterone levels.'

'Is that so? Baldness as a sex aid. I hadn't thought of that.'

'It's just me trying to cheer myself up. You'll never guess what I've got to do tomorrow.'

'Take the dog for a walk? Clean the car? Mow the lawn? Watch racing on TV? How many out of four have I scored?'

'Nil,' said Sam Dawson. He looked across at the whisky drinkers as they wrestled with an anagram, and wondered whether they were the retired rich or victims of the recession, like himself. The recession had changed everything and made situations difficult to read. Nobody seemed to know quite what was going to happen. While the Government talked of recovery, the banks were awaiting a fresh wave of bankruptcies. So while more people faced financial disaster, the politicians, finding that their political objective – winning an election – and their economic objective – bringing down inflation – were completely incompatible, lied and smiled, lied and smiled.

Above all, the recession was testing people in areas where they had not expected to be tested. Some found, to their surprise, that they were not as honest as they had always supposed. Desperate situations demanded desperate remedies, even if the normal standards of honour and morality were edged to one side.

When Sam Dawson was trying to sell his house and move west, he had a friend who was trying to sell his house to appease sundry creditors; the asking price was £100,000 – the least that he needed to put his affairs in order. Unfortunately, it was a figure that nobody wanted to pay. Potential buyers trooped through his house at regular intervals, admiring his kitchen and praising his garden, and then they rang up the estate agent with offers that made the man seethe. Desperate situations required desperate remedies and in the end the man invented his own buyer. A false birth certificate, a few bogus documents and a willing accomplice who only wanted a thousand pounds, and suddenly Sam's friend had a firm offer of £100,000 from a non-existent customer who had, on the strength of his forged credentials, received a hundred per cent mortgage. It wasn't hard to get; the building societies were desperate for customers. By the time that Sam Dawson's friend had banked his £100,000, the buyer had disappeared and the building society was re-possessing the unwanted house.

Another man he knew persuaded a friend to hire a car and smash it into his so that he could get from the insurance companies the money that he couldn't get for the car from anybody else.

Scams abounded. But Sam Dawson wasn't like that. He wrapped his honesty round him like a torn coat, and took what scraps the world threw at him. His house went for £20,000 less than he had originally asked and his new home in Somerset wasn't quite the rural mansion he had originally hoped.

He finished his cider and decided that enough was enough. There were things that he had to do, like find his suit and press it, clean his shoes and dig out his old leather briefcase.

'I'm off,' he said, getting down from his stool. 'They can't breathalyse pedestrians, can they?'

Outside the rain had stopped and the sun was in control again, drying the road so quickly that it raised tiny pillars of steam.

'You didn't tell me,' said Tim. 'What *are* you doing tomorrow?'

'I've got an interview for a job,' Sam told him.

In the grey Nissan Bluebird, Janice Dawson sped through country lanes separated from brown fields by drystone walls. In the fields were strange horizontal chimneys, relics of the old lead mines, and hundreds of sheep. At least here she would not face the customary hazard of rounding a bend to find her way blocked by a herd of cows.

Twenty minutes later she pulled up outside the offices of *The Clarion* and parked neatly on double yellow lines. In his room at the back, Leo the editor was idly surfing the Internet and chain-smoking French cigarettes. The arrival of Janice's column wasn't quite enough to drag him away immediately from his new toy, and for a few more moments he pushed keys and summoned up information that he would never need. He had a plump, self-satisfied face which suggested that he had not suffered the quota of pain and frustration that Janice thought everybody had to endure at some time, and which this man particularly deserved. Even in these cramped and unimpressive surroundings, he behaved as if the end product of his labours was one of the world's great newspapers instead of a downmarket freebie, replete with spelling mistakes, ungainly headlines, wandering apostrophes and sensational errors of fact which never merited fewer than two apologies a week.

'It's the Janice Dawson column,' he said, standing up at last. 'What are we getting at this week?'

'Out-of-town supermarkets. The death of the town. Can you read it in a hurry? I've got an appointment.'

'Of course you have, Janice. You never stay still.'

He took the column and read it standing in the

middle of the room. Like many bizarrely dressed men, he seemed to regard himself as an arbiter of fashion, flaunting today a leather waistcoat and pink trousers as if this was where the future lay. He was fifty-five.

'You write like you talk, Janice,' he said. 'There are no commas in your conversation, and none in your column, either.'

'If God had meant us to use commas, He wouldn't have given us editors. I don't want to make you redundant, Leo. Is it okay?'

'It's fine. Bloody supermarkets. What are they going to do when they've killed all the shops?'

'Put their prices up, of course. But you can't warn people. They won't listen.'

'Well, you've tried.'

Outside, a female traffic warden hovered malevo-lently over the Nissan, a threat which Janice immedi-ately quashed by chatting to the woman about her son's gifted drawings at the nursery school where she worked.

Her next stop, two hundred yards away, was the cake shop where she dropped off two specially ordered birthday cakes, and took orders for three more. After that there was some shopping, a little chore that was considerably prolonged by a chance meeting with a neighbour who had time to kill and stories to tell about her experiences with her doctor. And then she was ready for the second meeting of The Lunch Club.

6

Determined as she was to see the successful establishment of The Lunch Club, and therefore scrupulously prepared for every conceivable setback or hitch, Beverley Callard was nonetheless surprised and upset to discover that by the time of the second meeting there had already been two defections. A note conveying this unwelcome news was waiting for her at the hotel.

It hinted as delicately as such matters could be touched upon that Vera Selwood, the poet, and Davina Smith-Proctor, the erstwhile mountaineer, were now in the throes of a rumbustious lesbian relationship, a joyful and quite unexpected association that would take up what spare time they had. Neither felt that they had much to offer on the subject of men, a species they had little interest in unless they were privy to the mysteries of the car engine. They naturally wished the venture the best of good fortune.

'What do lesbians do, anyway?' asked Gemma Swan resentfully. Doleful experiences with three failed husbands had left her wondering what physical pleasures she had been missing.

'More than my husband, I hope,' said Laura Morton, who was dressed today in an elaborate bright yellow outfit with a flowery multi-coloured collar. 'There are five hundred and twenty-nine possible positions for sexual intercourse, and David knows only two of them. And one of those he hasn't quite mastered. The man is such a complete twerp that at the age of fifty-two he's still not entirely sure whether he's been circumcised.'

It was apparent to Beverley that Laura had been at the sherry before she arrived. She suggested helpfully: 'Buy him a book.'

'Farting against thunder, dear,' Laura Morton said regretfully. 'Ignorance on that scale is difficult to surmount.'

'It sounds to me as if you picked the wrong man in the first place,' said Monica Titchmarsh from her seat beside Beverley. They all looked at her thoughtfully. It was hard to imagine that she had fared any better in bed.

Laura Morton stared mistily into her wine. 'Perhaps I did,' she said. 'It was all so different then. We sat on the beach at Amalfi exchanging pledges that would die on the wind. None of us can see into the future with the clarity that we need.'

'Particularly if you're dealing with men,' said Gemma Swan with unnecessary vehemence. 'What *is* it with them? Even those who show some promise never fulfil it. They sort of sink back into a disgusting lethargy.'

'Lethargy's a word that Beverley and I would recognise,' said Janice Dawson. 'I sometimes think that if my husband died, it could be weeks before I noticed.'

Laura Morton finished her wine and absent-mindedly refilled the glass without offering the same service to anybody else. 'It's their deceit that gets me. They don't seem to realise that you can only lie to the same person once.'

'I had a boyfriend,' Gemma Swan told the table, 'who tried to fool people by putting dandruff on his toupee. Was he mad or vain?'

'Both,' said Monica Titchmarsh tersely. 'I'm surprised you had anything to do with him.'

The waiter appeared through a side door with a tray of salads. He served the food quickly and then withdrew as if he had been eavesdropping on the conversation and did not feel entirely safe in this company. His arrival, delivery and retreat were ignored.

'I'm beginning to see my husband's life as a great tragedy,' Janice Dawson said. 'It's been a story of wrong directions, and there'll be nothing at the end of it to suggest that there has been much point to it.'

Monica Titchmarsh managed a contemptuous shrug at this unnecessarily sympathetic résumé of Sam Dawson's career. 'Whose fault is that?' she demanded. 'They have all the advantages and then they muck it up.'

Laura Morton, ignoring the food but clutching her wine, nodded vigorously. 'They *do* have all the advantages, don't they? All the female sex demands is level killing fields.'

'I think the expression is level playing fields,' Beverley told her.

'I know what I meant. Where's my husband now? Flying a bloody Cessna. What chance have I had to learn to fly planes?'

The sympathy which she had expected to elicit at this deprivation was strangely absent from the faces of those round the table. They had seen her drinking and her driving and had no desire to see her flying. Only Beverley was disposed to encourage the ambition; Laura Morton was showing the right degree of hostility to the male sex and she didn't want her to be deterred.

'Book some lessons,' she said, 'and don't tell David.'

'I was at a cocktail party last week,' said Gemma Swan, feeling left out. 'I was talking to a woman about a job we're doing for her at the agency when there was a whistle from the other end of the room. "That's my whistle," she said. It turned out that her husband trains sheepdogs and he had a special whistle for her, too.'

'Did she brain him with a bottle?' Monica Titchmarsh asked hopefully.

'No, she left me and she left the party. She was a submissive little creature.'

'I think what we've got to focus on now is change,' said Beverley. 'It's no use our sitting here and just running men down.'

'Enjoyable though it is,' said Laura Morton.

'We've got to do something about these pathetic creatures. I'm with a man who hasn't earned fourpence this year. Janice is the same. Gemma's husband is permanently paralytic, Monica's hasn't spoken for six months, although he may be ill, and Laura's seems to lead a life of selfish self-indulgence that doesn't include her. I think the purpose of The Lunch Club is to right some of these wrongs, to put these men on the right track again. I mean, that's why we're here. The sods need help.'

'I quite agree with you,' said Monica Titchmarsh. 'In fact, so far as Mr Dawson is concerned, Janice and I have already made a start.'

Sitting on a plastic chair and confronting the huge bulk of Sheridan Barrett, Sam Dawson felt like a small boy who had been caught smoking behind the bike sheds. It was many years since he had submitted himself to the gruelling humiliation of a job interview, but he could remember now with limpid accuracy what a deeply unwelcome experience it was.

Sheridan Barrett was a man of seventeen or eighteen stone. His enormous, etiolated face, topped by greased black hair, seemed to block Sam's vision of the room in which they sat, and his large brown eyes slid regularly from Sam to the papers that lay before him on his small white desk. The eyes were flecked with a pain that suggested to Sam that a colossal bowel movement would be unambiguously welcomed.

'I've always been interested in food,' he said. 'I began my career during student travels as a short-order chef at a lunch counter in Omaha. I've stayed in touch with grub ever since.'

'My own retailing experience lies in a quite different direction,' Sam admitted. He wasn't sure what he was doing here. He didn't want the job. He wanted money, but he didn't want this job. Janice wanted him to get the job, which was strange because this was just the sort of out-of-town supermarket that she was railing against in her column this week.

'Experience is your most expensive asset, Mr Dawson,' said Sheridan Barrett. 'You've paid for it with time.'

'But my knowledge of food doesn't go much beyond the fact that you eat it. How did you come to approach me, anyway?'

Sheridan Barrett's eyes dropped to the papers on his desk. 'I don't know how you came to our attention,' he said. 'Somebody evidently knew your history and that you were available.' He looked up. 'The food thing doesn't matter. It helps if you can tell the difference between broccoli and spinach, but even if you can't you soon will. What we're talking about is the customer-service ethic which applied where you worked and applies where we work. Motivating people, generating sales, customer care, line management. It's the same everywhere. Baked beans or books. What's the difference?'

'I see,' said Sam.

'We want you to work for us, Mr Dawson. There

may be thousands of unemployed people out there, but when you get to interview them you find out why they're unemployed. The sixteen-year-olds can't write and the twenty-year-olds can't think. Most of the older ones were lucky they ever had a job to lose. You, on the other hand, have a proven track record.'

Sam Dawson was beginning to realise that this was the reverse of the normal job interview in which the applicant sought to persuade the interviewer, obsequiously if necessary, that he should be given the post. Sheridan Barrett was desperately anxious that he should accept it.

'What would my duties be, exactly?' Sam asked.

'Supervisory,' replied Sheridan Barrett promptly. 'It would cover all departments. Customer complaints, financial queries at the check-outs, quality control, seeing that the shelves are re-stacked when the marauding multitude has stripped them. Of course, you wouldn't have to fill the shelves yourself. You wouldn't be wheeling round trolleys of potatoes. But you'd keep an eye on the youngsters who do. Your position would be number two to me. I think you'd like it.'

He sat back, his salesman's spiel exhausted.

'What do you say?'

The dinner party that had been suggested by Janice Dawson and enthusiastically supported by Beverley Callard was approached with sombre misgivings by their men, who saw something sinister in this wilful rearrangement of their social agenda. The men met for golf and had a drink, the women met for lunch and had a talk. To mix these two separate routines – to subject Sam to the searing scrutiny of Beverley and expose Tim to the searching questions of Janice – would not, they suspected, help to produce the peace and contentment that they continually sought.

The chosen venue, a former inn converted now into an Italian restaurant with ancient flagstone floors, gigantic fireplaces and low ceilings that brought back the past, was in a picturesque village some miles from where they lived. But they arrived simultaneously, the Dawsons in the Nissan and Tim and Beverley in her dark blue Passat, and were ushered into a candlelit dining room with plain walls that reminded them of a monastery. The women had dressed up, Janice in a blue two-piece and Beverley in a colourful dress, and so the men had felt obliged to put on suits.

'We're celebrating,' Janice announced as a swarthy young man poured them a free introductory drink.

'Celebrating what?' Beverley asked, turning to Sam.

'I've no idea,' he said. 'It's news to me.'

'Oh Sam,' said Janice. 'We're celebrating the fact that you have finally got a job.'

The prospect of resuming a career that had been drastically foreshortened by the incompetence of Treasury ministers did not lift Sam's heart or seem to him to be cause for celebration, particularly as he would be working for exactly half the money he had once been paid.

'You've got a job, Sam?' Tim asked. 'You be

careful. They make you work when you get one of those.'

'All we've got to do now is find you one, dear,' said Beverley. 'Playing golf doesn't seem to fill the larder.'

A waiter arrived to distract them with menus and then insisted on reciting a list of items that were not on it. This ritual confused Tim Bonner who listened politely, forgot instantly and ordered lasagne from the menu.

'What have you been doing these last few months, Tim,' Janice asked when the waiter had taken their orders, 'apart from playing golf?'

'I think it's called trying to enjoy my life.'

'Why would you expect to do that?'

'I know,' said Tim. 'It's a pretty forlorn objective, isn't it? But I read somewhere that was what you were supposed to do.'

'He has these funny ideas,' Beverley said. Her thick eyebrows dipped towards her eyes in a gesture of disapproval.

Tim faked a laugh and looked at Sam. 'I didn't imagine we'd come here for a quick chat about quantum physics. What do you ladies all talk about at your Lunch Club?'

'Men,' said Janice, 'and how we can help them.'

'And how they've got one brain cell between them,' said Beverley. 'You get a good standard of conversation over lunch.'

Listening to Beverley's astringent tone, Sam Dawson wondered how Tim managed to stay so cheerful. He seemed to be closeted with a female terrorist and yet behaved as if he had the love and support of a gentle and understanding woman.

When their food arrived – a steak for Sam, spaghetti for the women – Janice moved into the conversational void. 'What I really wanted for Sam,' she said, 'was that he should make money. It wasn't that either of us relish luxury or even spend very much, but the money would have been good for him, good for his personality and character. He would have been able to shake off this awful feeling that he is a failure and be able to look the world in the face. The money shortage is a kind of malnutrition, pinching him up when he should have been expansive and sociable. I think that poverty's a blight that shrivels people. What he really needed was to be a millionaire – it's the only thing that would have relaxed him.'

Sam Dawson listened to this with a mixture of amusement and embarrassment. Janice was seldom so candid and never so sympathetic.

He said: 'I wanted to be a millionaire, but I seem to have this terrible job in a supermarket.'

'An interim measure,' said Janice, 'while we find out what you're good at.'

'What I'm good at?' said Sam. 'I've been working non-stop for more than twenty years.'

'Perhaps the best is yet to come,' said Beverley. 'Forty is not old.'

Tim filled their glasses and told them solemnly: 'My climb to the dizzy heights of extreme indigence began with childhood poverty on an epic scale. The shared clothes and the outside bucket. The junk food.'

'You are what you eat,' said Beverley. 'Anyway, your father was an accountant.'

'The memories become blurred,' said Tim, rubbing his forehead in affected concentration. 'I'm sure that deprivation and hardship were in there somewhere. One year Father Christmas couldn't afford a bicycle. It provided the spur which drove me towards the dream of riches.'

'What happened,' Janice asked, 'to the dream?' Tim Bonner, for all his boyish charm, seemed to her to lack the seriousness that she would want in a man of his age. At thirty-five he behaved like a twenty-year-old; she could understand Beverley's exasperation.

'I'm holding it,' he told her. 'I cling to it like a charm.'

'And what are you doing to bring it about?' Janice asked.

'I plot and I plan.'

'Then he pours a bucket of lager down his neck and falls over,' said Beverley. 'It makes you want to punch a wall.'

'Tell Janice about the Jesus Trail,' Sam said, worried about the impression that his wife was getting of his friend. 'Tim is a man who has ideas and he's put several of them into practice. He started a magazine, he opened a burger bar. He's an entrepreneur who hasn't hit his stride yet.'

'How long can the world wait?' Beverley asked,

forking her spaghetti. 'How long am I supposed to wait for my fifty-room castellated mansion?'

'What is the Jesus Trail?' Janice asked.

Tim, signally frantically for another bottle of wine, turned to her and smiled modestly. 'My latest idea which, like many of my other great ideas, has now been put to rest. At first I thought it would make a lot of money. After all, religion is big business in America. Why not here? But then Beverley poured enough cold water over it to give it pneumonia, and now I'm glad the thing is dead. Just organising it would age you twenty years. I'm hoping that a less ambitious project will occur to me one of these days.'

Beverley explained to a confused Janice: 'There is a story, a rumour, a legend or a myth that Jesus was brought to Somerset as a boy by his uncle, Joseph — a lead merchant who came here on business. Brainbox here thinks there is money to be made by organising a walk for visiting pilgrims along the track used by Jesus. What a prannet!'

Tim laughed at her language. 'Say what you really mean,' he suggested. 'Don't hold back.'

'And where exactly is the track used by Jesus?' Janice asked.

'That's where we run into difficulties. We don't even know where He landed.'

'Or *if* He landed,' said Beverley. 'The whole idea brings certain words to mind, like squad and fraud.'

'Not where the credulity of Christians is concerned,' said Janice. 'You'd be pushing at an open door.'

Tim brightened. 'You like the idea, do you?' he asked.

Janice nodded. 'I do.'

'There are a lot of people out there who are desperately in need of something,' Tim explained portentously. 'Hope, faith and the promise of eternal life. My thing would have helped them, and it sure as hell would have helped me. A thousand pilgrims a week at a hundred quid each. What's that — five million a year? We're talking serious boodle here.'

The waiter was at the table collecting plates, and they were left to contemplate the amazing figures that Tim, inspired by wine, had plucked from thin air. They sounded so impressive that even Beverley fell silent, and it took the production of a dessert menu to restore her power of speech. The women ordered ice cream, but the men decided that another bottle of wine would round off the meal nicely.

Tim, smiling now at the imaginative figures he had thrown across the table, asked: 'What did you say this job was?'

Sam thought for a moment. He was using a fingernail to nudge pieces of steak from between his teeth. He needed a toothpick, he decided, or even a trochilus. 'Assistant manager in a supermarket,' he muttered bleakly.

'I'm sorry to hear that,' Tim commiserated. 'How are we going to play golf?'

'Golf?' Sam repeated miserably. 'There isn't going to be any golf.'

'How did you come to get the job anyway? It doesn't sound like the gold mine we're after.'

'It isn't. How did I get it? The manager wrote to me and offered it.'

'Why did he write to you?'

'It's a mystery. I asked him, and he said they'd heard about me from somewhere.'

'Many are called but few are chosen,' said Janice.

'St Matthew,' said Tim. 'I'm becoming quite an expert on religious questions.'

Janice phoned Beverley at her shop.

'He's got to do it, Beverley,' she said urgently.

Beverley was polishing a silver brooch.

'Hallo Janice,' she said, putting down the work. 'Got to do what?'

'Tim. The Jesus Trail. The more I think about it, the better the idea seems. It wouldn't even cost much to launch.'

'Tim has ideas like that once a month. I've stopped taking them seriously.'

'Well, he said you'd poured cold water on this one, but listen. We're trying to get these bastards into work. I've got mine into a supermarket, and this is your opportunity. Who knows? It might be the money-spinner he suggested.'

'I must admit that when he mentioned the money I warmed to the idea a little. I've been turning it over in my mind ever since, and I'm glad to hear your opinion.'

'Push him, encourage him — if necessary, kick him.'

'You sound very strong on this, Janice.'

'I am. It's just the sort of crazy idea that could come off, and I decided I had to ring you to try to get you to support it. Now he's got no one to play golf with, he'll just drink. He's a nice chap, but if he doesn't have a purpose he'll come apart at the seams. I know the type. Anyway, I think it's a wonderful idea. Jesus in Somerset? It could be huge.'

'He won't be here personally, unfortunately. We're in the land of fable and superstition.'

'That's where religion lives, Beverley. Go for it. Get him off his backside.'

Beverley picked up the brooch again and began to smile.

'Okay,' she said. 'I'll activate him.'

7

Tim Bonner no longer read newspaper columns headed YOUR MONEY because he knew they were talking about something that didn't exist. But he was still a dedicated peruser of the financial pages with their gloomy prognostications and mysterious graphs. He read them as a small boy reads an adventure story — stirring tales of fearless heroes who succeed against daunting odds and make all things seem possible to the poor unsuccessful reader. But some people were making too much money:

> Sir Richard Sykes, chief
> executive of drugs giant Glaxo
> Wellcome, is set to pick up a
> bonus of £5.6 million.

Tim read this with an indignation that made his heart palpitate. He hurried away from such egregious excess and took refuge in another page.

> Peter Dawe's paper worth is
> £22 million, and because his
> shareholding in the Internet
> company Unipalm is likely to
> be bought out soon, his actual
> wealth is likely to be £22
> million, too.

Every bastard was making money except him. Even young women were making money:

> Petra Doring, who turned
> £100,000 into a personal
> fortune of £25 million,
> is writing a book. The
> glamorous Doring, 34, made
> her money after starting the
> Cabouchon jewellery business
> in 1990 to sell costume
> jewellery in the same way as
> Tupperware and Avon.

People he had never heard of were becoming preposterously rich every day. They slipped into the newspapers and then out of them, disappearing with their mansions and their millions. He hoped that it brought them heartache and misery, along with boredom, alcoholism, divorce and stupendous bills from therapists and psychiatrists, hired for ridiculous fees to reassemble their broken lives. It was the least he could hope for.

He put the papers to one side and turned on the television to keep his daily date with Teletext. He read:

DAHMER CREMATED EXCEPT FOR BRAIN.

It seemed an appropriate note to end the day on, and he made his way upstairs, a journey that Beverley had undertaken more than an hour ago. As usual, he looked in on Chloë in her little pink room that was crowded with picture books and dolls. He was surprised to find her awake but then realised that he had woken her.

'Daddy,' she said. 'Why does a frog say "rivet, rivet, rivet"?'

'I don't know, darling,' he said. 'Why does a frog say "rivet, rivet, rivet"?'

''Cos it can't say "bollocks".'

She watched him to see whether this was funny. It was clear that she had no idea what she had said, but was repeating something that she had heard somewhere.

'Very good, Chloë,' he said doubtfully. Not for the first time he thought that there should be classes somewhere for parents, with specific tuition in how to deal with surprises like this.

Beverley wasn't asleep either. She lay in bed nude, reading her latest book, a biography of Auden. He glanced over but she did not look up. Other women read Jackie Collins or Catherine Cookson. She read a biography of Auden. He sometimes forgot how educated she was. As a cherished only child she had been sent to a famous public school in Sussex where she had sailed through exams that brought down lesser girls. But when the moment came to choose from the horde of universities that were clamouring for her presence, she returned to Somerset and rode horses in competitions, a hobby she had thankfully given up. Now that the world seemed to be filled by people with ambition but no talent, Tim had to recognise that he was shacked up with a lady who had talent but no ambition.

When he slipped into bed beside her he ran his hand up her leg, but nothing that he could construe as encouragement followed this gesture. He nodded at her book.

'Have we found a man that we can admire?' he asked.

'Not exactly,' she said, without lowering the book. 'He used to stop outside the royal palaces and fellate sentrymen as they stood in their sentry boxes.'

Tim was fascinated. 'I didn't realise you were reading filth. I thought you were engaged on an intellectual exercise.'

'He also took Benzedrine every morning for twenty years.'

'Another flawed male then?'

'Afraid so, Tim.'

He lay back on his pillow and stared at the ceiling as she returned to her book.

'Do you think he took the Benzedrine to get the taste out of his mouth?' he asked. 'I mean, if he was a consummate gobble artist—'

'Tim, it's not something I want to dwell on.'

'Oh, sorry. You brought it up and it's a gruesome picture. If the cost of a few poems is some plonker on his hands and knees in the Mall giving blow jobs to complete strangers, we've got to ask ourselves whether we're paying too much for our literature. Lose a few poems and be spared the grisly spectacle of—'

'Shut up, Tim.'

'Why can't I be allowed to finish a bloody—'

'Go to sleep, Tim.'

For a while he tried, but he had drunk no alcohol today, Beverley was obviously in no mood for a romantic interlude, and so he endured the insomnia of the celibate non-drinker who has nothing to lure himself towards sleep.

Eventually the book was laid down and the light switched off.

'I've been thinking,' she said, lying on her back beside him, 'about the Jesus Trail.'

He opened his eyes. 'And?'

'I was wrong. It's a good idea. It might even be a brilliant idea. You ought to try it. After all, you've got nothing else to do. Perhaps it'll take off.'

'This *is* a volte-face. What made you change your mind?'

'I've just been thinking about it since we had dinner with the Dawsons. I've begun to see its possibilities. How would you set it up?'

'It's a somewhat incomplete concept at the moment,' Tim admitted reluctantly. 'You sort of knocked it on the head.'

'Well, luckily for you I've been giving it some thought. This is what I think. You do a deal with all the local hotels and get a special rate, and then you do the same thing with the local coach companies, who will take the visitors from their hotels to the start of the walk, and pick them up at the end of it, and take them back to their hotels. When you know what the hotels and the coaches are going to charge you, add your fee and you've got a price. All you've got to do then is advertise in all the religious newspapers and magazines and you're reaching the right people straight away. Would they come from abroad?'

'You're ahead of me, kid.'

'I think they would. They fly to Fatima in Portugal from all over the world, and to Lourdes. The pilgrims pay you and you pay the hotels and coaches. Get on to it, will you?'

'Beverley, you're so businesslike.'

'One of us has got to be,' she said, turning her back on him and closing her eyes. 'It will all be quite simple. Once you've lined up the hotels and the coaches, all you have to organise is the walk itself. You'll be the guide, pointing out the places of religious significance and selling them baubles at exorbitant prices.'

Her airy summary of what he was required to do frightened him. His whimsical idea had been turned into a gruelling undertaking.

'It's a tall order,' he suggested, as he imagined an endless programme of planning, organisation, negotia-tions and investment.

'A tall order, but not beyond you.'

Tim closed his eyes but felt that sleep had now moved even further away. He had been quite happy to drop the

Jesus Trail idea, but there was no chance of dropping it now. He owed Beverley the effort.

He lay there, seeing himself surrounded by hundreds of pilgrims from all over the world — the old, the sick, the mentally disturbed — and all of them waving candles and crucifixes and singing obscure hymns. Onerous burdens loomed.

But soon his thoughts drifted on to the financial rewards that might lie at the end of this ordeal, and he began to feel quite jaunty.

'Hey,' he said, 'this could put Jesus on the map. The trouble is, I don't know exactly where on the map to put Him.'

But Beverley was asleep.

Sam Dawson was prowling the aisles of the supermarket, feeling like a misfit with no trolley to push. He had been instructed to familiarise himself with the shop's layout, and appreciate the subtle conjunction of one item with another. As a customer he had been infuriated by the apparently arbitrary placement of goods, and had spent much time hunting down items on Janice's lists. To hear now that there was an intention and design in where each product sat came as a shock, and he was trying to understand the thinking behind it. Why was jam at one end of the store and syrup at the other? Why was the sugar always stacked on its own?

Many times he had returned home without sugar, having failed to find it, but now he tried to think his way into the minds of the supermarket bosses. His search for logic and reasoning wasn't entirely successful but he continued to prowl and observe and try to make the connections which he had been told were there.

Concentration was difficult because he was mostly preoccupied with trying to identify the mistake he had made somewhere in his life which had dumped him in this absurd occupation. In the aisle with him were lonely-looking men who behaved as if they had been plunged into an alien environment, children who felt free to bawl at the tops of their voices, and serious housewives who checked calorie, fat and cholesterol contents, and then compared costs and studied sell-by dates before primly dropping anything into their baskets.

They had been hit at the door by a massive display of videos and magazines, and now made their way through a minefield of cut-price offers, this week's bargains and buy-one-and-get-one-free enticements. There was hardly a price on show that didn't have a line through it and a lower one alongside. At the same time, now he came to study it, Sam couldn't help being impressed by the exhaustive nature of the stock. Everything was here, from air fresheners to L-plates. Whether the bargains were genuine bargains he wasn't qualified to say.

At eleven o'clock he accepted Sheridan Barrett's invitation to a coffee in his office.

'How is it?' the fat man asked, lolling back in his chair. 'Have you worked out where everything is?'

'I'm getting the picture,' Sam said, stirring his coffee. 'I'm not sure I've worked out why it is where it is, though. Is there some deep psychological reason that leads people naturally from tea bags to toilet rolls?'

'If there is, I haven't been told it,' said Sheridan Barrett. 'But the whole thing is based on research carried out by Head Office, and we have to follow the plan.'

'Why do you have two lots of frozen meat pies at different ends of the shop? Two lots of several things, actually, on offer in different places?'

'You haven't worked that out?'

'Not yet,' said Sam miserably.

'One is our own brand, Sam. That's the one we want them to notice first. Bigger profit margin.'

'I never found the sugar, but then I never do.'

'End of aisle nine,' said Sheridan Barrett. Sam nod-ded. He hadn't even known the aisles were numbered. 'You'll soon get used to it. Carry on having a look round this morning, and this afternoon we'll introduce you to a spot of paperwork. You'll be surprised at how much they spend in here every week.'

Sam wanted to say that if the figure was truly impres-sive he might require an immediate salary improve-ment, but as he had only been in the place three hours and provided absolutely no evidence that he was suited to the job, such thoughts were probably premature.

'I imagine it's a gold mine,' he said.

'No need to go anywhere else, unless you want a television or a pair of trousers. And how often do you buy a television or a pair of trousers?' He leaned over his desk. 'By the way, do you know the County Councillor, Monica Titchmarsh?'

Sam stared at him blankly. 'I can't say that I do. Why?'

'I've tracked down the recommendation that brought you to us. It was from Monica Titchmarsh.'

'Well, that's odd,' Sam said. 'I've never even heard of her.'

'She spoke well of you to one of my superiors. I was told "Get Dawson".'

'And that's why I'm here? Curiouser and curiouser.'

'It *is* strange,' Sheridan Barrett conceded. 'Perhaps you have a secret admirer.'

If Jesus came to Somerset, where did He land?

This was the question that began to nag at Tim Bonner, because if he didn't have an answer he didn't have a Jesus Trail and the lucrative dream fell apart. The Trail had to start at the point where Jesus first stepped on land, but the paparazzi weren't there on that day and the truth was impossible to discover.

'Are you sure people were travelling those distances by sea at that time?' Sam Dawson asked when Tim raised the subject of his problem. 'Boats seem more recent somehow.'

'Caesar came to Britain in 55BC,' said Tim. 'He was an Italian gentleman, you may remember. How do you suppose he got here? Think he swam?'

'Weren't we joined to Europe then? Perhaps he walked here.'

'Britain had been an island for six thousand years by then, old man. Don't go on *Mastermind*. It got warmer — it used to be bloody freezing round here — the ice melted, the sea level lifted, we weren't connected to France any more and the Europhobe was born. There were naval battles before the birth of Christ. Antony and Cleopatra lost one, didn't they? They practically had roll-on, roll-off ferries.'

'Why did it take them another fifteen hundred years to find America then?'

'These were gentlemen of taste and discernment, Sam. They mixed in exalted circles. They dined in the royal courts, seeking patronage for their expeditions. What did they want with hamburgers and horror movies? They could see all too clearly where it would lead.'

Shocked by Sam's ignorance, Tim took himself off to the public library hoping that the gaps in his knowledge would be filled by the secrets that nestled on its shelves. For more than an hour he bounced from the History section to the Religious section, poring over pages of impenetrable prose that filled him with despair. He shared an ill-lit room that had depressingly dark wooden walls with an old man who repeatedly removed his false teeth as he studied a huge and dusty volume that somebody must have placed there for him.

Surely, among the millions of words that now surrounded him, the information that Tim needed could be found? Occasionally the scent grew warm and he seemed to be on to something, but then the chronicle veered off in another direction to recount historical facts that were of no use to him.

Eventually, bemused by antiquity and the sagas of bygone times, it became necessary for him to do the sensible thing and enlist the help of a member of the staff. She was a pretty girl in her mid-twenties who wore a badge on her left breast that announced her name: Jill Hack.

To her, Tim confided his interest in the story that Jesus had visited Somerset as a boy, and his curiosity about where He might have landed. Would He have come up the Severn, and disembarked at Bristol? And what chance was there of discovering where this journey, if it took place, began? He didn't mention the Jesus Trail, and tried to create the impression that he was a mature student at work on a thesis. It was a situation with which Jill Hack was very familiar.

'I'll bring you some books if you find yourself a table,' she said. 'You've been looking in the wrong section. You want Local History.'

Tim Bonner found himself another table where the visiting readers showed no proclivity to remove their teeth, and thought that his entire venture now rested in the hands of Jill Hack. It was a quarter of an hour before she reappeared. She carried four large books under her chin, in each of which she had placed a sheet of paper to guide him to the relevant page. When she spoke, he only just restrained himself from jumping up and kissing her.

'You're overlooking one thing,' she told him with

a stern smile. 'When Jesus was alive, the Somerset Levels were underwater. Lowland Somerset was a marshy sea. That's why the Levels are flat, you see. In fact, sea flooding reached the foot of the Tor as recently as 1607. Jesus, if He came, wouldn't have disembarked in Bristol. He would have sailed right here, and in one of the books it tells you where. Okay?'

'Jill Hack,' said Tim. 'You're a genius.'

'I do my best,' said Jill Hack, gliding off in search of fresh inquiries.

Tim Bonner got out his notebook and his pen and turned to the first book. There was no hopeless quest now for elusive information. Jill Hack's bookmark led him straight to what he wanted to know.

The information on Joseph of Arimathea, who was now described as the great-uncle of Jesus, was unequivocal: *'His boat sailed up the swampy inlets and landed him at Wearyall Hill where his staff took root and blossomed out into a flowering thorn which still mysteriously blooms twice a year.'*

The next book he consulted confirmed another fact: *'Joseph sailed to the West Country to buy Cornish tin and Somerset copper and lead, bringing his great-nephew Jesus as a shipwright.'*

Tim could hardly contain his excitement. Wearyall Hill was within a mile of where he was sitting, and would turn the Jesus Trail into the short walk that he needed it to be! The pilgrims would only have to walk down the hill and along the road to the

ruins of Glastonbury Abbey, a suitable ending point
for the Trail.

He sat at the table, filling his book with notes, feeling
like a man who has solved an insoluble crime. All the
facts were here for somebody who was prepared to
look. In the Lady Chapel at nearby Pilton Church, he
learned, there was a banner showing Jesus in a red and
gold garment with Glastonbury Tor in the background.
What more did he need?

But there was more. Because when he opened the last
volume that Jill Hack had brought him he found out, to
his astonishment and delight, where this voyage began.
Joseph of Arimathea had sailed to Britain, he read, from
Tyre, a seaport in the Lebanon just south of Beirut and
still on today's maps.

When he had finished writing, he looked through
his wallet and found a £50 note that he didn't know
he had. As he went out he slid it discreetly into Jill
Hack's hand.

'Buy yourself something,' he said grandly. But she
pushed it straight back at him as if money would
contaminate her. 'I'm only doing my duty,' she said.

He walked out into the hot sunshine, marvelling at
how productive a spell in a library could be. He had
spent many hours in bars and pubs seeking inspiration
and ideas, but had to admit now that the only piercing
insight he had brought back to the real world from
these brainstorming sessions was that lager was regal
backwards.

8

A pinhead as hot as the sun could kill somebody standing ninety miles away. Janice Dawson relayed this information to about thirty pensioners in a church hall in the Polden Hills and wondered why, at this stage of their lives, they had developed a curiosity about the universe. Perhaps they were contemplating their next move, which they imagined was going to take them out of here and up there somewhere. 'At its centre the sun is fifteen million degrees Centigrade, or one hundred and fifty thousand times hotter than boiling water.'

As she watched them sitting in rapt attention on rows of uncomfortable wooden seats, she realised why it was that this group of senior citizens who were attached in some way to the local church had eagerly ordered her talk on the universe. They wanted company and in this hall they found it, both from the friends who were sitting alongside them and afterwards with Janice who always stayed behind to chat. They had already heard her other talks and had wanted her to come back and talk to them again, whatever the subject.

But 'The Universe' was her least favourite offering because of its infinite possibilities. She dreaded questions on quasars and pulsars and black holes. New discoveries with new telescopes produced a steady flow of extra information and it was an effort to keep up. Space probes were sending back fresh facts every day. They had even discovered a new mini-planet called Chiron, orbiting the sun between Saturn and Uranus. Janice Dawson wasn't sure that she needed it.

'Mercury whizzes round the sun in eighty-eight days, but Pluto takes two hundred and forty-seven years, which must make for a long winter,' she said. The old folk smiled at the idea of it. Behind her as usual she had pinned maps, charts and figures to the wall but it was unclear whether the eyesight of this elderly audience was taking them in. Her impression was that they would respond gratefully whatever she spoke about, so long as she stayed clear of hospices and crematoria. They were just glad that she had come to see them.

But today she had something else on her mind, and when they gathered round to thank her afterwards and coax a few more answers out of her on the subject of galaxies and the radio waves they emitted, she was keen to get away. Once she had pocketed the vicar's cheque, she made her apologies and slipped out of the door.

A small event the previous evening had started to

worry her, and she knew very well what she was going to find when she got home.

She had been writing her column for *The Clarion*, a five-hundred word ramble on the mysteries of planning permissions — who could build an extension on their house and who couldn't — and was speculating on the possibility of a relaxation in the rules, given the huge open spaces that confronted a visitor to Somerset and the increasing demand for homes.

Sam, as usual, picked up the pages and read what she had written. Normally he made a helpful suggestion; often he wondered aloud where she got her ideas from. But last night he had stared at her column and said nothing. He put the pages down and went over to turn on the television.

Perplexed by his reaction, Janice nevertheless typed on. Writing the column was not a job that delayed her for long, and there was dinner to get. The words poured out — Leo could rearrange them in a more felicitous order if he felt the need — and then she went to the kitchen. By the time that she returned with a pie, Sam was immersed in a game of football. He dragged himself to the table to eat.

'Who's Monica Titchmarsh?' he asked.

'Who?'

'You quote her in your column about planning appeals.'

'Oh yes. She's a County Councillor — didn't I say that in the column?'

'Yes, you did. But how do you know her?'

'She comes to The Lunch Club. A wonderful old dear.'

Sam Dawson didn't say anything else, but moved his chair slightly to take in the developments on the football field.

And when she drove home from her talk on the universe, Janice found what she expected. Sam — no longer in his suit, but wearing old jeans and a grubby short-sleeve shirt — was in the garden playing with a stick with Footprint. A deckchair on the lawn suggested that he had been home for some time. He threw the stick into the air and Footprint, jumping, caught it before it could hit the ground.

'Well, hallo,' said Janice, coming round the side of the house. 'Don't supermarkets require staff any more?'

'I expect they do,' said Sam, turning to face her. 'How did the talk go?'

'Very well,' said Janice, flopping into the deckchair as Footprint ran up to welcome her. 'They always go well. But what about you? Did they give you a half-day for good behaviour?'

'I've left,' said Sam. 'I don't work there any more.'

'What?' said Janice.

'It was very kind of you to fix me up with a job, Janice, awful though it was. But I'm not too keen on being manipulated, or moved round the board like a pawn. For some reason it didn't dawn on me that I had been dumped in a bloody supermarket purely as a result of your efforts.'

'You needed work.'

'Maybe I did, but you could have told me. If Sheridan Barrett hadn't mentioned Monica Titchmarsh the other day I'd have gone on believing that I'd got the job on my track record. It's humiliating, Janice. Am I so pathetic now that it takes my wife to get me a job? You made me look a fool.' He threw the stick a final time and turned to leave. 'I'm going out for a drink.'

Janice sat in the deckchair for a long time and didn't move. Such prolonged inactivity was quite uncharacteristic, but she was bruised by what he had said. Of course he was not supposed to hear about the Monica Titchmarsh connection, and his reaction, now that he had, was exactly what she would have expected. She felt crushed and defeated: it was an unfamiliar feeling. Her plans normally advanced smoothly, achieving their intended objectives; for one to unravel this quickly was a new and chastening experience.

When she got up it was only to go indoors and upstairs to lie on the bed. Footprint followed her and lay on the bedroom floor, patiently waiting for attention. Janice was usually all noise and movement, and this strange inertia confused him.

For a miserable half-hour she lay there, her eyes open, and then, strengthened by an unaccustomed rest, she began to brighten. Intuition, that belief that arrived without reason, told her that Tim Bonner's religious idea was going to make him a lot more money than a man could earn in a supermarket. It was a disparity that would have plunged her husband into an even deeper pit of gloom. The supermarket, an idea that had emerged during a conversation with Monica Titchmarsh, was the wrong place for Sam. What was needed was an idea like Tim's, an idea that would push him in the direction of real money.

She got off the bed and examined her face in the mirror. Her eyes looked sad as well as tired and she wasn't sure that anybody would put her age as young as thirty-eight today. Soon she would be looking neurotically for grey hairs. She took off her dress, creased now by the spell on the bed, and took a shower. The shower always invigorated her and often produced ideas – for her column or the nursery school or just for the everyday details of living. But no idea came.

She put on a tartan shirt and a pair of jeans and went downstairs to the kitchen to feed the dog.

'One good idea is all I want, Footprint,' she told him. 'Perhaps a sherry will help.'

She poured herself one and sat down doubtfully. If alcohol produced ideas, her husband should be a ferment of them. Soon he would be wandering in, morose, slightly drunk, and out of work again. She could feel the burden of his presence. To change the mood she picked up the small portable radio on the kitchen table and looked for some music. For the first time she noticed a sticker on the front that said *Made in Malaysia*.

The music took her away from her search for an idea, and she started to think back to her talk that afternoon to the pensioners in the hall. The most powerful impression that she had brought away with her was how grateful they were to have something that filled their empty lives.

She sipped her sherry. She had her idea.

Strolling down a country lane that had on either side fields filled with lambs, Tim Bonner was hauled back from a reverie about the pleasant surroundings in which he lived by a question from his daughter, who was walking thoughtfully beside him.

'Daddy,' she said, sucking one thumb, 'why doesn't Mummy like me?'

Some questions from Chloë, who possessed an endless supply of them, barely reached the first level of his consciousness. She could ask 'Why don't old women have long hair?' or 'Why do dogs chase cats?' and answers sprang from his lips without troubling his brain. But this question, which arrived with an accompanying expression of abject misery, brought his stroll to a halt.

'What?' he said.

'Mummy doesn't like me. Why doesn't she?'

His heart sank as he addressed this question because he could see why she had asked. Beverley's attitude to her daughter wasn't entirely normal. She didn't seem to have the time for her that another mother would have for an only daughter, and she didn't have the patience.

'She *does* love you,' he stalled.

'She hates me,' said Chloë emphatically. 'She wishes I wasn't there.' She was wearing a little sun hat which she now pulled over her face so that he couldn't see her. She said something else but the hat muffled the message.

'What?' said Time.

She took off the hat. 'Mummy doesn't like children,' she said.

He talked quickly. 'You mustn't say things like that, Chloë. Mummy loves you very much. But she's very busy earning money so that she can buy you food and toys and clothes. Sometimes she's so busy that she can't spend as much time with you as she would like to. I'm no help, you see. I'm not earning any money. It's all my fault, but it will be all right soon.'

The child seemed vaguely gratified by his acceptance of guilt, and he felt that he had achieved something.

'Why don't you work, Daddy?' she asked. 'We need money, don't we?'

One man and his dog marched in the opposite direction and the man slowed as if he would like to hear the answer to this. Tim acknowledged him, as people did round here, but denied him the pleasure of his reply. Instead, he asked her: 'Would you like a lemonade?'

Chloë's need for a lemonade turned out to be less urgent than his own for a pint of lager, but he persuaded her that it was a good idea by throwing in a promise of crisps. She followed him into the saloon bar of a roadside pub that he had seldom used.

To his surprise, Sam Dawson was slumped across a

seat in the corner in what looked like a state of nervous prostration.

'What are you doing in here?' Tim asked. 'Are you hiding from me?'

'Needed a little time to think,' Sam said.

'And then I bust in?'

'Seems like it,' said Sam, sitting up. 'Hallo, Chloë.'

Chloe eyed him warily but didn't respond. Tim hurried off to get the lemonade and the crisps that would keep her happy for perhaps ten minutes, and then went back for two pints of lager.

'This necessity to think,' he said, when all needs were catered for, 'what's all that about?'

'I gave up the job today,' Sam told him. 'I'm out of work and available for midweek golf.'

'Was that wise?' asked Tim. 'Golf is golf, but wages are wages.'

Sam picked up the new pint and drank copiously. 'It turns out I only got the job because Janice fixed it behind my back. The mysterious letter I received inviting me to apply had been arranged by her.'

'The bitch,' said Tim. 'The scheming cow.'

'Steady on,' said Sam. 'That's my wife you're talking about.'

'Okay, you have a pop at her first and I'll come in behind you.'

'Am I so pathetic that I need my wife to get me a job, Tim?'

'Well,' said Tim, thinking carefully, 'how many jobs have you got lately without her help?'

'None.'

'Seems to wrap the question up,' Tim decided judi-cially, but Sam needed expressive gestures from both hands to convey adequately the depth of his indigna-tion.

'I feel manipulated, controlled, dominated.'

'Married is another word,' said Tim. 'You don't think you've been a little impetuous here? What the hell does it matter who got you the job?'

'It's not the getting of the job,' said Sam, picking up his drink again. 'It's the furtive machinations in the background that I wasn't supposed to know about. A man could be made to look a damn fool.' He emptied the glass without moving it from his lips. 'One more?'

'Make it quick. I'm in charge of a small person here.'

Sam Dawson shuffled over to the counter. He had already drunk more than his usual allocation and felt mildly drunk. This pleased him. It represented an escape from the slavery of the supermarket: he was free again.

Standing at the bar and waiting to be served, he considered the sad story of his life and, helped by the drink, imagined how different it might have been. Service was a long time coming and he was able to construct a much more attractive alternative life story in compelling detail. After expulsion from a minor public school for running a drugs ring, he could have joined the Army and been sent to Northern Ireland to wage war on terrorism. Uncertain of his allegiances, he could have vanished into the Irish mist with a green-eyed nymphomaniac and spent a blissful summer on the shores of Donegal Bay. Overtaken by sexual exhaustion, he could have worked his way on to some commercial vessel and wound up in one of the exciting cities on America's east coast. In Boston or Philadelphia he might easily have found work as a disc jockey who spent his nights in smoky clubs drinking Tennessee sour mash bourbon, and resisting or succumbing to the flagrant attractions of oil heiresses or rising starlets who were enraptured by his accent, now seductively enhanced by his Irish exile. The jump from here to the beau monde was easy to imagine. Seductions and propositions in elegant salons, friendships with the famous, and introductions to men who knew how the money moved, would have transformed him into a mysterious Gatsby-like figure who was sought out and envied. Exclusive parties, cultural diversions, financial adventures, bacchanalian evenings and sexual trysts with senators' wives would all have been his. And then, rich and sated, he could have flown home at thirty, a quite different man.

He reached for the new drinks and belched like a camel. The story was someone else's.

'I've led a hamster-wheel existence,' he announced when he returned with the lager. 'It could all have been so different, but today I am a free man.'

'And about to become a full-time piss artist, by the look of it,' Tim said. 'You've got the restless energy of a terrapin, old man. Wealth does not lie that way.'

'Well, you're not exactly off to the office at half-past seven every morning. When are you proposing to give up all this rest and recreation?'

Tim drank his lager and looked at his daughter who was beginning to exhibit every sign of restlessness. Two beer mats were already shredded. 'Tomorrow,' he said. 'I'm going to walk in the footsteps of Jesus. Care to join me?'

'I might do that,' said Sam, 'if I'm capable of walking tomorrow. I can see that now Beverley is behind this scheme you're really motivated.'

'All I've got to do now is motivate the bank manager. How do you think he'll react if I ask him to back the Jesus Trail?'

'Cynically,' said Sam. 'God and Mammon never did get on.'

Tim sat back and lit a cigarette. 'Actually I'm accumulating some quite impressive evidence that ought to convince people like bank managers. Why, for instance, was Glastonbury Abbey the first Christian sanctuary in the British Isles, if not Europe, if it wasn't because Jesus came here?'

But Sam had another idea. 'If Beverley's so hot on the project now, perhaps she's got some money to fund it.'

'She's got more than me, that's for sure, but all that's going to change when the devout multitudes start flying in with their dollars and pesos and gourdes and zloties. This little pilgrimage is going to be big, big, big.'

Sam drank his lager and smiled. Tim made it sound

as if what Jesus had lacked until now was a man with Tim's grasp of publicity and promotion, an impression that was reinforced when he said: 'I'm going to do for Jesus what Colonel Parker did for Elvis Presley.'

'God'll be tickled,' said Sam. 'A sainthood in the new millennium Honours List at the very least, I should think.'

Tim exhaled cigarette smoke in a very relaxed way. 'You still don't take it seriously, do you Sam?'

'The last I heard, you didn't even believe in God.'

'What's God got to do with it? I believe in Jesus. He was a very remarkable man. Dead at thirty-three and the most famous person ever to set foot on this earth. This will be a celebration of His life.'

'But you don't believe He's up there, watching your crafty manoeuvres?'

'Unfortunately not. But I'm going to meet a lot of people who do, and that's what counts.'

He finished his lager and beamed contentedly at Sam, as if all financial problems were now in the past and the supreme idea of his life, which would banish further tribulation, had definitely arrived.

'Have you heard of Wearyall Hill?' he asked, tapping cigarette ash. 'You drive past it every week.'

'Which hill is that?'

'It runs alongside the Street road from Glastonbury, opposite the sheepskin tannery. There are usually a few cows gathered on it.'

'I know it. What about it?'

Tim leaned forward in his seat, as if he didn't want

to be overheard. 'That's where Jesus landed. The Levels were underwater then – a fact that you and I completely overlooked.'

'Who says that's where He landed?'

'It's in books,' said Tim. 'It's perfect. It means the Jesus Trail would be no more than half a mile. Down the hill, along the road and into the grounds of the Abbey.'

'Tim, have you heard of ethics?'

'Yes, it's between Kent and Thuffolk. Are you coming up the hill with me tomorrow or what?'

'I'll try,' said Sam. 'I'll certainly try.'

When Tim and Chloë had gone he had another pint, finding no good reason not to, except that with every drink he slid reluctantly towards the conclusion that his departure from the supermarket had perhaps been a little hasty. He was too old for the reckless gesture and the impulsive dash for freedom. He no longer had the options of a younger man. As Tim had said, golf is golf, but wages are wages. It was a depressing truth that confined him to the hamster-wheel. His confidence was misplaced, anyway. Like many insecure men, he had always worked more hours than he had to, as if an ostensible devotion to duty could somehow compensate for his failure to become genuinely involved.

He walked home with difficulty, discovering an involuntary tendency to move to his left, like a supermarket trolley with a faulty wheel. Collisions with a bus stop and two dustbins helped to concentrate his mind and eventually he made it.

A big surprise awaited him. Janice was drunk, too!

She sat at the kitchen table with a champagne bottle that was already half-empty.

'Hallo, lover,' she said, far too loudly. 'Have I got news for you!'

The sight of his wife under the influence sobered him a little. Janice hardly drank at all, having far too many other things to do. He reached the table and sat down heavily beside her.

'What's going on?' he asked.

'Problem solved,' said Janice, pouring champagne into an empty glass for him. 'You're going to be rich.'

'I am?' said Sam.

'That's why I'm celebrating.'

Drunk as he was, Sam could see that his wife had delivered this last word without the third letter, but slurred speech from Janice was such a novelty that he decided not to mention it, particularly as his own attempts at pronunciation were unlikely to be more successful.

'Cheers,' he said and drank some champagne.

'I sat down and thought, Sam doesn't want to work in a supermarket. Fair enough. You don't get rich working in a supermarket. So I had a drink and a think.'

'A think?' said Sam.

'And a drink. Cooking sherry, actually. I didn't open the champagne until after I'd had the idea. I needed a drink to celebrate then.'

'It was a fruitful think?'

'Very,' said Janice. 'I don't usually have time to think.' She refilled both their glasses and discovered to her disappointment that this emptied the bottle. 'No matter. We'll soon be buying by the flagon, or is it the jeroboam?'

Sam sipped the champagne and realised that there was no immediate prospect of dinner. His wife had been thinking, not cooking. They were on a different schedule this evening and he knew how champagne affected his wife and where it would lead.

'So,' he said, 'what's the big idea?'

Janice leaned forward, both hands flat on the table. 'In the old days, Britain used to make things. Cars, motor-bikes, television sets, cameras. You bought something in a shop and it said *Made in Britain* on it.'

'Yes,' said Sam. The drink, as usual, was beginning to make him sleepy and he struggled to tether a mind that was already beginning to stray.

'Well,' said Janice, 'that doesn't happen today. It says *Made in Taiwan* or *Made in Korea*. It says *Made in Malaysia* on that radio there. It's made in China, made in Thailand, made in Poland, made in Hong Kong, made in bloody Borneo. The footballs the kids play with are made in Pakistan by other kids. What happened to Britain? Are we all watching *Neighbours*?'

'I think the problem,' said Sam, staring at his empty glass, 'is cheap labour.'

'Right,' said Janice.

'We don't have any.'

'Wrong,' said Janice. 'We have plenty of cheap

labour in this country just waiting for somebody to mobilise it. And that somebody is going to be you.'

'Is this your idea?' Sam asked, puzzled.

Janice stood up gracefully and held out both hands to him.

'It is, but it's too important to discuss when we're drunk. Champagne always gives me other ideas, anyway.'

He got up quickly at this news. He was too drunk for a complicated discussion himself and Janice's new idea interested him more than her first one. He took her hands.

'Are you going to have your way with me?' he asked. 'I didn't want dinner anyway.'

9

Tim Bonner stood on Wearyall Hill and tried to imagine the moment a couple of thousand years ago when Jesus arrived in a boat. Was it summer or winter? Day or night? Was journey's end greeted with bright sunshine, or a hostile wind off the marshes? Were Somerset's famous apples waiting to be plucked by the young visitor? Did people gather round suspiciously at this strange arrival of foreigners?

Tim Bonner wished that he had the answer to some of these questions because soon, in the exalted role of pilot and guide, shepherd and chaperon, he would be surrounded by hundreds of cash-paying customers who were accustomed to certainties and would not be happy to be fobbed off with the conjecture and guesswork of which he was capable.

'It was a brilliantly sunny day when the small boat that carried Joseph of Arimathea and the Boy Jesus reached landfall on Wearyall Hill,' he tried. 'They had travelled for two weeks, three weeks, four weeks

– how long would it have taken them to sail here from the Mediterranean?'

Sam Dawson was sitting on the grass in the sun. The excesses of the previous day had turned his legs to sponge.

'Six weeks,' he said. 'Be positive. Who can contradict you?'

'Exactly. I'm a historian; I've studied the period. People believe historians. When they tell you that the slaves revolted in Sicily in 104BC, nobody says "No, they didn't" or "Pull the other one, you plonker".'

'Quite so,' said Sam. 'Please proceed.'

'They had been travelling for six weeks and the Bay of Biscay had been particularly rough, with twelve-foot waves and a continuous swell.'

'I'd leave the Bay of Biscay out of it if I were you,' said Sam. 'It had another name then.'

'I think it was called the Roman Sinus Aquitanicus, but we know it as the Bay of Biscay.'

'It doesn't sound right. I'd skirt over the journey or you'll start chatting about their duty-frees. Start the story here.'

'The apples were red on the trees and the young Jesus, like all small boys, was hungry.'

'That's the stuff,' said Sam.

From the top of the hill they could see Glastonbury Tor across an expanse of fields that were filled with cows. The hill, too, long and straggling and shaped like a cat's back, had recently accommodated them: cowpats were everywhere. From the road it hadn't seemed like much of a hill, but from the top they could see for miles. To the north they looked down on an industrial estate and a petrol station; to the west were the flat Somerset Levels, the green fields that had been under water when Jesus arrived. Much later the Romans had established vineyards on the southern slopes of the hill, but there was nothing growing here today except for the Glastonbury Thorn surrounded by protective railing. The legend was that when Joseph of Arimathea arrived with his companions he thrust his staff into the ground and it took root. A flowering thorn tree grew and still blossomed once a year. There were other explanations for the Glastonbury Thorn, but this was the one that Tim would be promoting. The thorn was not native to Britain, but was a Levantine variety from Syria, a fact that was definitely in his favour.

Looking down towards Glastonbury they could see the ruins of the Abbey, the stark remains of one of the greatest monasteries of medieval England. The legend here was that Joseph and the Boy Jesus built the first church of wattle and daub in honour of the Virgin Mary on the site of the later Lady Chapel, making Glastonbury the cradle of Christianity in England and Europe.

Tim felt that he was not short of material that would legitimise his Trail. He could construct a most persuasive talk from what he knew already, and there were more books that he had yet to read.

'What we have to work out now,' he said, 'is

the Trail itself. How far do you think the Abbey ruins are?'

'As you thought, no more than half a mile,' said Sam, upright now and gazing down the hill.

'Let's walk there.'

At the bottom of the hill was a stile and a chained gate. They climbed over the stile and found themselves on a steep narrow road that led down to the town. The homes on either side were cheap and unattractive. Many had been converted into flats.

At the bottom of the hill they turned left into Fisher's Hill which led quite quickly into Magdalene Street in the town where the entrance to the Abbey ruins was. The buildings in the street looked sadly neglected, as if not a lot had happened here since the Big Visit. Tim liked this: it gave the Trail an authenticity which would have been destroyed by the huge new buildings that had ruined other towns. Down here in Glastonbury, among the earth mysteries and the ancient cults, the myths and the legends and the ley lines, people were so relaxed that Tim wondered whether some of them had ever seen a big new building. The notices in some shop windows said: *Open Around Noon.*

It cost two pounds to enter the Abbey grounds, a fee that Tim saw as an expense to set against future profits.

'If you're going to arrive here with two hundred singing pilgrims every day I should negotiate a special rate,' said Sam. 'A penny saved is a penny earned.'

'I thought the same thing myself,' said Tim. 'There's no point in throwing it about.' He stopped and looked round. 'So that's the way Jesus came. Down the hill, down Fisher's Hill, along Magdalene Street and into the grounds where the Abbey would be built.'

'Are you sure?'

'Would I lie to you?'

They went in. The remains of the Abbey and its outbuildings were scattered over 36 acres of grounds: chapels, halls, kitchens and a refectory. The Abbot's Kitchen was the best preserved, a square building with fireplaces and chimneys. According to a notice inside, the meals that were served here consisted of plain food, plenty of bread and a pint of wine.

'Drunk monk,' said Sam.

'What else did they have?' asked Tim.

They walked across the neatly kept grass from which jutted the strange brown remnants of old buildings. The south side of the Lady Chapel still stood, with ornamental geometrical patterns of foliage and tendrils. The Abbey barn, used to store grain, was intact.

The end of the monastery, they gathered, was a violent affair. The last Abbot, a frail old man, was dragged up the Tor and beheaded on the orders of Henry VIII. His quartered body was subsequently displayed in Bridgwater, Ilchester, Bath and Wells.

'Plenty of room here for a final farewell to my clients,' said Tim. 'Cup of tea and a cake, then I bung them back on their coaches.'

'After you've flogged them a few sacred memen-toes. Why don't you sell little boxes of earth from Wearyall Hill?'

'Sam, I think you're beginning to get the hang of this. I may take you on the pay-roll.'

'No need,' said Sam. 'My wife has plans for me. She's going to make me rich, or so she was hinting last night when the drink overtook her.'

'Drink? Janice?'

'She was celebrating this idea she's had. Unfortu-nately she celebrated so much she forgot to tell me what it was.'

They walked out into the street.

'My God,' said Tim. 'What a miserable, bloodthirsty bunch of sadistic lunatics they were in those days. The past is another world, isn't it?'

'The present isn't too wonderful,' Sam remarked.

'Ah, but the future is bright. For you, too, if Janice is to be relied upon when she's full of liquor. Shall we have a drop ourselves to celebrate this impending wealth?'

'Lead me to it,' said Sam gratefully.

Somerset today, sliced off from its largest city, Bath, by the capricious boundary changes of a tarnished Tory government, was a little-known rural county that was tentatively seeking to replace the lost prosperity of its traditional industries by a flirtation with tourism. Quaint charms were being deployed to attract visitors with money.

To this extent, thought Sam Dawson as he walked home in the sun — he had declined a lift, he had time to kill — Tim Bonner was riding a wave by tapping into the local thirst for legend. Jesus at Glastonbury had more promising financial possibilities than the Witch of Wookey, the Beast of Exmoor or the Flying Dragon of Norton Fitzwarren, and the appeal reached beyond Somerset, beyond Britain, beyond Europe.

Sam, on the other hand, was at a disadvantage in being here. Cheaper homes were balanced by lower wages, even if you could find a job. Not that he had made the most of his situation when he lived in a more prosperous part of the country. Much of what he saw among his neighbours then was a mystery to him. The fastidious commuters who never missed the 6.59; the thrusting executives with their six-figure salaries and share options; the Range-Rovers and Mercedes that sprouted suddenly in other people's driveways — all belonged to another world that he never really understood. He felt curiosity, not envy, when he met people who had money. Where on earth had they got it from?

He took off his shirt and walked on in the simmering heat. He had never been so brown, which he saw as testimony to his idle summer. When he reached the Levels he stopped to look for the unusual birds which visited here. It was one of the most popular destinations in the country for them. In the summer they flew in to breed from Africa, and in the winter they flocked here from as far away as the Arctic. Sam never saw the black-tailed godwits or the Bewick's swans, and he was still looking for the Redshank and the snipe, but he had grown accustomed to the herons, buzzards and kestrels and enjoyed watching them, except on the sad occasion when he had seen a buzzard snatch a skylark in midair.

A car pulled up behind him.

'Want a lift, sir?'

It was Janice, fresh from casting precious gems of knowledge about some arcane subject before a presumably grateful audience of housewives at Wedmore.

'I'm not used to picking up half-naked men in the country, but I thought I'd make an exception in your case.'

She seemed very perky, Sam thought as he put on his shirt. Perhaps they should make love more often. But when he recalled how weak and hungover he had felt that morning he wasn't sure that this was one of his best ideas.

'How was the talk?' he asked.

'The talk was fine. How was the walk?'

'It's all there. That bastard is going to make a lot of money. He's even going to sell boxes of earth from Wearyall Hill.'

'Brilliant,' said Janice. 'Why can't you have ideas like that?'

'It was my idea, actually.'

'There's hope for you yet, darling. Hope for us. I see a big house in the country with conservatory, tennis courts and swimming pool. I see a garage for four cars. I see an orchard and a stable block.'

'You have astonishing eyesight.'

'You can always sell and move down. What we want to do is buy and move up.' She braked for a herd of cows and smiled at him. 'Over dinner tonight I want your undivided attention.'

But once they were home there were other things to do. Footprint needed a walk, Sam needed a shower, and Janice had enough work preparing dinner in the kitchen. It was roast chicken with roast potatoes and so it was two hours later that they sat down in the dining room and were finally able to talk without interruption.

'Tim might make money from his Jesus Trail, but you can make more,' Janice announced when she had filled her glass with Evian water. 'Much more.'

'Is this it?' asked Sam. 'Is this the idea?' He refilled his own glass with red wine, and resolved to concentrate.

'This is it,' said Janice. 'See what you think.' She took a sip of water and began to talk, watching Sam for his reaction. 'The other day I gave a talk to thirty pensioners in a church hall. They were lovely people and so pleased to have someone come to see them. I don't even know whether they were interested in the talk. It was the idea of someone who had the time to visit them and fill one of many blank hours in their lives that pleased them. How many pensioners are there in Britain? Six million? The vast majority aren't in their nineties, needing help with every daily task. They're alert and capable people in their sixties and seventies who once held good jobs. They've got knowledge and talents, and they're on the scrapheap. They're frustrated, and many of them are lonely. Invite them out to a warm hall where they're given a meal and the company of other people and they'll turn out in droves. And there's another thing. Many of them are short of money. Pension funds that were started years ago have been killed by inflation, and many of them don't have pension funds anyway. So this was my idea. Supposing these people were given something to do? The warm hall, the meal, the company. They'd be delighted. You'd pay them something, of course, but money wouldn't be why they were there. They'd be flattered and delighted that somebody thought they were still useful, and if they got a bit of pocket money at the end of it that would be a bonus. What do you think of it so far?'

It still surprised Sam that he had such a serious wife. The words poured out of her but they were never going to be about cosmetics or shopping or the merits of seaweed as a face-pack. Her eye was eternally fixed on more important matters.

'Okay so far,' he said. 'We've got six million pensioners sitting in halls all over Britain. What are they doing?'

Janice had discarded the dress that she wore for her talk that afternoon and reverted to the jeans and denim shirt that she was happier in at home. It gave her a businesslike air, an almost masculine drive, and she hammered home her points as if she was dealing with an obtuse pupil. Sam felt as if he was back in the classroom himself, struggling to assimilate the complex details of an exercise that he had to master.

'They could be doing anything,' Janice said, with a gesture which indicated limitless possibilities. 'They could be stuffing and sewing teddy bears, making poppies for Poppy Day, putting toys together, or plastic goods that need screwing up and bolting. They could make circuit boards, or the framework that houses electronic equipment. They could paint toy soldiers or any other dolls. They could sew on buttons, put in screws, fill envelopes or pack things. What about fan heaters and portable radios? Somebody has to assemble them and it's not difficult. We're talking about jobs that a thousand Chinese children do in a factory for a bowl of rice, but with our system you don't have to pay to bring the end product halfway round the world. You need to find the labour-intensive industries, where the labour cost is the major cost. Tell firms that you can get their costs down and increase their productivity which is lagging behind overseas rivals, so I read. Find out who the suppliers are who make the components. The work has to be straightforward, but not too boring. Make the old feel productive! All that knowledge and expertise being wasted!'

'I think I should be taking notes,' said Sam, ruefully contemplating the scale of organisation that his wife was envisaging. It seemed to him then that it would take at least three government departments to make the arrangements that Janice's plan required. 'Have you any ideas how I should set about this?' he asked. 'It seems a little — well, ambitious.'

'Mailshots, telephone calls, personal visits,' Janice rapped out. 'Take the Nissan. I'll hire a runaround. After you've talked to the firms, you need to contact the Parish Councils who run all those empty village halls, and whatever the senior citizens' organisation is. When it's up and running you could have a roving nurse who would visit the old folk in the halls where they are working. You could organise coach trips for days off. And what you'd do quite early on is hire several of the younger pensioners as your assistants who would supervise the operation in their area. Delegate, Sam. In the end the whole thing would be making you money without you doing very much. Just like a conventional millionaire!'

Sam sat back and tried to picture the scheme that his wife had devised. It probably seemed an exercise of breathtaking simplicity for a woman who could handle four or five jobs at once while thinking about something else. To Sam it appeared a nightmare of organisation and negotiation that was quite outside anything that he had experienced in his years at work where he had never had to concentrate on more than one thing at a time and sometimes not even that.

His wife looked at his disconsolate face.

'Do you sincerely want to be rich, Sam, as you told me all those years ago? Because the men who are didn't get that way by sitting down with the sort of expression you've got on your face at the moment. They got up and got cracking. They used energy and initiative. But if you think it's all beyond you, please say so.'

Sam Dawson reacted with indignation. He recognised a last chance when he saw it, and he had been idle, he knew, for too long.

'Of course it's not beyond me,' he said. 'I'll start tomorrow.'

A buoyant atmosphere of achievement and success prevailed in the back room of the hotel at the next meeting of The Lunch Club when the guests listened with quiet satisfaction to the stories of Janice and Beverley.

'We've kick-started the lazy sods,' Beverley announced with pride. 'Tim is actually putting a lot of hours into his little project.'

Janice, who had arrived in a very old Volkswagen Polo, hired cheaply for a month while Sam travelled the country in the Nissan, said: 'My idea might not be one of the great ones, like fish and chips, thermal vests or artificial hip joints, but Sam has really taken to it.'

It was true. Galvanised into furious activity by the mordant taunts of his wife, he had reacted with unexpected determination to her teasing. He had so far phoned her from Cardiff, Birmingham, Nottingham, Liverpool and Hull, and was still, at the last call, heading north for Middlesbrough, Sunderland and places in Scotland that he had never seen. It wasn't entirely clear what these journeys were achieving — phone calls to Janice were apt to transform the caller into the listener — but that Sam was putting a lot of energy into the venture was undeniable.

'It's a remarkable thing,' said Monica Titchmarsh, tentatively dissecting a meat pie. 'I thought you had two lost causes on your hands and suddenly they've sprung to life.'

'"Life" might be an exaggeration,' Beverley said. 'But they're moving around a bit like tortoises coming out of hibernation.'

Laura Morton, flamboyant again today in a candy-pink satin shirt and Chinese jacket, waved an admonitory finger at Beverley when she said this.

'You mustn't be so dismissive, Beverley. I'm very impressed with what your men are doing. Perhaps we've been too harsh on them. I'm beginning to think that feminism has knocked an awful lot out of men. They used to run things, then they were told that they didn't, so now they don't. Who can blame them?'

Beverley didn't want to hear this. 'I suppose a few thousand years ago when we all lived in caves they were useful for going out and slaying some creature for supper. But today? I work and earn money. I fetch the food from the supermarket. I even cook it. Increasingly I wonder whether we need men at all.'

But Laura Morton's line had softened appreciably on hearing about the efforts of Tim and Sam. 'I know women say that,' she said. 'They ask what men are for. Well, they're not for anything. They're just here without having been consulted like the rest of us, trying to enjoy their lives.'

'Well, I've married three of the bastards,' cried Gemma Swan in a high-pitched voice that fixed everybody's attention. She was appalled at what she was hearing. 'In my opinion they're unfeeling, lazy, selfish, frivolous, destructive, hostile, troublesome, disorganised, dogmatic and self-indulgent.'

'The question is, my dear,' said Monica Titchmarsh, who was more accustomed to rancorous debate than the others, 'if your opinion of them is so low, how did you come to marry three of them?'

'Obviously I was sustained by an optimism you rarely see outside a madhouse,' Gemma Swan admitted. 'But I've learned my lesson now, and my sympathies are entirely with Beverley. I shan't be marrying again. I agree with Roseanne Barr. The fastest way to a man's heart is through his chest.'

'I'm not sure optimism comes into it,' said Laura Morton. 'If your first husband was a serial adulterer, your second a homicidal maniac and your third an impotent drunk, one has to consider the possibility that you're not a very good judge of people.'

'But they were none of those things when I met and

married them,' Gemma Swan protested. 'How was I to know?'

'The signs are always there, waiting for you to recognise them,' said Monica Titchmarsh. 'It's why we have female intuition. On the other hand, I have to agree that the ideal mate we all dreamed about is as rare as a ballet dancer's wife.'

'How's Gerry?' asked Beverley. 'Broken his silence yet?'

'No, he's still on strike,' said Monica Titchmarsh.

Listening to this, Janice Dawson began to wonder whether she had the makings of a column here. She doubted whether anywhere else in the region had a secret feminist cell dispensing such bile and vitriolic abuse at half the population. It could arouse interest and provoke letters, two gratifying developments the column seldom produced.

But then she thought of Sam, haring round the country in pursuit of a dream, and began to feel guilty about the company she was keeping and the thoughts she was hearing expressed. After the sudden explosion of energy that had driven him halfway across Britain, Sam deserved better than this behind-the-scenes carping, let alone newspaper coverage of it. She addressed more pertinent matters.

'Monica, I want you to do me a favour,' she said. 'You must have in the Council offices a register of all the pensioners' organisations and a list of all the village halls in the county and their caretakers.'

'The information is there somewhere,' said Monica Titchmarsh. 'Do you want it?'

'I do,' said Janice. 'Sam will need some help. He's only a man, poor bastard.'

10

Climbing into his second-hand two-door Honda Prelude, Tim Bonner tried to gauge what degree of affability and bonhomie it would be necessary for him to drag from the shadowy recesses of his personality to win over the dour businessmen he was obliged to confront this morning. None of them, he knew, would be remotely cheerful. Battered by the recession and alarmed at the collapse in their profits, they would offer him the sort of welcome that you normally received from a funeral director.

In the notebook in his briefcase which lay alongside him on the front seat, he had a succession of appointments that would take him three days to complete and had taken him five days on the phone to arrange. Hotel managers came first, followed by the spiky gentlemen who owned the district's coach firms. After that he had to talk to the travel firms if only to pick their brains, the Tourist Office and the dedicated folk who were in charge of what was left of Glastonbury Abbey.

He was borne along on a tide of optimism that was greatly reinforced when he reminded himself that he was bringing good news to these unfortunate people in the shape of money and regular business. They should throw themselves at his feet (the saviour who produced customers in a recession), ply him with drinks and offer him remunerative seats on their boards.

But the chief reaction at his first meeting was a mistrustful perplexity.

'Jesus in Somerset?' said Mr Proctor, pulling with finger and thumb at a nose of purest magenta. 'It's the first I've heard of it.'

'Neverthless,' Tim affirmed steadily, 'the evidence is there.'

Mr Proctor owned a splendid hotel in the country with thirty bedrooms, twenty acres and half a dozen tennis courts. He was fat and forty but his hotel had a good reputation, and Tim didn't intend to get sidetracked into a debate about the Jesus Trail which was no concern of Mr Proctor's, who abandoned his nose now and said: 'It's a good angle.'

Alarmed again, Tim Bonner felt that he had to stamp right away on the implication that there was something unethical in what he proposed, and on the other man's smiling assumption that they were colluding in a disreputable hoax.

'He landed on Wearyall Hill, Mr Proctor,' he said with a conviction that he was beginning to feel himself. 'It's all in the library. But what I want to talk to you about is rooms and discounts. I plan to fill your hotel many times, over the next few months. You'll be given plenty of notice of the bookings so it won't disrupt any you already have. It's going to be boom-time for hotels round here — or, at any rate, those who come up with the right price.'

'I see,' said Mr Proctor. 'And who would these people be?'

'Foreigners, mostly. Religious, obviously. And therefore well-behaved and unlikely to trash your excellent hotel.'

'And what sort of discount did you have in mind?'

'Fifty per cent,' said Tim.

'In this climate I might just accept that,' said Mr Proctor gloomily.

Driving to his next appointment, Tim felt a twinge of irritation that the first reaction of his first business collaborator had been a scarcely concealed scepticism. Faced by today's harsh and distasteful realities, there seemed to be a growing minority who clung desperately to convictions that were self-evidently loopy. Some thought they were going to win the lottery, others believed in poltergeists or telepathy or embraced mystical beliefs that suggested mental instability. In Glastonbury, a notorious centre for far-fetched conceptions, the University of Avalon offered courses in magical herbalism, dowsing, Tarot and runes. There should be no difficulty in finding an audience that would accept the yarn that Tim was meticulously assembling, and the last thing he wanted was crude cynicism from an associate.

Fortunately his second call, to the manager of a large hotel in the town that belonged to a national chain, produced a committed Christian who was familiar with the story of Wearyall Hill.

'Marvellous idea, Mr Bonner,' said Mr Keating. 'A great help to the church and, dare I say, the tourist industry.'

Contrary to Sam's observation, God and Mammon sat side by side in Mr Keating's office. A crucifix on the wall was accompanied by a chart showing the top saving rates with building societies, national savings accounts, Tessa accounts, guaranteed income bonds and cash unit trusts. He said: 'I'm interested in money, and I'd love to do business with you.'

Mr Keating was a small man with a small moustache and a permanent smile that was in stark contrast to the more sombre expression of Mr Proctor. Tim wondered whether this was because Mr Keating was an employee and not the owner with his life savings invested in a creaking business, or whether it was his faith that made him appear so cheerful. Either way, the desire to do business was mutual – Mr Keating's hotel had more than a hundred bedrooms.

He sat at a small green desk beneath the crucifix and asked: 'What's the turn-round time?'

Tim Bonner, drastically self-prepared for every conceivable question, found himself at a loss here. 'The what?' he asked.

'How long would they stay?'

'Ah. Two nights, three days. They'd be brought

here on day one, we'd do the walk on day two, and they'd fly home on day three. But by day three, I hope, more would be flying in, so the demand for bedrooms would be continuous.'

'Of course, not all would be flying in. You'd have pilgrims who live in Britain?'

'I certainly hope so, and they'd need hotels as well. I've yet to find out. Frankly, Mr Keating, my first job is to get the accommodation and transport in place and work out my costs.'

'Naturally,' said Mr Keating. 'Well, I can promise you a considerable discount. I might even come on the walk myself.'

'I can promise *you* a considerable discount,' Tim assured him.

His burgeoning optimism was only slightly dented by his first encounter with the owner of a coach firm who raised a problem that he had completely overlooked. The coach-firm owner was called Rowland and he sat in a grimy office at the back of a hanger-like building that must have held at least forty coaches which were not, at this moment, being used. His attitude to Tim's proposal was quiet amusement.

'The Jesus Trail, eh?' he said, in a rich Somerset accent. He had in his time ferried pop fans, football hooligans, Women's Institutes, schoolchildren, sports teams, Masonic lodges, pub landlords, concert-goers, opera lovers and theatre addicts, but pilgrims were something new. 'What'll they do?' he asked. 'Sit in the back singing hymns?'

'They'll be very well behaved, that's for sure,' said Tim.

Mr Rowland was a young man and Tim imagined that there was a semi-retired father somewhere in the background. 'Coaches don't come cheap,' he said. 'There are a lot of ancillary expenses.'

'Like petrol,' said Tim.

'And the rest. All you'd want is for us to go round the hotels, pick them up and take them to the Hill, then pick them up from the Abbey and take them back to the hotels?'

'That's it,' said Tim. 'At a very competitive rate because of all the business I'm going to bring you.'

'You're overlooking something,' said Mr Rowland.

'What's that?'

'How do these poor bastards get from Heathrow to Glastonbury? It's not exactly a straightforward journey, and if you're seventy-five and you've just flown in from Seattle or Auckland it's a lot to ask.'

'You're right,' said Tim, crestfallen. 'I had overlooked that.'

'No problem. We could cover the airport for you. If we organise it right, we'd pick one lot up as we drop one lot off.'

'The trouble is they're going to arrive at different times.'

'We could cut down the waiting time by doing two or three pick-ups a day.'

'I like what you're saying, Mr Rowland, but will I like what you're charging?'

Mr Rowland consulted a Sharp pocket calculator on his desk. 'You might do,' he said. 'I've no idea what figures you have in mind.' He punched buttons and looked at the results. 'Here's the deal, Mr Bonner. Take it or leave it. We'd charge you forty quid a person. That takes in everything from Heathrow to the hotels, the hill and the Abbey.'

Tim Bonner, deprived of a pocket calculator, did sums in his head. He could see that Mr Rowland would be earning £1,600 for each forty-seater coach, but what would Tim be making? He took a notebook and pen from his briefcase and wrote down some figures – more to impress Mr Rowland than to satisfy any need of his own.

The sums were quite clear. If he charged each pilgrim £100, and paid the hotels £20 for each of the two nights and Mr Rowland the £40 he wanted, he would have £20 for himself from each devout customer. If he had fifty pilgrims a week, he would make £1000. If he had five hundred, he would make £10,000. If he had . . .

'Let's shake hands on that, Mr Rowland,' he said.

Beverley's shop was empty. She sat at the back in a gaudy yellow shirt and jeans, reading a book. Tim found a chair and sat down too.

'Why does Chloë think you don't like her?' he asked.

They were always able to have conversations in the shop that they never could at home with Chloë's constant presence. When Beverley put down her book and looked up, he thought it was a long time since he had seen her look really happy.

'Does Chloë say that?' she asked.

'That's what she told me. She said you hated her.'

Beverley's expression transmitted nothing more than impatience. 'You know what children are. They'll say anything to get attention.'

'She went on to say that you hate children, not just her.'

Beverley's shift this time was towards the evasive. 'And you now take the opinion of a three-year-old as being cast-iron fact, do you? Come on, Tim, she's a baby.'

'Out of the mouths of babes and sucklings.'

'For an atheist, you're showing a remarkable command of the Bible these days. How did it go?'

'It went very well. I've still got a lot of people to see, but the hotel and coach costs fit in perfectly. I think we could make a lot of money.'

Beverley stood up and turned on a kettle at the back of the shop. 'Your next job will be the most difficult. Tea?'

He nodded. 'What job is that?'

'Finding the customers.'

The optimism that had been building up inside him drained a little when Beverley said that. It was a problem that had been worrying Tim, and the worry mingled now with a frustration at the way she had managed to change the subject.

'Any ideas?' he asked hopefully. After all, she had urged him to embark on this venture and effectively staunched his doubts with alluring talk of banknotes. Let her pick up the ball and run with it.

'Melissa's brother,' said Beverley, handing him a mug of tea.

'Melissa, your single-parent assistant?'

'Has a brother. Who works for an advertising agency in Sloane Street or somewhere. Talk to him. How much money have you got?'

'Why?'

Beverley sat down with her tea. 'You've got to advertise in all the religious papers and journals in those countries that are still Christian. There must be some. An advertising agency will not only design the advert but place it for you in the right papers. So you'll get just one bill from the ad agency.'

'All we want then is money. What on earth will it cost?'

'Probably less than you think. It's not like trying to advertise in a national newspaper with five million readers. These religious publications have quite small circulations – but every reader will be very enthusiastic about Jesus. You won't be wasting your money talking to atheists or Moslems. You'll be hitting the target audience every time.'

'Well, never mind how much money *I've* got. How much money have *we* got?'

'On the basis of what's thine's mine? I don't recall our getting married.'

Tim finished his tea. 'I thought you might like to become a shareholder, seeing as how you pushed me into this thing.'

'You'll work harder if you invest your own money,' said Beverley. 'Or so they say. You must have a few thousand left.'

She collected the mugs and went out to a washroom behind the shop. Tim, determined not to be thrown by a strange new feeling of isolation, picked up the book she had been reading. It was Myles's *Textbook for Midwives*. The bookmark left in it took him straight to post-natal depression.

Psychiatric disorders occur in about one in a thousand births, he read. *Fifteen per cent are during the pregnancy, and most in the two weeks that follow the birth. Depression is the most common manifestation and if it persists requires specialist attention.*

He replaced the book as Beverley returned, and stood up.

'It's time to pick up Chloë,' he said.

'You pick her up,' said Beverley. 'No point in arriving in two cars.'

Janice Dawson was working at the playgroup when he got there.

'How's Sam?' he asked. 'Has he left you?'

'Nobody's that lucky, Tim,' she said with a weary smile. 'No, I mustn't be cruel. The poor sod's working quite hard.'

'What's he doing?'

'At the moment he seems to be driving round Scotland.'

'Very nice at this time of the year,' Tim said. 'It doesn't sound like work to me.'

Janice was beginning to wonder herself. The daily phone calls had dwindled to one every three days, and she could picture him cruising through the Highlands with a nubile hitchhiker flashing her brown thighs at his side, stopping occasionally to enjoy the native products of fresh salmon, wild raspberries, Scotch beef and malt whisky. In fifteen years of marriage he had never before gone off on his own and she was beginning to develop doubts about how he would cope with this unfamiliar freedom. He could discover a taste for it and never be seen again.

She told Tim: 'He's not touring, he's working, if the shock doesn't kill him. We had a little commercial idea and he's supposed to be exploring its possibilities. How's your little commercial idea coming along?'

'It's looking good,' said Tim. 'Boodle in large quantities is what I'm anticipating.'

The children, engaged in a game at the end of the hall that involved hoops and balls, were suddenly dismissed, and Chloë ran the length of the room to embrace her father. Tim worried that such a show of affection after so short a separation signified a feeling of insecurity. He picked her up.

'Alex wants to marry me,' she told him.

'Does he have any money?'

Chloë laughed. 'Children don't have money, Daddy.'

'Sometimes daddies don't have money either,' he told her. 'Let's go home and play hotels.'

Left on her own to lock up the hall, Janice ran through her usual crowded diary in her head. There was the column to be written for delivery in the morning when she was also supposed to be doing a stint in the charity shop. There were two cakes to make, the ingredients for which she had not yet bought. There was other shopping to do if she was going to eat tonight. There was also the tedious duty of cleaning Jake's bedroom; he was home soon for the half-term holiday.

It was a long time since she had had a holiday herself and she was beginning to feel that she really needed one. Perhaps the Dolomites, with their Renaissance palazzi and Gothic arcades. Perhaps Brighton. She smiled. There would be no holiday, she knew. The little jobs stretched in a never-ending line into the unforeseeable future.

She arrived home laden with shopping as the phone started to ring. The old Polo had made various ominous noises on the journey home and she had crept back at half her usual speed, fearful that she was about to be stranded in the Somerset hills while the frozen food melted in her sweltering boot. But it coughed its way into the drive and she hurried in with her shopping to answer the phone before it stopped ringing.

Sam said: 'Where have you been? I've rung three times.'

She was relieved to hear his voice. Her picture of

the hitchhiker and her brown thighs had become quite vivid.

'I've been working, Sam. Where are you?'

'Paisley. It's in Scotland.'

'Yes, I know that, Sam. How has it gone?'

'Amazing is the word. The response has been extraordinary. I've now called on thirty-two firms, and eighteen want to use us.'

'Is eighteen enough?'

'They've each got a hell of a lot of work for us. It's a great start.'

'Well, that's terrific, darling,' said Janice. 'When are you coming home?'

Sam, sitting on his single bed in a cheap hotel where the bathroom only had a shower and the faded picture on the wall was the Forth Bridge, consulted his list of engagements.

'I need two days in London. If I could pick up half a dozen firms there we would be thriving from Day One. These people think our idea is wonderful. They wonder why nobody has thought of it before.'

'Whose idea?' said Janice.

'Okay, your idea. Anyway, I'll drive home from London on Friday. When's Jake's half-term?'

'Friday.'

'See you then, kid. How are you?'

'I'm fine. Sam — did you meet any hitchhikers?'

'Hitchhikers?' said Sam. 'I haven't had time to talk to hitchhikers.'

11

The golf course — its grass still a verdant green from prodigal watering — was too popular on this hot afternoon so they lay on the ground and watched the ineffectual exertions of others.

'Let me get this right,' said Tim Bonner, lying on his back with his eyes firmly shut. 'You're going to mobilise an army of pensioners and set them to work for peanuts?'

'That's not how I'd put it,' Sam Dawson said, pulling a new white golfing cap that he had bought in Scotland over his face. The sun that beat down threatened to take the skin off their noses without the intervening warning of a tan.

'I can see the headlines. JOBLESS MAN EXPLOITS THE OLDIES. SLAVERY FOR THE OVER-SEVENTIES. Are you sure you've got the PR right on this, old man?'

Tim's voice was friendly and concerned, but Sam felt vaguely disturbed by what he was saying. He hit back: 'They could run the story alongside one about the shyster who conned the Faithful into believing that Jesus was partial to holidays in the West Country.'

Tim opened his eyes. 'I've got books on my side. I didn't invent the story myself. There's even a drawing of Jesus in a boat with Glastonbury Tor in the background.'

'Drawings don't prove a lot. You want photographs.'

'Unfortunately the first photograph didn't come along until about 1820 so I've had to get by without them.'

Sam raised himself on an elbow. 'Let me disabuse you of a few misguided ideas, Tim. The old people, and many of them not that old at all, who are going to take part in my scheme, are going to do so not only willingly but with considerable pleasure. They're bored, lonely, rejected and wasted. This will revolutionise their lives and their social lives. It's not compulsory, you know.'

Tim grunted doubtfully. 'I'm not suggesting that they are going to be driven into village halls all over the country by whips and dogs. But the money is a problem, isn't it? I hear talk of a minimum wage.'

Sam lay down again and wished that he were on a beach. Lying in the sun fully dressed was an English eccentricity, and it was so hot that it seemed to be melting the wax in his ears.

'Money has got nothing to do with it — they'd work for no wages,' he said. 'This is therapeutic. It's going to give their sad, empty lives some purpose, and if they pick up a pound or two to augment their pension it's a wonderful bonus for them.'

'I do hope for your sake that's how the tabloid Press see it. SLAVES, AGED 70 isn't a pretty headline.'

'You said something like that just now.'

'Did I? This sun's cooking my brains. Let's go and drink lemonade in the shade.'

The previous afternoon, when Sam had arrived home in what felt very much like triumph, thoughts of tabloid headlines were far from his mind. In London he had signed up eight more firms who were happy to send lorryloads of simple but repetitive work to Somerset on the promise that it would be done for half their usual costs.

Janice greeted him with the sort of effusive welcome that he hadn't enjoyed for years. Jake, whose expensive education had now enabled him to master the difficult art of playing the guitar with his teeth, managed to congratulate him.

'Many dads who are made redundant go ga-ga,' he announced authoritatively. 'They send off literally hundreds of letters for jobs, get no response or are told they're too old, and then they sink into a sort of trance.'

'They do?' said Sam. 'How do you know that?'

'Kids at school,' said Jake. 'Two dads have committed suicide this term already.'

'What happens to the kids?' Janice asked, horrified at what she was hearing.

'Oh, they leave,' said Jake. 'They can't take the jokes.'

'Jokes?' said Sam.

'Kids pretending to hang themselves with towels and all that.' He held his tie above his head as if he had been hanged. His tongue lolled out at a grotesque angle.

'Stop it,' said Janice.

Over dinner Sam delivered an interminable account of his odyssey into the hinterland of Britain, and his earnest conversations with suspicious businessmen, distrustful designers, unimaginative trinket merchants and cautious industrialists who were reluctant to stray a few feet from the path they already knew. In shabby offices that proclaimed with their peeling paint and damaged furniture the pain of the recession, he developed powers of persuasion he never knew he possessed, gripping his listeners in the matched causes of compassion for the elderly and cut-price commissions. Many brushed his invitation aside in accents he could barely understand; others, perhaps with ancient relatives of their own, saw advantages that weren't entirely mercenary. Encouraged by one success, he would arrive in high spirits at his next appointment, presenting a case that was difficult to spurn. Dismayed by rejection, he took time to remind himself of the number of people who would benefit if he transformed this idea into a successful enterprise. The experience had been a revelation to him, exposing depths and talents he didn't know he had, and he was left wondering what he might have achieved if he had abandoned the security of the shop many years ago and attempted something more adventurous.

'So we're up and running?' said Janice. 'I may have to cut down on some of my jobs.'

'There's still a lot to be done,' said Sam. 'Like finding the halls and the people.'

'I've enlisted the help of our wonderful County Council on that,' Janice said. 'We'll soon have all the information we need.'

'Why are you two doing this, anyway?' Jake asked.

'We're trying to pay your school fees,' Sam told him.

'You realise we're being controlled?' said Tim when they had established themselves with pints of lemonade at a table in the shade.

'Controlled?'

'By women. It was Beverley and Janice who pushed us into these crazy ventures. We could be drinking and playing golf. We could be loafing.'

'It was Janice's idea. I'm just the factotum.'

'Well, the Jesus Trail was my idea. Then she got hold of it and demanded action.'

'You were quite happy to leave the idea lying there?'

'Why not? It's what happens to most ideas. Instead I'm plunged into a nightmare of organisation, with the prospect of steering hundreds of mad foreigners up a bloody hill and worrying about torrential rain, broken legs, crashed coaches, unsatisfactory hotels, disgruntled clients, bouncing cheques and diverted aircraft. Why couldn't she leave me in peace?'

'My impression is,' said Sam, 'that when she gets her hands on you it's like a bird getting hold of a snail.'

'I can't work out whether it's that men are such nice creatures they try to be co-operative, or that they're so feeble any woman can kick them around.'

'Beverley Callard,' said Sam. 'Mentor or tormentor? How is she these days, anyway?'

Tim looked glum. 'Terrible. Her daughter thinks she hates her, and I'm certain she hates me. When your bed shakes it's probably because you're having sex. When our bed shakes it's because the cat's scratching itself. Beverley's in the grip of a depression I don't really understand.'

'Talk to a doctor. Get a book.'

'Do a runner. Why are women so complicated, Sam?'

'They're not complicated. If you do what they tell you they work perfectly. Another lemonade?'

A vestigial sense of parental duty took the Dawson family to the coast the following day. It was clear that a trip to the sea was not their son's dearest wish, but Sam and Janice took him anyway as it gave them a chance to study him at close quarters without his disappearing. Evanescent at home, he could somehow contrive to vanish in mid-conversation before the sound of music surfaced in another part of the house, or other noises, connected to ball games, arrived from the garden.

Sam had a jaundiced view of the English coast, feeling that where people had impinged upon it they had destroyed it, with tacky shops, grubby take-away eating joints and litter-strewn amusement arcades. Only in parts of Devon and Cornwall, with their harbours and their boats and their smart seafood restaurants, had the natural attractions been enhanced.

But the coast to which they were obliged to drive from where they lived was neither one thing nor the other — an almost neglected stretch of land facing the Bristol Channel and Bridgwater Bay. It was like stepping back in time. From Weston-super-Mare in the north to Burnham in the south, nothing seemed to have changed in fifty years. The beach in front of a row of ancient hotels presented the same picture that appeared on antique postcards in the shops.

'We're stepping into a space — time continuum,' said Sam. 'The ice creams should cost tuppence.'

'This was your father's era,' Janice told Jake.

'Absolutely,' said Sam. 'I remember the trolley bus and the tram in London. I can remember starting a car with a starting handle.'

'He remembers Marilyn Monroe, but has never heard of Madonna. It's the same with all these old men. The past is engraved on their brains, but they can't remember what happened yesterday.'

On the crowded beach they sat on a plaid rug that they found in the boot of the car, and considered the future of Jake. His parents hoped that the constrictions of a boarding school had concentrated his mind on study and the possibilities that it opened up for him, but when pressed on his future he betrayed no hint of ambition, no interest in a career. He sat on the rug in old jeans and a T-shirt whose logo referred to an American baseball team. He removed his Velcro-fastened shoes and buried his feet in the sand.

'The people I envy are the hedge monkeys,' he said.

'The who?' asked Janice.

'People they call New Age travellers. Drifting round the country in their old vans and keeping out of the rat race.'

'The ones we all keep with our taxes by staying in the rat race?' Sam asked. 'What is there to admire about them?'

Jake looked at him almost contemptuously and corrected the trick question. 'I didn't say I admired them. I said I envied them.'

'Why are they called New Age travellers, anyway?' Sam asked. 'Some people have chosen to live like that since time began. What's new about it?' The prospect of his son throwing in his lot with the itinerant riffraff he had seen boiling kettles at the side of the road filled him with dismay when he considered the soaring cost of his school fees.

'It takes a lot of courage to turn your back on society like that,' Jake said, kicking sand.

'Not when society gives you a cheque every Friday,' Sam said. 'Anyway, what are you going to do when you leave school?'

The school reports did not suggest that he was going to Oxford. The subjects that he was best at − art, poetry, acting − were precisely those activities which, if developed into a career and pursued diligently and with burning dedication, would bring him professional frustration, private misery, enduring poverty and probably a nervous breakdown, if not an occasional attempt at suicide.

'I haven't decided yet, Dad,' said Jake. 'Did you know what you were going to do when you were fifteen?'

Sam, reluctant to admit that he didn't, lay back on the rug. From somebody's radio nearby, James Taylor was singing *You've got a free-und*.

Janice said: 'When you've had enough of this sun, we should sample the epicurean delights of Weston-super-Mare.'

'They call it fish and chips,' said Sam, slowly deliquescing in the heat.

'Smashing,' said Jake.

Sunday mornings, which should have been filled by unbroken sunshine, leisurely smiles, trilling birds and the amiable murmur of neighbours' lawn mowers, were notably despondent affairs these days and it took some time for Tim Bonner to work out why. After all, no day was exactly packed with unbridled merriment, but Sundays seemed to carry a special cargo of gloom which pervaded the whole house.

Eventually he tumbled to it: this was the lottery hangover, the period when the hopelessly optimistic dreams, secretly built up through Friday and Saturday, lay in wreckage at their feet. Beverley's addiction to the forty-nine balls in the spinning drum defied rational explanation. She actually expected to win and her failure to do so came as a devastating setback every week, because every week she had won the money before the first ball fell.

'We're not going to spend it, we're going to invest it,' she said. (The lottery winnings were to be shared because Tim paid for the ticket.) 'If there were two winners we'd get about four million. If we invested it, what would we get every week?'

'I don't know,' Tim said. 'Interest rates are pretty low at the moment. At least six thousand before tax, I suppose.'

'We could live on that.'

'I'm glad to hear it.'

'And the four million would remain untouched.'

It worried Tim that Beverley's plans were so advanced; she seemed to be only a step or two away from declaring this bountiful interest to the Inland Revenue. Reality had fled. And then came Saturday evenings and the flattening realisation that the money had gone elsewhere – to a Bangladeshi waiter from Ealing, a well-heeled money broker belching champagne in a Chelsea penthouse, or, even more unworthily, to an out-of-work felon with a drugs habit who had abandoned his seven kids.

But usually you were never told who the winners were. Cosseted by advisers who were employed by the organisers of this weekly heartache, they were spirited away to open secret bank accounts so that the news would not leak out in their own home town, and you were left to watch your neighbours suspiciously for any sudden and uncharacteristic extravagance.

So Sundays were low now, and it was often Wednesday before Beverley could be lifted back to her usual level of routine discontent. On Wednesday she chose the lottery numbers and hope began again.

Taking Sam Dawson's advice, Tim bought a book. It had been self-published in America by a woman who had endured the agonies of post-baby depression and wanted to share her experiences and discoveries with those who were similarly afflicted. There were, the book said, more than 100,000 cases every year in America alone. They had found that post-partum depression wasn't a two-week inconvenience but an on-going nightmare that could run into years.

He read about mothers who were too depressed to do the washing-up, mothers who lived on tranquillizers and anti-depressants, and others who spent months in psychiatric wards being laboriously coaxed back to normality. They had doubts about their ability as a mother, and resentment about the freedom they had lost; but all such thoughts were the consequence and not the cause. Depression was a physical illness, and the changes the body had been through during childbirth had placed a stress on the nervous system so that the body lacked energy and strength. The body's needs had to be met — with vitamins, minerals, rest and exercise — before the depression would lift.

Tim had another theory and after dutifully working his way through the book he chucked it in the bin.

Beverley's arrival at the next meeting of The Lunch Club was greeted with the news of another defection. Laura Morton had left a message on pink notepaper telling them that she had been given a part in a television play, and would be filming in Wales for at least six weeks. She thought that this was therefore an appropriate moment for her to sever her connection with the club, whose conversation she had greatly enjoyed.

'The lying cow,' said Gemma Swan. 'She never was one of us. Did you hear what she said the last time she was here? "Feminism has knocked an awful lot out of men"! She was gun-running to the enemy.'

'Perhaps the fact that David has just given her £1,300 to have her teeth veneered had something to do with it,' said Monica Titchmarsh. 'Bless his high-cholesterol heart.'

'Even if he is a selfish, dominating bastard with the sex appetite of a panda,' said Gemma Swan.

Beverley nodded approval of these criticisms and wished that she had never invited Laura Morton in the first place. Defections unsettled the others, and threatened to raise doubts in their own minds.

'It is true that Laura was dominated by her husband,' she said. 'She put on a little act for us, but then she's an actress. David made her study the piano, learn to ride horses and then take bloody ballet lessons. He imposed all this on her and squashed her individuality. She's a sad case.'

'She can set fire to her bum for all I care,' said Gemma Swan, whose harassed life had today given her the wide eyes of an insomniac frog.

The four survivors considered the menu carefully. Janice Dawson led the way, choosing lamb with an onion and caper sauce, and the others, perhaps reluctant to make further waves, said they would have it too. The young waiter took their orders with his customary nervousness, as if he privately harboured the direst misgivings about what fiendish plot this secret cabal was hatching.

'I see you've got your car back,' said Monica Titchmarsh, when he had gone. She occasionally spoke with an unnecessarily forceful delivery, picked up during years in the Council chamber. Janice thought that she could make "hallo" sound like a challenge, and "good morning" a threat.

'Yes, Sam is home,' she said. 'He had a very productive trip. I thought he'd forgotten how to work but it all seemed to come back to him.'

Monica Titchmarsh put on her glasses and pulled sheaves of paper from her bag. 'This is the stuff you wanted. Halls, their caretakers, and all the pensioners' organisations. Good luck to you. Can you give my Gerry a job?'

'Is he speaking yet?'

'Not a dicky bird.'

'What does the doctor say?' asked Janice, curious about this prolonged silence.

'He can't find anything wrong with him.'

'That must be a male doctor,' Beverley said. 'Bring Gerry in here. We'll find something wrong with him.'

'Actually I'm beginning to find the silence quite restful,' said Monica Titchmarsh. 'When he did talk he seldom stopped moaning, but men are like that, aren't they? And their abiding characteristic is that they blame everybody except themselves.'

The others recognised this as being a great truth.

'It's because they can't bring themselves to admit that they were wrong,' Janice said. 'It interferes with their masculinity somehow.'

'It's because of the giant inferiority complex they work so hard to conceal,' said Beverley. 'The reason they've got an inferiority complex is because they're inferior.'

This collective denunciation seemed to enliven Gemma Swan, who told them: 'Saskia's violent father, my second husband, was so impatient he once tried to widen the hole in an egg-timer.'

'As a joke?' asked Janice.

'I don't believe so,' said Gemma. 'He wasn't strong on humour. He was just going quietly round the twist.'

When their food had arrived, Janice said: 'This third husband of yours, the one with the thirst. What's his name?'

'Alastair.'

'Does he work?'

'Good God, no. He worked for an export-import agency and they paid him off a couple of years ago. He's shown no inclination since to return to the fray.'

Janice looked at her thoughtfully, unwilling to delve too deeply into the fiascos and frustrations of Gemma Swan's private life. But she had now had time to look at the endless lists of halls, caretakers and managers, and the numerous organisations that were connected in some way to the elderly, which Monica Titchmarsh had given her, and she could see that Sam was going to need assistance.

'Can he work?' she asked. 'I mean, is he ever sober enough to work, or is his life spent in a permanent alcoholic stupor?'

Curiously, Gemma Swan seemed to resent this. She evidently held, as the suffering spouse, exclusive rights in belittling her husband, and it was not a game that anyone could join.

'He's not a dribbling dotard, if that's what you mean,' she said. 'His cerebral cortex is still in working order.'

'Do you think he would be interested in a little part-time work?' Janice asked. 'It's of a charitable nature so the pay wouldn't be too generous.'

'We can only try,' said Gemma. 'I think boredom's his problem frankly.'

'That would be marvellous,' said Monica Titchmarsh. 'If The Lunch Club can get Gemma's husband back to work it really will be achieving miracles.'

'The real miracle will be when we don't have to

work ourselves,' said Beverley. 'Are you still doing four jobs at once, Janice?'

'You've reminded me,' said Janice. 'I've got to write my column this afternoon. Is there no end to it?'

12

Trying to write a column that might divert the casual readers of a free newspaper while at the same time making two cakes, preparing for a two-hour stint in the charity shop and attempting to convince her grumbling son that the world wanted and loved him, persuaded Janice Dawson that if her husband's efforts paid off she would shed these nagging duties and approach life from a quite different angle. The pleasures of other more fortunate women — travel, cruises, shopping — had never appealed to her because she had not had time to acquire the taste for them; but now they beckoned.

Jake, whose reaction to half-term was an aggrieved boredom, presented a particular problem. He sat around the house like a challenge, defying anybody to entertain him. Extricated by his father from his slough of sloth, he retired to the television where he watched obscure videos of unimaginable violence. Janice, adept at so many things, did not have the experience to deal with him. Nor, she sometimes thought, the time, patience or desire. If this was a transitory pubertal phase he had to pass through before becoming a proper human being, let him get on with it.

Fired by dreams of riches — of travel, cruises, shopping — she wrote in less than twenty minutes a column on 'If I won the lottery'. The syncopation of her two-finger typing took her into a delightful world where wishes were granted and luxuries bought without a qualm.

'Wonderful,' said Leo, when she delivered it at *The Clarion* offices. 'Just what the reader is talking about every week.'

'Don't forget to put the commas in,' said Janice, sitting on the corner of his desk. 'Just sprinkle them around as you think fit.'

Leo sat back, his French cigarette producing acrid smoke that twisted lazily round his head, and announced: 'I've got a story. At least, I think I have.'

'I hope so, Leo. No newspaper should be without one.'

'Apparently there's some madman at large who thinks that Jesus came to Somerset. I was talking to Rowland, the coach man, and he said this chap is planning to swamp the area with pilgrims who'll want to walk in the footsteps of Christ.'

'What's wrong with that?' Janice asked warily.

'Phoney as a two-pound note,' Leo replied briskly.

'And you're planning to write about it?'

'It's a gift, isn't it?' said Leo. 'You don't get a

lot of opportunities for exposés and probing inquiries round here. People don't want to read stories about rustic bestiality over their Coco Pops according to my postbag, and there's not much else.'

Janice stood up, alarmed at what Leo was saying. Her line was clear.

'I should think carefully about that, Leo, if I were you. Anybody who is about to fill all the hotels, and provide the shops with hundreds of customers, is going to be a bit of a hero. Your friend Rowland will be making a packet, too. If you start knocking it, you'll be dead in the water.'

'Think so?' Leo asked doubtfully. He drew on his cigarette and looked at her thoughtfully.

'The editor who killed the tourist business? They'll run you out of town. At the very least, your advertising will disappear.'

This last threat took some of the colour out of the editor's plump face. Talk of being run out of town was meat and drink to an efficient journalist, but the suggestion of vanishing adverts made the blood run cold.

'Best not be too precipitate, you think?'

'Banish the word,' said Janice. 'This madman, as you call him, might be about to produce the prosperity this place needs, and it will reach everybody. Busy shops will be able to take space in *The Clarion*. You might even be in a position to give yourself a rise.'

Leo stood up, tugging a smart new yellow waistcoat over his bulging waistline, and wrestled with a residual objection. 'But Jesus didn't come to Somerset. My newspaper deals in truth.'

'Like the time you said Fergie was getting bonked stupid by a toe-sucking farmer in Staple Fitzpaine? And what about the tiger at large in Cheddar Gorge?'

'Both stories came from an impeccable source.'

'It didn't stop them being dead wrong, Leo. Anyway, can you prove that Jesus *didn't* come to Somerset?'

'I can't even prove He was born in a stable.'

'Well, there you are then. Drop it, Leo. You'll live longer.'

Leo extinguished his cigarette in a pink ashtray and immediately reached for his packet to light another. He gave Janice a long look. 'I suppose it's beyond the bounds of possibility that this madman – this chap – might be known to you? That he might be a friend of yours?'

Unable to lie and unwilling to confess, Janice adopted a more truculent tone. 'When I give people advice, Leo, it's the best advice I can give. It's not coloured by other considerations. If you plan to mock the biggest tourist initiative for years, your paper will be dead in a year. You can take my advice or ignore it, but I always give it sincerely.'

'You do know him then,' Leo said, with a smile of satisfaction.

'Unfortunately I can't stand here chatting to you all day. I'm due at the charity shop five minutes ago.'

She picked up her bag and moved towards the door.

'Next week I'll have a real story for you,' she said.
'What's that?'

'My husband's working again.'

Leo scowled. 'Sensational. I'll make room on the front.'

'No, Leo. It's what he's doing that will make news, not that he's doing it. It's a story that will interest all your readers who are over sixty. It's a story that will eventually reach the national papers, but you will have it first.'

'And all I have to do to get this marvellous scoop is to forget the Jesus in Somerset nonsense?'

'Sounds like a deal,' said Janice.

Beverley's home, with its four bedrooms, two unproductive acres, and empty stable blocks and tack rooms, seemed somewhat underused, but Tim now moved in on the fourth bedroom and converted it into a throbbing powerhouse of activity, with a new desk, a filing cabinet, a word processor, an extra telephone line with answer machine and, best of all, a fax.

From this new toy one morning there stuttered a dozen advertisements for the Jesus Trail, designed in London and intended for the pious readers of religious publications he had never heard of that appeared in countries he could barely find on a map. THE JESUS TRAIL, they said. THE SPIRITUAL EXPERIENCE OF A LIFETIME. Some were ambitiously illustrated with the Boy Jesus standing amid swirling mists on the Tor at Glastonbury; others attempted to represent the boat which had brought Joseph of Arimathea on his commercial mission from the Mediterranean. The ones Tim liked stuck to the facts — the financial facts, the cost of this once-in-a-lifetime experience. He phoned the advertising agency in London, selected three, and extracted a promise that they would all be on their way to their distant destinations by evening. Then he went to the bank and opened a new account to accommodate the cruzados, escudos, korunas, lira, pesos and roubles which he now expected to flow in his direction. The bank manager listened to his project in wide-eyed wonderment, studied the advertisements with a sardonic grin, and then granted the new account an immediate overdraft facility of £10,000 for the start-up costs which would be largely swallowed by the advertising agency.

Tim Bonner drove home convinced that patience was all he now needed to obtain a financial security he had always dreamed about. He went up to his new office, the hub now of his empire, and lit a cigarette while he tried to envisage the Trail itself and what he would need on it. Huge signs would have to be painted, seats and food stops provided. A souvenir stall was essential, perhaps with tiny models of Jesus in a boat. There could be a hymn-singing corner to break the journey, and he would certainly sell the franchise for photographs to some grasping lensman.

Sitting there, he had the fanciful notion that the Jesus Trail could lead straight through a supermarket, so that the pilgrims were obliged to pick up a basket at one end and buy things as they moved through the store. He was sure that he could do a deal with the manager, who would pay him a percentage for delivering so many captive customers on a regular basis. The problem was that although there was a Safeway supermarket in the vicinity, it wasn't quite on the route, and the detour might appear exploitive.

He ditched this idea reluctantly and considered next whether he should have a clergyman in attendance, a man of God in appropriate priestly garb, to give the occasion an air of sanctity that it might otherwise lack. This was the most troubling thought of all. He had kept well away from priests for most of his life, and wasn't sure that he knew how to deal with them. Some of them, he didn't doubt, would do anything for money, but he might stumble across one who refused to accept the premise on which the whole enterprise was based.

In the end, and with relief, he dropped this idea, too. The Christian faith was split into so many warring factions that any priest he hired could alienate more than half his customers. Catholics flying in from Portugal would not be pleased to find a Methodist preacher presiding over their devotions, and Protestants arriving from Northern Ireland would be less than delighted to find themselves listening to a stringent homily from a representative of the Pope.

He decided to steer clear of professional churchmen. What did Jesus in Somerset have to do with them, anyway?

*   *   *

Sam Dawson had also commandeered a bedroom, but, apart from a second telephone, lacked the technology with which Tim had smoothly surrounded himself. Ironically, Sam needed it more than Tim: the list of manufacturers, their addresses and phone numbers, the available halls and their managers and caretakers, and the many organisations that catered in one way or another for the elderly, all amounted to a pile of paperwork which in more competent hands would be consigned to the retentive memory of a computer. Deprived of the know-how, Sam devised a card filing system and waited for help to arrive.

Janice, he understood, had spoken to one of her friends at The Lunch Club, a hyperactive lady called Gemma Swan whose husband was a part-time alcoholic, but allegedly bright when sober. He arrived at noon.

He stood on the doorstep in grey slacks and a blue blazer with a regimental badge stitched to the top pocket. He looked like a two-bottles-of-red-wine-for-breakfast man, with heavy eyes, a shiny red face and a drooping moustache. All this was topped by a shock of ginger hair.

'Mr Swan?' said Sam, extending a hand. The visitor appeared to be sober.

'Alastair Ford,' said the man, accepting the hand-shake. 'I'm afraid my wife is marooned for profes-sional purposes on the second of the four surnames she has so far had. She opened the Gemma Swan Secretarial Agency when she was Gemma Swan, you see. Bit like Liz Taylor. No point in keep changing her name.'

'Of course not,' said Sam. 'Please come in, Mr Ford.'

'Alastair,' said Alastair Ford. 'Call me Alastair.'

He followed Sam upstairs to the bedroom which was already beginning to look a little cluttered, and sat at a table that had been provided for him. Sam sat at his desk in the corner and wondered where to begin.

'Has she stopped now?' he asked, hesitant about plunging straight into work. 'This quest for new surnames?'

'I'm hoping so,' said Alastair Ford, who looked as if he would be good fun in a non-working environment. 'She's good for me. Although, of course, the older a man gets, the younger the woman he needs, don't you find? But I wouldn't want to lose Gemma. Love at first sight. What I admired about her was her natural elegance, her innate beauty, her burning intelligence and her enormous bazoomas. But will she stick with a dissolute-looking cove like me?'

'Why not?' said Sam.

Alastair Ford shrugged. 'I think I'm perceived to be a man of intelligence and sensitivity,' he said, farting loudly and disastrously at the moment when he most needed aplomb, 'but you can never tell with women. Clearly this is not a lady who is frightened by divorce.'

'I'm sure she'll stick around,' said Sam, reassuringly. It was, he felt, time to move on. 'The first thing we should discuss here, Alastair, is money. I don't know how much you know about the venture that we're embarking on—'

Alastair held up one hand. 'Forget money,' he said. He had the mellifluous voice of a serious drinker. 'To tell you the truth, money isn't important. I have a fat pension. No, the object of the exercise here is to keep me out of mischief. I probably couldn't get a conventional job any more, but if you can keep me busy here you'll be doing us both a favour. Fact is, when I've got nothing to do I'm apt to reach for the bottle.'

Sam hoped that his expression reflected the right degree of disbelief at this confession.

'Gemma got me to join the Mendip farmers' skittles league to keep me out of trouble, but it turned out that they drank more than I did. What a disaster that was. Got home two days later without my shoes.'

'I'm afraid that alcohol will be hard to find in here,' Sam said. 'For a few weeks we're going to be very busy. In the end, I hope, the whole thing will run itself, but setting it up in the first place is going to be pretty hectic.'

'Tell me about it,' said Alastair Ford.

For an hour Sam described the plans that he had. He told Alastair Ford about his trip round Britain and the reactions he had received in factories up and down the country. He showed him the long lists he had accumulated of pensioners' organisations, and explained the need to find many more if the project was to spread beyond the West Country.

'Here's the work,' said Sam, holding up one hand, 'and here are the people,' he said, holding up the other. 'All we have to do is introduce them.'

'And arrange venues and hot lunches,' said Alastair Ford. 'A very worthwhile venture, if I may say so.'

'Do you think you can handle it?' asked Sam.

'It's right up my alley,' said Alastair. 'All I need is a phone.'

Sam placed the second phone on Alastair Ford's table, and provided him with lists, pads and pens.

'I'm hoping to start a month today,' he said, 'so we want to fill all the days from that date. When we've got the people and the halls lined up, I can get back to the manufacturers.'

'Let's go,' said Alastair, picking up the phone.

Sam watched him anxiously, half-expecting a bottle of something to be secretly extracted from a blazer pocket, or Alastair himself to pitch forward on the table, finally overtaken by liquid nourishment consumed before he arrived at the Dawsons' house. But it was soon apparent that before indolence and alcohol intervened, Alastair Ford was an efficient machine. Most importantly, without the distraction of drink, he could hold three ideas in his head and do two things at the same time. Sam could tell quite quickly that Alastair, having worked once in a more competitive world, was actually more efficient than he was.

His spirits rose.

Beverley Callard was sitting in her shop polishing

a silver coffee pot. Two customers examined a gold bracelet on a shelf near the door. On the other side of the window, tanned tourists paused, peered and wandered on. Chloë, ignored, sat on the floor, methodically dismantling a doll. There was no playgroup today, Melissa was away, Tim claimed that he was going to be busy, and so Beverley had Chloë to look after while she ran the shop.

She wished that she was a thousand miles away. She would have liked to be stranded on a deserted beach in the Indian Ocean. She wished, above all, that she wanted to be here.

Chloë held up the result of her work. The doll had endured some gruesome surgery.

'Daddy's going to meet Jesus,' she said, 'on a hill.'

'Are you sure?' asked Beverley.

'Daddy said so. Jesus is coming in a boat.'

'Well, that will be nice.'

Chloë looked puzzled. 'I thought they nailed Jesus to a cross?'

'He must have got off again,' said Beverley, who was rescued suddenly from this difficult inquisition by the ringing of the phone. To her surprise, it was her mother calling from Spain.

'How are you, Bev?' she asked. It sounded as if she was in the next room.

'All right.'

'You don't sound all right.'

'How are *you*, anyway? How's Dad?'

'Bloody hot.'

'It's hot here.'

'It's hotter here. We need a break from it. We're coming over till the Spanish heat subsides. Is that okay?'

Beverley wasn't sure whether she wanted an invasion by her parents at this moment, but as she was living in their house she could only welcome them. There would be the usual diffident inquiries about why she hadn't married yet, and sad little explanations about where exactly this placed Chloë. Her father would have quiet words with Tim, none of which would ever be reported back to her. And then there was the Jesus Trail, which didn't need the interruption of visitors at this moment.

'It would be lovely, Mum,' she said. 'When are you coming?'

'Couple of weeks. Your dad's in some golfing tournament first. He sends his love, by the way. How's business?'

When she had got rid of her mother with a noisy exchange of kisses, Beverley dialled Tim to warn him about the impending visit.

'J.T. Ltd,' he said.

'Tim? What are you talking about?' she asked.

'Oh, hallo Miss Callard,' said Tim. 'I've formed a company and opened a bank account for it. It's all go round here.'

'What does J.T. stand for?'

'What do you think it stands for? Jesus Trail. I just managed at the last minute to get J.T. Ltd in the adverts, so the cheques are made out to the right account. Clever, eh?'

'Mum rang,' said Beverley. 'They're coming over in a couple of weeks.'

'I thought they were practising atheists,' said Tim, whose head was filled now with plans for his venture.

'No, they're coming to *stay*. Spain's too hot at this time of the year, apparently.'

'Fine,' said Tim. 'I may be too busy to give them my full attention, or to thrash your father at golf, but I'm sure they'll understand. Tell you what, though. You'd better make certain that our little daughter doesn't start telling her grandparents that you hate her.'

Beverley replaced the phone and realised with a tremor of concern that Tim was right. This was not the sort of announcement that would go down well with her parents. She looked at the little girl, who was now curled up like a cat and fast asleep on the carpet with her arms round the broken doll.

'I love you, Chloë,' she said.

Part Two

Every man who is high up likes to
feel that he has done it all himself;
and the wife smiles, and lets it go at
that. It's our only joke. Every woman
knows that.

Sir James Barrie
What Every Woman Knows

13

There was no respite from the heat. Sweltering days were followed by torrid nights, and people who for years had found conversational possibilities in the disappointments of the British climate were reduced to a welcome silence.

At his new desk, Tim Bonner found that the sweat that ran down his forehead and then down the bridge of his nose before dropping on to his multiplying paperwork turned his mind to the pleasures of the golf course; but a bill for nearly £10,000 from his advertising agency helped bring his wandering thoughts back to the uncertain fate of the Jesus Trail. He was in this now, and only an infusion of pilgrims who carried credit cards along with their crucifixes would get him out of it. In distant corners of the world, subscribers to religious journals were now studying his advertisement and asking themselves, he imagined, whether this was an experience they could afford to miss.

He reached for his new cheque book, as if thought

transference could urge them towards their next move. In the corner of each cheque it said *T. Bonner, J.T. Ltd.* Using the facility provided by the bank he wrote a cheque to the advertising agency and then sat, sweating in the heat, and considered his new overdraft. Debt, he had once read, is a great motivator.

A week later, sitting at the same desk and enduring the same uncomfortable heat, he was disturbed by a thunderous knocking on the front door. The doorbell had ceased to work, and there was no knocker, so it was necessary for visitors to rouse the inhabitants by hitting the door with whatever came to hand.

In this strange waiting period, Tim had found himself sitting dutifully in his office without actually having anything useful to do. Occasionally J.T. Ltd drifted from his mind completely, and he thought instead about Beverley, his moody co-habitee, and how her increasingly surly demeanour would strike her parents, who were now poised for flight to Britain.

The book that he had read about depressed women had clarified his thoughts on the subject, but not quite in the way that the writer intended. The writer herself had seemed unsure of her ground because having ascribed a physical cause to the depression, she had gone on to discuss mental cures.

Tim was now certain that only depressed women became post-natally depressed. The women he had known who had suffered serious unhappiness after the birth of a child had had deep reservations about the way their life was going before the baby was born.

The women who were happily married and throughly delighted with their lives didn't know what serious post-natal depression was.

It therefore followed that Beverley was deeply dissatisfied about something, and had been before Chloë was born. All he had to do was track down this secret source of unhappiness and eliminate it. Dispensing thus with years of professional research based on the carefully documented case histories of hundreds of real-life victims, gave him a palpable boost. Cutting through the crap was the secret of success in this world.

He lit a cigarette as the clattering on the front door began, and went downstairs, resolving again to get the doorbell mended. Their friendly postman stood on the step, but instead of clutching a parcel that he couldn't get through the letter-box, or a Registered letter that required a signature on delivery, he offered Tim a sack.

'A bit of post for you today, Mr Bonner,' he said. 'It's all in this sack.'

Temporarily mystified, Tim took the sack, emptied the contents on the sitting-room floor, and returned the sack to the postman who said: 'You're not a secret pop star, are you?'

When he returned to the mail, scattered over quite a large area of the carpet, its brightly coloured international stamps and blue air-mail stickers removed all doubts about what had arrived for him this morning. It was money of many denominations.

He sat on the floor like a child with new toys

and began to open the envelopes. Each contained a filled-in form that had appeared in the advertisement, and each contained a cheque. There were cheques for 150 dollars, for 18,000 pesetas, for 560 rand and for 760 French francs. There were cheques that brought him Finnish markka, Austrian schillings, Irish punts, Swedish krona, Canadian dollars, Swiss francs, German marks and Portuguese escudos. There were four-figure cheques from Belgium, five-figure cheques from Spain and six-figure cheques from Italy.

He gazed in awe at this windfall, paralysed briefly by the size of the response, and then he got a grip on himself and counted envelopes. There were 734. Strewn around him on the floor, he guessed, was £73,400.

His first reaction was fear. Could he organise the event that would satisfy the customers who had replied so eagerly to his advert? Were these people going to fly home satisfied that they had received value for money, or was he about to preside over a fiasco?

He opened a couple more envelopes nervously and realised that he had made a serious miscalculation.

Confused by the foreign currencies, he hadn't realised that many of the applications were for pairs. They were coming in couples. The money on the floor was a lot *more* than £73,400. He collected all the envelopes, put them in a box and took them to his new office, working out, as he went, that his share of even £73,400 was £14,680.

Then, fearful about what he had started, he jumped into his Honda and drove to Beverley's shop. He drove erratically, distracted by the task which now faced him. What did this fearsome army, fuelled by a religious zealotry he couldn't even imagine, expect to find when it ended its long journey in Somerset?

Beverley, in jeans and a pink top, was engaged in some prolonged haggling over the price of a silver bracelet with a young man who had a ponytail, and Tim was obliged to hang on to his news while the trading took place. Impatient to talk to someone, he rang Sam Dawson.

'I want to buy you a drink,' he said.

'You're lucky to catch me in,' Sam said. 'It's bedlam here. We're nearly ready to go.'

'Marvellous,' said Tim. 'I, too, have news.'

'Save it for the pub,' said Sam. 'I'm creating an empire here.'

'A busy child is a happy child. The Crossed Wires at six.'

Beverley broke off her negotiations with the pony-tailed customer with an impressive display of contempt, suggesting that he might be more at home with mail-order shopping, or possibly find what he was looking for in Woolworth.

'Are you always so rude to your customers?' Tim asked, surprised.

'He's a dealer,' said Beverley. 'He knew it was worth more than I was charging him, but he still tried to beat me down.' It was astonishing how cool she looked, even in the present heatwave.

'Fat chance,' said Tim. 'Tea?'

'I'll put the kettle on. Why aren't you working?'

He sat on a table and took her hands.

'How many replies do you think I got this morning?'

'Two?'

'Seven hundred and thirty-four. That's at least seventy-three thousand pounds, kid, and it's actually more than that because most of them aren't coming on their own. They're coming in pairs!'

'Good God,' said Beverley and sat down. 'Janice was right.'

'Janice?'

'She sort of persuaded me that this idea would produce a big response. Can you handle it?'

Tim grimaced at the doubts which Beverley obviously entertained. 'A question I'm asking myself at the moment,' he admitted. 'I suppose it will all be a question of sorting out dates and bringing them in two hundred at a time.'

She looked up at him and as he studied her face a barely-remembered expression spread over her sun-tanned features: she looked happy.

'Tim, this could mean real money!'

He nodded. The shock of the postal response was beginning to wear off, and her smile had restored his confidence. 'It looks that way,' he said. 'We could be rich.'

She jumped up and threw her arms round his neck and, just as suddenly, disentangled herself. 'I'll put the kettle on.'

He stood there, examining his surprise. This was as affectionate as Beverley had been for some time. His theory was right. Her depression had been brought on by other things and now he knew what had caused it. She had been worried sick about money.

She bounced back in with two cups of tea and sat down with a new friendly smile on her face.

'This shop can go for a start,' she said.

'I thought you enjoyed it?' he asked.

'It's a prison. No, it's too small for that. It's a cell.'

'Flog it, kid. Hitch your wagon to a star.'

Sam Dawson was becoming accustomed to Somerset's pubs, their mysteries and their mores. In darkened rooms with dim lights in mock-gas brackets, men preferred to shuffle dominoes than play darts, the beer was cheap and potent, and there was always an indoor skittles alley at the back that would have been incongruous in any other part of the country. The customers at the bar were no longer the solicitors or bank officials that he had once drunk with, but farriers or cider-makers or men who worked on the land.

He and Tim had found a new one. It was called The Crossed Swords, but the impenetrability of the landlord, a wiry refugee from the north with a penchant for producing the wrong drink, had persuaded them to rename it The Crossed Wires. Sitting at the counter and waiting for Tim, Sam listened to a big man, who sucked remorselessly on a briar, remind the room that although hay was now £2 a bale, it had cost more during the great snows of 1963. It wasn't a conversation that he had ever expected to eavesdrop, and for a while it had a certain novelty value, but his thoughts returned inevitably to the great project that Alastair Ford was working on in his upstairs bedroom. He had not only been in touch with every senior citizen's organisation he could find, but had also placed card advertisements in every newsagent in the county. The response arrived with every post and they were close to choosing a start date.

Sam was on his second pint when Tim Bonner arrived looking like a man who had won the lottery jackpot and wasn't worried about anonymity.

'You can't guess what has happened,' he said, taking the next stool.

'I don't have to,' said Sam. 'You're going to tell me just as soon as you have bought the promised drink.'

'Drinks can wait,' said Tim. 'Listen to this. I had seven hundred and thirty-four replies today from all over the world. Five hundred were for couples, no doubt married couples. That's a hundred thousand pounds. The rest are singles, which is another twenty-three thousand. I've just been through every ruddy envelope – and that's just the first post.'

'Remind me,' said Sam. 'What's your cut after you've paid for the hotels and coaches?'

'Twenty a head. Don't worry – I've worked it out. My take so far is nearly twenty-five thousand pounds. Isn't that amazing?'

Sam drank his beer and wondered whether his

own enterprise would be able to match Tim's success. 'Not really,' he said. 'How many countries did you advertise in?'

'At least twenty, judging by the postage stamps.'

'Your agency found religious journals in twenty countries?'

'No, they found some international ones, particularly Catholic, that are published in London and New York and then go all over the world. It simplified their task somewhat.'

'Well, it isn't amazing at all,' Sam decided. 'Those aren't people who are being hit by an advert for cars or holidays they didn't know they wanted. They're deeply religious folk who are suddenly offered an experience they mustn't miss. That response is less than forty per country. My advice is prepare for a deluge.'

'My God,' said Tim. 'Do you think so?'

'I'm certain of it,' said Sam. 'But I think there's something you've overlooked.'

'Oh no,' Tim said, looking worried. It was what Rowland had said to him at the coach garage, and it was a sentence that he didn't want to hear. 'What is it?' he asked, steeling himself.

'How are you going to get these people to the top of the hill in the first place? Chances are the average age of your clientèle is fifty-plus. People take an interest in religion when they're staring at the morgue. You could be surrounded by heart attacks.'

Tim looked shocked. 'Do you know, I hadn't thought of that.'

'If the walk starts at the top of the hill, you've got to get them there in the first place. It's a pretty steep hill, I seem to remember, and some might not enjoy the climb.'

Tim looked unexpectedly downcast now, but managed to produce his wallet and order the drinks.

'This is what worries me,' he said. 'What else have I overlooked? I could be battered to death with a thousand Bibles.' He pulled out his cigarettes, and was so concerned at the gaps and flaws which he now thought were waiting to be exposed in his planning that he offered Sam one.

'I gave up smoking when I left school,' he said, not for the first time. 'A brilliant organiser like you, wrestling with the complex details of an elaborate undertaking like the Jesus Trail, should be able to remember something like that.'

'I need help,' said Tim, sipping his drink with unusual slowness. 'You wouldn't care to join me, I suppose? I can pay great money.'

'That's a laugh, isn't it? Now I'm up to my ears in work he offers me a job. Where were you when I needed you?'

'I believe we were playing golf together.'

'Well, I have to organise thousands of pensioners, and make sure they get to the right hall where the right job is waiting for them. I've got to organise all their lunches and daily payments, and this scene is going to be taking place in fifty different halls simultaneously. It makes taking two hundred people up a hill look like brushing your teeth.'

Tim considered this intimidating schedule with equanimity. 'If you're so clever, old man, do me a favour and tell me how I'm going to get these bastards to the top of Wearyall Hill. Helicopters?'

'Golf buggies,' said Sam. 'You can hire them from the golf club.'

Janice's story about her husband's plans to bring purpose and responsibility into the lives of countless pensioners ran to a thousand words, although she could see that there might be some shrinkage after Leo had wielded his blue pencil.

He sat at his desk, sifting through the standard fare of traffic protesters, quarry protesters and bypass protesters, while at the same time indulging a newly acquired taste for obscure Cajun music with a small cassette player on the floor. The usual pungent aroma of French cigarettes pervaded the office.

'Is this the promised scoop?' he asked, when she arrived with several sheets of paper.

'That's it,' said Janice, dropping them on his desk.

Leo bent to the floor to turn off his music, inspected the sheets, presumably for coffee stains or burn marks, and then read aloud: '"Thousands of pensioners in the West Country who sit at home all day feeling lonely and unwanted are about to be given the chance to do something about it".'

'You don't have to read it out loud,' said Janice. 'I already know what it says.'

Leo grunted and read on in silence. His ensemble

today included a pink waistcoat and a polka-dot bow tie. Janice studied his plump face for some indication of what he thought about the story. Leo liked to create the impression that what emerged from his rickety office was accepted by the world outside as great literature, and he was consequently obliged to treat incoming copy as if it was the latest instalment of a Dickens novel, still wet with ink from the master's quill pen. He finished reading, laid the sheets carefully on his desk and sucked on his Gauloise.

'Help the aged,' he said. 'Put the buggers to work! What's this enterprise called? Exploit the elderly? Ponce off a pensioner?'

'Leo, you're so cynical you ought to be a journalist,' Janice said. 'Don't you see the possibilities?'

'For whom?' asked Leo, picking up the story again. 'Who's getting paid what here?'

'Everybody's getting paid something,' Janice told him 'Of course, Sam will have certain administrative costs.'

'Of course,' said Leo. 'Clever, that. He can pay himself tax-free money. And what do these ancient slaves get — a bowl of gruel? What's going on round here? One man's trying to convince the cerebrally challenged that Jesus took His summer holidays in Somerset, while another is busily rounding up the happily retired and whipping them into sweatshops.'

'You mean you wish you'd thought of the idea yourself,' said Janice, sitting on the corner of Leo's desk. 'I suggest you wait until you've seen the response before you pass judgment. The retired aren't going to be whipped into sweatshops. They'll arrive of their own accord and be highly delighted about it, because they're desperate for something to do. What will you say when they turn up in their hundreds and thousands?'

'I'll say I wish I'd had the idea. It's a good one. Yours, I suppose?'

Janice nodded. 'A little scheme that occurred to me after talking to some old folk one afternoon. I've brought a photo of Sam, by the way, to go with the story. As you can see, he looks a picture of moral rectitude.' She handed Leo a photograph which she had taken earlier that summer in the garden. Sam, leaning on a lawn mower, smiled confidently into the camera.

'We can cut out the lawn mower and do a head and shoulders,' said Leo. 'I trust you haven't forgotten your column?'

Janice delved into her bag and produced more sheets of paper. 'It's on the same subject, I'm afraid. I'm urging the oldies to sign up.'

'Handy, really,' said Leo, 'working for the local paper when you've an axe to grind.'

'Well, I certainly don't do it for the money,' said Janice. 'Which, incidentally, is what all those pension-ers will be saying.'

Driving to Bristol Airport in her Passat, Beverley Callard envisaged a sexual tableau which made every fibre of her body tingle. Her long legs were wrapped round the naked body of a muscular young man with blond hair who bore a considerable resemblance to Tim. This resurgence of sexual desire took her by surprise and was difficult to explain, but it was real enough to send her the wrong way twice during her thirty-mile dash to the airport.

Her parents were due in at noon. They would arrive grinning, with their preposterous sun-tans and their duty frees, and the endless responsibilities their presence imposed on her would make spare time rare and daylight sex impossible. She parked the car and headed for the arrivals lounge.

Her father, Howard, was a busy little man with white hair and glasses who had spent his life doing deals in the silver business, with a sideline in watercolours and antiques. At one time he owned six shops, but after a heart murmur he decided one morning never to work again. He sold five shops, bought an apartment in the south of Spain, and gave the sixth shop and the house to his only child.

Her mother, Doris, was a plump, short lady with curly hair who was quite unlike her tall, slim daughter. Her abiding characteristic was that she adored her husband, supported him through good times and bad, had helped in the shops and readily agreed when he announced that he wanted to live in another country. Beverley secretly felt that such devotion was almost demeaning, and yearned for the day when her mother would assert herself more; but she had to acknowledge that her parents were that rare commodity, a happily married couple.

They appeared with a trolley that was piled so high with cases that at first she couldn't see them. The cases trundled towards her and then her father jumped out from behind them.

'Bev, darling!' he said, giving her a hug. He wore white slacks and a white short-sleeve shirt with sandals. His face was nut brown and Beverley wondered what sort of temperatures they had been living with in Spain if they expected to cool down in Britain's heat.

'How are you, darling?' said her mother, kissing her on the cheek. 'How's Timmy?'

'Timmy?' said Beverley. 'You make him sound like a cat.'

'I don't suppose he's actually got a job yet?' asked Howard, resuming his trolley-pushing.

'Not yet,' said Beverley. 'But he's got plans.'

'That boy always had plans,' said Howard. 'What he didn't have was a job. How's the shop?'

'He may surprise you,' said Beverley as they walked towards the car. 'The shop's fine. What have you both been doing all summer while I've been working?'

'Polishing my top spin cross-court forehand,' said Howard, lifting cases. His athletic appearance suggested that his reaction to the heart murmur had been unduly pessimistic.

'Flirting with his Meryls, Cheryls and Beryls,' said Doris, getting into the car. She was as informally dressed as her husband in a simple white dress, but once in the car she began to fan herself with a map that lay on the back seat. 'I thought we'd come here to escape the heat?'

'I did warn you,' said Beverley, starting the engine. 'How's your Spanish coming along?'

'You know my attitude to foreign languages, dear,' said her mother. 'Why can't they all speak English and stop being silly?'

Busy as he was, Tim Bonner was waiting to greet them at the front door, having kept a vigilant eye on the drive from his office window. Replying to applicants and offering them dates was proving to be an enormous task. Just addressing envelopes seemed to fill the day, and then there were hotels to ring and bedrooms to reserve. It was not, he now thought, a one-man operation.

Howard approached him with his usual wide grin and offered his hand.

'How are you, Tim?' he asked. 'I hear you've had another idea.'

'A big one — I think we'll save it for dinner,' Tim said. 'Let me carry your cases.'

He would have felt more at ease with Howard if he was married to his daughter and not just living with her in their house. He didn't know whether Howard was aware that this was an arrangement of his daughter's choosing.

'Where's Chloë?' asked Doris, giving him a peck on the cheek.

'She's at playgroup, Mum,' Beverley said, lifting cases.

Tim was curious about what sort of life this couple lived in the south of Spain. Their Christmas card always arrived in November, which he took to be a sign of boredom rather than dazzling organisation, and yet the postcards they occasionally sent and the phone calls managed to suggest a fun-filled stress-free existence.

Later, over drinks, he took the old man out to the patio, mercifully shaded now, and watched him light a series of small cigars with cheap Costa del Sol lighters that always featured a matador or a flamenco dancer.

'We thought Bev has been sounding a bit depressed,' confided Howard, man-to-man. 'Anything we ought to know about?'

Prepared for a polite low-key chat about nothing very much, Tim found himself unsettled by this question, which seemed to carry with it the suggestion that if Beverley was unhappy somebody must be causing it.

'Puerperal psychosis,' he said immediately.

Howard looked at him as if he had been invited to take part in the three-card trick. 'What?' he said. 'What in hell's that?'

'It's a disorder that sometimes occurs in women after childbirth. Characterised by a deep depression. But I think you'll find she's over it now.'

'Over it?'

'She's been a different girl lately.'

'And are the two of you going to get married?'

'She won't have me. I *have* suggested it.'

Howard chuckled to himself at this news which

seemed to cheer him up. 'She always was a contrary lady,' he said. 'You have to be firm with her.'

From what Tim had seen, Howard had never been firm with Beverley in his life, but he nodded solemnly as if important information was being revealed here. He had no intention of being firm with Beverley himself, preferring to let her fly and delight him occasionally with moments of shared enjoyment. These moments had been rare in recent months, but Tim was now afflicted with an irrepressible optimism. The number of replies to his advertisements had topped one thousand.

They were called in to dinner by Chloë, who said that she had been helping her mother and grandmother prepare it in the kitchen. It turned out to be a joint of rolled sirloin and more vegetables than Tim could count. There was an advantage in having guests, he thought: the grub improved.

'I eat to live, she lives to eat,' said Howard, as his wife filled her plate.

'You should see him demolish a paella,' said Doris happily. 'God, it's nice to be back in the countryside again. Things are green.'

Through the open French windows they could glimpse meadows and cows, cowsheds and pylons, and, in the middle, the River Brue, banked on either side to prevent the flooding which threatened the flat, low fields every year.

'Not as green as they were,' said Beverley. She was still in jeans, but as a concession to the visitors was wearing over a white blouse a rather flashy waistcoat, intricately embroidered with hand-stitched seashells and beads.

Chloë, feeling ignored, announced: 'Daddy's going to meet Jesus.'

The effect on Howard startled them. He dropped his knife and fork and said: 'What's she talking about, Tim? You ill?'

'She's talking about Tim's idea,' said Beverley. 'You'd better tell them about it, Tim. I'm interested in how they'll react.'

Slowly, over the next twenty minutes, Tim told their guests about the theory that Jesus had visited Somerset and how he had come up with the idea of the Jesus Trail. He told them about the negotiations with hotels and coach firms, about the bank loan and his advertising, and finally, as his *coup de grâce*, revealed the size of the response he had had.

'So far,' he told them, 'more than £150,000 has come through the front door.'

Howard, who had listened somewhat mistily to the story about Jesus, and actually yawned at the mention of advertising agencies, jack-knifed into hair-trigger alertness at the reference to money and emitted a low whistle which frightened the cat. The old dealer's brain, which had spent a lifetime trimming percentages and gauging profits, was only temporarily nonplussed by the size of the figure quoted. Soon he was back in touch, enthralled by the extraordinary potential which appeared to lie before them.

The remains of his dinner were abandoned. The red

wine, the third bottle of which was being moved round the table, was picked up and emptied absent-mindedly into his own glass.

He leaned over the table. 'It's the best idea I ever heard,' he said. 'We must cancel our return flight and stay and help you.'

14

In the bedroom, Beverley whispered: 'We'll never get rid of them.'

'I don't mind,' Tim said. 'Do you?'

Her blue eyes glowered as she sat on the bed. 'I do,' she said. 'We used to make passionate love on the lawn. You can't do that if you have house guests.'

Tim looked at her attractive, pouting face, surprised at the message he was receiving.

'Beverley, we haven't made love on the lawn for months,' he said, 'passionate or otherwise. I don't see their presence changing anything.'

She removed her blouse and her bra and strolled topless to the en-suite bathroom which had been lavishly furnished during the conversion with every modern aid to personal cleanliness. 'I haven't been feeling well,' she said over her shoulder. 'I've been depressed.'

'I know you have,' said Tim, taking off his shirt. 'You've been worrying about money.'

'And you,' she said, pausing at the door. 'I was

worried about you not working and drinking all the time. I was worried about where your life was going.'

'This is worried, past tense?' he asked.

'Yes, I can see where you're going now. You're going to make a million.'

'Do you really think so?'

She winked, which astonished him. She had never winked before. 'I'm going to make sure of it.'

She vanished into the bathroom, leaving him standing by the bed. He knew now that his analysis was correct, and that her depression had lifted with the glimmering promise of financial security. Money as an aphrodisiac! Perhaps he should cover the pink duvet with banknotes, or rouse her to peaks of frenzy with a collection of platinum credit cards. Perhaps he should fill the bed with commemorative two-pound coins and see where they all ended up.

Once, in a gîte in the Dordogne, he had enjoyed a protracted sexual encounter with a girl from Médecins sans Frontières who, deliberately or otherwise, managed to cover the sheets with potato crisps. Like a copulating animal, she betrayed no hint of pleasure when they made love, but afterwards, scrabbling round their bodies for the remains of the crisps, she had become notably excited.

His conception of women as unpredictable creatures who were difficult to read had been formed in that gîte, and not a lot had happened since to clarify the picture. They were never quite on the wavelength he imagined, their thoughts wandered when he most expected them to be focused, and the closer they got the more distant they seemed.

Beverley appeared suddenly and glided naked to the bed as if walking on clouds. She was brown all over, he realised with surprise. Some nude sunbathing must have been taking place while he was struggling heroically on the golf course. When she slipped into bed he took off his clothes and got in beside her. Her body was red hot and he felt that touching her would scald his skin, but his hand moved without consulting him and cupped a breast.

'Are your breasts getting bigger, or are my hands getting smaller?' he asked.

But stimulated by her fantasy in the car, Beverley had only one thing on her mind tonight. 'Do you think you can remember how to do it?' she asked.

'Hang on,' he said. 'I've got a book somewhere.'

'Don't worry,' she told him. 'My memory is excellent.'

Afterwards as she lay beside him, her mouth slightly open in a smile, he pulled her on top of him and did it again, lying on his back.

'What are you?' she asked. 'Some sort of sex maniac?'

'I've been saving it up,' he said.

'Well, now you've got some interest.'

Without the constant intake of alcohol, Alastair Ford's appearance had begun to improve. The red face was not so red, the heavy eyes were not so heavy and even sparkled a little. The moustache still drooped, but a moustache was an external artefact beyond the reach of diets and self-restraint. Invigorated by this unexpected temperance, he revealed an enthusiastic commitment to Sam's project and succeeded in convincing him, against Sam's natural instinct, that he was going to have to spend a lot more money if it was going to succeed.

Expenditure had always frightened Sam, and speculative expenditure petrified him, but he was persuaded by Alastair, now the very picture of acumen and efficiency, to talk to his bank manager, register the firm, and make sure that funds would always be available. Luckily for Sam, his meeting with the bank manager, McAllister, took place on the day after Janice's story about the venture had appeared in *The Clarion*, and the manager, impressed by the coverage and beguiled by the idea, was delighted to give him whatever he wanted. It was the height, or the depth, of the recession, the banks were laden with money that people were too frightened or too pessimistic to borrow, and to discover a customer who actually wanted some was now regarded as a triumph for a bank manager.

Alastair set about disbursing this loot with feverish abandon. A fax machine was installed almost immediately, followed by an answering machine for the phone. Next came a Dell Pentium personal computer costing £1,500, which Alastair then devoted himself to for four days while Sam struggled to understand what he was doing.

'It's all in there,' said Alastair when he had finished. 'You can call it up any time.'

'We can?'

'You were fighting a war with pea-shooters, Sam.'

'What have we got now?'

'Cruise missiles. Welcome to the twentieth century. You only just made it.'

When Janice dropped in on this preoccupied couple with coffee and biscuits, she was impressed with their tireless industry. The idea that she had dreamed up seemed suddenly to be too big and too complicated for anybody outside a major conglomerate to handle, but the two of them sat there, writing letters, sending faxes and making endless phone calls which she listened to with anxiety and admiration.

'Stuffing and sewing teddy bears?' said Sam one morning. 'Right up our street. How many teddy bears? Ten thousand? Okay, we can do that.'

'Ford are telling their suppliers to keep costs down to their present prices for five years,' said Alastair into the other phone. 'We can help you there . . . Yes, well we're helping Britain's balance of payments and you don't want the stuff stuck on a boat for six weeks. Quick turn round, that's it.'

'Lots of screwing and bolting? That's perfect,' said Sam on his next call. 'Half a million light switches. We can handle that.'

'Painting toy soldiers?' Alastair was saying. 'It's what we're good at. Two hundred thousand?' He raised his eyebrows at Sam. 'You have a deal.'

'The work's there,' said Sam, when the phone calls stopped. 'Let's hope to God the workers are.'

'You men are working a miracle,' Janice said. 'It makes me tired just listening to you.'

'You had a clever idea, Mrs Dawson,' said Alastair, stroking his moustache. 'Any fool can work, but ideas are gold dust.'

'Would you care to join us, dear? Pull up a chair and discover what you've landed us with.'

'Not me,' said Janice, retreating hastily. 'I've got a date at The Lunch Club.'

The Lunch Club was breaking up for the summer in an atmosphere of mutual congratulations. Both Monica Titchmarsh and Gemma Swan had holidays planned, but the main reason for the hiatus was that Beverley and Janice were about to become immersed in the ventures they had urged on their men, and there would be no time for these leisurely meetings which sometimes went on until mid-afternoon.

The fact that three of their four men were now spending more time working than drinking was regarded as a triumphant vindication of the club. Only Gerry Titchmarsh, whose continuing silence posed an intractable problem, had escaped their rigorous scrutiny and reforming zeal.

'A season of considerable achievement,' decided Monica Titchmarsh over a seafood salad. The weather was so hot that cooked food was going out of fashion. Even the wine had been replaced by thirst-quenching fruit juices. 'We set ourselves some objectives and we achieved them. I wish I had you people with me on the County Council.'

'One of the things we've achieved is to restore my faith,' Janice admitted. 'I was beginning to think that giving a man a brain was rather a waste, like giving a crash helmet to a kamikaze pilot, but the men have surprised me. Were we wrong about them?'

Beverley moved quickly to suppress the notion that her Lunch Club had been founded on a misapprehension about the male sex. 'Absolutely not,' she retorted. 'They've only surprised you because we kicked them into action. Without our intervention they'd still be wallowing in the pub. Take the credit you deserve, Janice.'

'You certainly get the credit for taking Alastair off my hands,' said Gemma Swan. 'It's wonderful. I'm taking Saskia to France for three weeks and Alastair won't be able to come! He always spoils holidays, anyway, by getting drunk and belching and farting when I'm trying to introduce him to new people, but now he'll be too busy with Sam to leave the country.'

'And are these men of yours going to make money?' asked Monica Titchmarsh, surveying the table doubt-fully. 'I always thought the idea was to reintroduce these idlers to honest work and a regular pay packet, not to make them obscenely rich?'

'Sometimes the riches flow from the work,' Beverley replied, almost apologetically. 'Certainly Tim's crazy idea is producing foreign currency at a frightening rate.'

'And what about Sam? Is he going to make money, too?' asked Monica Titchmarsh, looking only slightly put out.

'I don't know,' Janice told her. 'He might do, or it might go horribly wrong. The logistics of the thing are terrifying. All the lorries have got to turn up at the right time at the right hall from far-flung destinations, the halls have got to be ready, and the pensioners have got to show up in sufficient numbers to make the whole thing work. Alastair has been brilliant, Gemma. He's put everything on to a computer, and even Sam understands it.'

'So far as I'm concerned, getting that drunken sot to buckle down has been our greatest success,' Gemma Swan declared with baleful satisfaction.

Beverley sat back, her salad finished, and cast an appreciative eye round the table. She never thought when the idea of a lunch club first came to her that they would achieve so much in so short a time. It wasn't clear what more they could do if they met in the autumn, but she wasn't really expecting The Lunch Club to meet again. If the Jesus Trail fulfilled the potential that was now being realistically suggested by the daily postbag, she might have better things to do with her time than sit in this decidedly downmarket hotel.

In his bedroom office, surrounded by graphs, charts, lists and folders, Tim Bonner lit a cigarette and played disbelievingly with his pocket calculator. Plans for the

Jesus Trail had been finalised, and his calculator told him an incredible tale.

Two hundred pilgrims would arrive on Mondays, most of them by air. They would go home on Wednesdays, when another two hundred would fly in. This second group would fly home on Fridays. The Jesus Trail itself would take place every Tuesday and Thursday.

This weekly influx of visitors would produce £40,000, of which £8,000 would belong to Tim. His pocket calculator said this put his annual income at £416,000, making him, according to the financial guidelines that prevailed, a paper millionaire.

While he sat gaping at those figures in blissful stupefaction, other people were doing the work.

Beverley, having closed the shop 'for holidays' but secretly intending never to open it again, was liaising with students at a local art college to produce the brightly painted banners and signs which would festoon the hill.

Her mother had taken over the responsibility for food, and was arranging food stalls and refreshment bars that would be on the hill and on the road down to the ruins of the Abbey where the Jesus Trail would end.

Howard had designated himself director of baubles and was arranging the printing of posters and postcards. He was also having thousands of tiny cardboard boxes made with a specially printed label attached. These, no bigger than a matchbox, would contain earth from Wearyall Hill, and costing no more than a penny to produce, would sell for a pound. Candles, crucifixes

229

and small plastic models of the Boy Jesus in a boat were ordered, and all would end up on the souvenir stall that Howard was to run. It had been agreed, after some not very strenuous negotiations, that Howard and Doris would keep whatever money they made.

Most of Tim's time was spent in confirming arrangements with the hotels and coach firm. Both were being provided with new lists every day of dates and the people who would be arriving on them.

He could see now that the arrival of Beverley's parents, with their nose for work and their commercial experience, had saved the whole venture from embarrassing failure. He would never have been able to organise it all himself, and if he had to recruit outsiders he would be plunged into the timewasting world of an employer, with forms to fill in, tax to be deducted and sent off, health insurance to be paid and God knew what else.

He puffed happily on his cigarette and decided that he deserved a drink. He rang Sam, who said: 'Did you see my picture in the paper? Very Paul Newman, I thought, apart from the hair.'

'Paper?' said Tim. 'I don't get time to read the papers. What did they get you for? Drunk and disorderly, or flashing?'

'Read it,' said Sam. 'You'll understand what we're about, here at Workfare. The next time I'm in the papers, it'll probably be a knighthood.'

This idea, wrapped up as a joke, came at Tim as a real possibility. Whereas his own venture carried within it the risk of opprobrium or ridicule, Sam could easily be hailed as the man who liberated a million pensioners, and the next thing they knew, it would be Sir Samuel Dawson — 'for services to the elderly'.

'Workfare?' he said. 'What's that?'

'That's what we're calling it. Read the paper.'

As soon as he had finished the call, Tim went to find the newspaper. Sam's smiling face, exuding a stirring mixture of firmness and compassion, was at the top of the front page with a headline that said SAVIOUR OF THE ELDERLY. A smaller headline underneath said: *Sam's plans to brighten pensioners' lives.* These headlines didn't have quite the zing that Tim found in his tabloid every morning, but he had heard that the editor was a vain, chain-smoking hack who thought he was James Joyce.

He headed for The Crossed Wires in his Honda, anxious to impress upon Sam Dawson that although he might not be getting the publicity, and had scant chance of a knighthood, he was nevertheless on the verge of a significant financial triumph. But Sam had beaten him to the pub and was drinking with his assistant, Alastair Ford, who was not only slightly drunk already, but also looked to Tim like the type of man you found hanging around at second-hand car auctions.

'My wife goes along to those lunches your girlfriend organises,' he said, when Sam had introduced them. 'They're a pretty seditionary clique.'

'Well,' said Tim, 'they seem to have got us three back to work.'

'That's what I mean,' said Alastair, gripping a large whisky. 'What happened to fun? I used to have time to look at girls with large breasts, now I'm manacled to Sam's computer.'

'Alastair has a thing about large breasts,' Sam explained. 'Can I buy you a lager?'

'Young beautiful girls with gargantuan knockers who will make themselves available for the bizarre sexual predilections of complete strangers,' Alastair elaborated with great seriousness.

'Do you find any?' Tim asked, taking his drink from Sam.

'None,' said Alastair sadly, 'much to Gemma's relief. She can't understand my tastes, but I told her: "It's not me, it's nature. Nature doesn't know about the Pill. Nature's never heard of the condom. Nature directs me to a young girl with big breasts because she is best suited for motherhood." It'd be an odd thing if nature sent me scuttling after a menopausal fifty-five-year-old with my trousers round my ankles, wouldn't it? Nature knows. You can't argue with her. She's got us all this far.'

'It's hard to imagine a nice chap like you prowling the streets with a lust you can barely control,' said Sam. 'Why don't you give it up and join the golf club?'

'A load of toffs, a gaggle of parvenus and a few beer-dazed journalists who sit under their apple trees with their Apple Macs and give the world a fearful bollocking once a week by the magic of the facsimile machine. Why would I want to mix with them?' He finished his large whisky, ordered himself another one, and turned to Tim. 'This Jesus caper. Bit of an earner, is it?'

Tim was programmed to resent now the creeping perception that the Jesus Trail was some sort of racket, impelled by profit and quite untouched by such considerations as faith and history.

'It's a spiritual experience that has to pay for itself,' he said with what gravity he could muster.

'I've heard some crap in my time, but this is de luxe quality,' Alastair remarked cheerfully. 'You could bag it up, and flog it to a garden centre.'

'Your friend drinks,' said Tim. 'I can tell by his conversation.'

'Has been known,' Alastair admitted. 'I don't have the financial consolations of you gentlemen.'

'We don't have financial consolations at the moment. We have financial worries,' said Sam. 'Will the old folk turn up? Will they be able to handle the jobs that are thrown at them? Tense times, Tim.'

Tim interpreted this cautious assessment as a façade, designed to conceal the size of Sam's coming triumph. He had never seen the old man look so pleased, and he wanted to tell him that the Jesus Trail was on course to pay him nearly half a million pounds a year. But after the sanctimonious response he had been obliged to deliver to Alastair Ford, such boasting would leave him vulnerable to remarks about profit and greed that he didn't want to hear.

Sam's visible pleasure was more to do with the smooth way that his operation was moving forward rather than expectation of financial success. The computer and Alastair Ford had brought the idea to the brink of life, but he was still at the mercy of thousands of pensioners who might be smitten with rheumatism or arthritis or other things that were even less pleasant when they should have been arriving, hungry for work, at their austere village hall. At each hall there would be an operative or manager who had been briefed by Sam during dozens of car journeys across the West Country; meal deliveries had been arranged; even a nurse would be paying regular visits to each hall. It seemed to Sam that there was not much more he could do beyond crossing his fingers.

He ordered them all drinks and proposed a toast to their forthcoming success. It was a ceremony to which Tim brought ambivalent feelings after the spurious disinterest he had been compelled to show in profit.

'All we can do now is wait,' he said, sipping his drink soberly.

15

From the top of Wearyall Hill, Tim Bonner watched five coaches, glimmering in a heat haze, thread their laborious way through the lanes of Somerset. He was wearing a new suit of clerical grey with a sober blue shirt and black tie, feeling that he had somehow cobbled together a civilian's sartorial equivalent of a clergyman's togs. He was frightened to death.

As the coaches approached the agreed dropping-off point at the foot of the hill, he decided that he could hardly hail his visitors from here, and clambered down to meet them. They climbed out of the coaches and stood on the grass gazing nervously up at Wearyall Hill as if Jesus still loitered among its sun-baked cowpats. Rowland Coaches had entered into the spirit of the occasion by fixing stickers to the back of the drivers' seats saying GOD IS MY PILOT. I AM ONLY A CO-PILOT.

'Hallo everybody!' Tim shouted. 'Welcome to Wearyall Hill. There are golf buggies over there that will take those of you who don't want to climb to the top.'

It occurred to him somewhat late in the day that he should probably be saying this in three or four languages, but the message seemed to have been received, for some of the older folk walked over to the buggies while the others followed Tim's example and climbed.

The sight at the top was impressive. A twenty-foot plastic banner with blue letters on a white background said THE JESUS TRAIL. The poles that held it up were wrapped in red ribbons and gold braid. Scattered around were dozens of chairs and tables that were covered with free leaflets containing a map showing the Trail's route.

Not far away, Howard, dressed identically to Tim, presided over an immense stall that was covered with every souvenir they had been able to think up, and ten yards away, nearer the stile that would take them off the grass of the hill and out to the road, Doris, in a black two-piece with a demure blue blouse, stood behind a stall crammed with chocolate bars, cakes, sandwiches, sausage rolls, tortilla chips, biscuits, sweets, milk shakes and ten different varieties of soft drinks in cans.

A bookstall with volumes of religious lore had been provided and manned by a local bookshop, and Tim was amused to discover that up here on Wearyall Hill, credit cards were accepted.

Brightly coloured flags in the ground showed the route from the top of the hill, but Tim had been unable to get permission to continue the line of flags when the journey reached the road. For the same reason he had been forced to abandon an ambitious scheme to cover the entire Trail with the white plastic footprints of Jesus. 'We don't want those coming down the main road,' said a planning official. 'Anyway, what size shoes did He take?'

Jettisoned, too, was an idea of Beverley's to mark the point of landfall with flags, bunting and streamers. Initially it had seemed a natural move, but second thoughts suggested that such dogmatic precision might invite scepticism that wouldn't otherwise be there.

Dominating the hill was a gigantic reproduction of the famous picture of Jesus in a boat with Glastonbury Tor in the background, which Tim had taken the precaution of having a poster firm reproduce to reassure any doubters.

Studying the scene, Tim decided that all his preparations had been worthwhile. People had travelled many miles for one shining moment on this hill, and he didn't want to disappoint them. The setting was magnificent, and the country smells — ordure or verdure?—seemed appropriate to the occasion.

He went over to check that Howard and Doris were prepared for the rush that was about to engulf them.

'We're ready, boss,' said Howard with a wink. 'I've got another four hundred boxes of earth under the table.'

'I'm ready to feed the five thousand,' said Doris, 'but not with loaves and fishes.'

At the top of the hill now the visitors were queuing to have their pictures taken on this historic spot. Beverley, in a virginal white blouse and modest black ankle-length skirt, was taking the photographs with a newly-bought camera. Individuals and pairs were invited to stand in front of the big banner, and they were no sooner photographed than another pair was ushered on to the same spot. Later that day she would take the prints to the hotels where the pilgrims were staying and sell them a personal memento that they would cherish. Perhaps uniquely on this hill, the motive was not money. In fact, the exercise was going to be more trouble than it was worth. But Beverley had decided that it had to be done. It was a service the customer would appreciate, it was one more diversion that helped to fill the programme, and when the photographs were taken back and shown around or, better still, published at home they might produce new bookings.

While the pictures were being taken − while old ladies suffused with devotion and God-fearing men, who suddenly felt appreciably closer to their Maker, smiled blindly at the zoom lens of Beverley's Canon − Tim mingled with the people who were now his clients, dispensing handshakes and goodwill, and trying to find out, while he did it, who they were and where they had come from. He had feared an invasion of militant believers, psalm-chanting born-again revival-ists or carpet-chewing fundamentalists who had no compunction about inflicting pain or worse on any heathens, infidels or barbarians they came across. The Jesus Trail, he had been warned, could attract that type of person. There were 600 new religious movements in Britain today, but less than three per cent of the population went to church on Sundays. The reason for these contradictory statistics was a warning to him about the sort of customer he could expect. Today's Christians wanted mystical experiences, divine inter-ventions, healed sick and, if possible, raised dead. They hadn't got the patience for the Church of England's mechanical repetitions. They wanted drama.

But as he moved among them and introduced himself while they recovered from their climb, he was relieved to discover that the majority of them were quite normal. Mostly they were the retired couples Tim had expected because at that age they had the time, the money and a revived interest in God. But others surprised him and brightened his day.

There was a bus driver from Ipswich who had once been a Tibetan monk in an Eastern temple, and a small, saturnine monk from an abbey near Gloucester who had once been a taxi driver in Cleethorpes. There was a young man with the full set of earrings, ponytail and tattoo, who seemed to have broken out of a 1960s casket and kept saying 'Peace, man'; and there was a former professional electric boogie dancer from Tallahassee in a mini-skirt who said that what she wanted was excitement in her religion, and then fondled Tim's thigh so that there should be no misapprehension about what sort of excitement she had in mind. There was a short and energetic American businessman in a snap-brim fedora who lived in New Jersey and told Tim that he had let Jesus into his life 'on a trial basis'; and a lecturer in practical theology from

Scotland who said he was researching a book on Jesus. One of Tim's favourites was a solemn but attractive waitress from a Swiss Mövenpick who revealed that she had once chatted to the Virgin Mary in Locarno. There was a seaweed farmer from the South Atlantic, a pilot from Portugal and an oil man from Dar-es-Salaam. There were Anabaptists, Adventists and Anglicans, Catholics, Calvinists and Congregationalists, Methodists and Mormons, Ritualists and Rosicrucians.

For all of these people a few minutes later Tim contrived a theatrical performance of dissimulated joy, stationing himself at the peak of the hill and allowing them to gather round to hear his words. He wondered whether a lambent flame should be flickering in the vicinity, or even whether he himself should have appeared through a hole in the ground to the strains of a mighty Wurlitzer. But it was too late for that: he swallowed hard and delivered his much-rehearsed oration.

'It was a brilliantly sunny day when the small boat that carried Joseph of Arimathea and the Boy Jesus reached landfall here on Wearyall Hill. They had been travelling for six weeks since leaving the port of Tyre in the Mediterranean, and were glad to set foot on firm ground again. The apples were red on the trees, and the young Jesus, like all small boys, was hungry . . .'

Nothing but gratified smiles greeted this imaginative evocation of an event that nobody was sure took place and some people were quite certain hadn't, and Tim pressed on, hugely encouraged, with an account of how Jesus passed His time while His great-uncle

conducted his business deal with local lead merchants.
(He eschewed local girls, but made friends with the
animals was the gist of it.)

'At the end of the Trail,' he told them in conclusion,
'we shall see in the ruins of Glastonbury Abbey – the
first Christian sanctuary in the British Isles – the site
of Glastonbury's first church of wattle and daub which
Joseph and Jesus built in honour of the Virgin Mary.
The title, Our Lady St Mary of Glastonbury, has
survived to this day, and in a few minutes you will
be passing a church bearing that name. I think, now,
that we should start the walk which will bring us to
that hallowed site.'

He stepped down to murmurs of approbation and
some scattered applause and saw that a TV news
camera was following his move. Men with notebooks
and cameras were also hanging around on the fringe of
the crowd, and he wondered what publicity was in store
for him. But there was too much to do for it to concern
him now. He led the way across the top of the hill as
slowly as he could so that all could keep up, and then
stopped at the stalls to allow people to spend money.

Howard and Doris were soon frantically busy, and
not helped by a multiplicity of languages. While Tim
waited for his party, feeling faintly embarrassed at the
money changing hands, Sam Dawson appeared from
the crowd.

'It's going well,' he said.

'What's a pagan like you doing here?'

'Just curious, Tim. You're handling it brilliantly, if

I may say so. But aren't you worried that one of them is going to come up and ask how you can prove all this apocryphal stuff?'

Tim laughed. He knew his market now. 'It won't happen,' he said. 'They want to believe it. They wouldn't have flown halfway round the world if they had any doubts.'

Janice came up with an older couple and introduced them to today's star.

'Tim, this is Monica Titchmarsh, the County Councillor, and her husband Gerry.'

'A very impressive performance, Mr Bonner,' said Monica Titchmarsh doubtfully. 'A tremendous boost for local tourism.'

Her husband, a small balding man with a worried expression on his pinched face, said: 'Are there any toilets on this Jesus Trail?'

The effect of this on Monica Titchmarsh was electrifying. She yelped loudly, threw her hands into the air, and wheeled round on Janice who was knocked to one side in the excitement.

'He spoke! That's the first time he's spoken in over eight months. My God, Gerry — are you okay?'

'Fine, dear,' said Gerry. 'I'd like to find a toilet, though.'

But Gerry's bladder was the least of their concerns.

'It's a miracle,' said Monica Titchmarsh firmly. 'We've witnessed a miracle here. Where's Leo? You must tell him.'

'Ask him where the toilet is,' said Gerry Titchmarsh.

But Tim had other things to think about. The pilgrims were gathering around him now, ready to move on, and he led them down to the stile which would bring them out on to the road.

A late addition to the occasion had been provided by Beverley, who had produced a choir of ten young girls in pink taffeta dresses to stand by the stile and sing *What a Friend We Have in Jesus* as the pilgrims walked by. This proved to be such an attractive sight that the walk ground to a halt until the singing had finished.

They followed Tim out to the road then, clutching their souvenirs and glancing round to see exactly where the Abbey ruins were. From this height there was still a view. Almost all of them seemed to be carrying a plastic model of Jesus in a boat, but the boxes of Wearyall Hill earth had also been a big seller.

A woman with hair like a tea cosy and a badge on her black lapel that declared JESUS IS MY BEST FRIEND fell into step beside him.

'What language was Jesus talking when He was in Somerset?' she asked.

She was testing him to see how genuine his knowledge was, he thought, and he blessed the time he had spent in the public library.

'Aramaic,' he told her.

'That's probably right,' said the woman, sounding disappointed. 'I represent Prayer Against Alcohol.'

'A very laudable movement,' said Tim, who was dying for a drink. Clearly, in this ambient mood of piety, no nonsense was too outrageous to win his grudging support.

He marched on down the road to the town. The pilgrims straggled behind him, some of them singing hymns, others carrying candles that Howard had sold them. He had inquired about the possibility of selling votive lamps but hadn't liked the look of the figures.

Some way back, Janice had found Leo. The editor, in a yellow suit, was walking along with the pilgrims while attempting to make it clear that he was not part of the pilgrimage. The usual French cigarette protruded from the centre of his mouth.

'I've got a story for you, Leo,' Janice said, and told him about Gerry Titchmarsh.

Leo listened to the tale with a barely concealed derision. 'What did he say?' he asked.

'He wanted to know where the toilets are, actually.'

'He broke eight months' silence to say he wanted a piss? Not exactly Oscar Wilde, is he?'

'What he said isn't important, Leo,' Janice protested.

'It was fairly important to him, by the sound of it.'

Other journalists gathered round, aware of who Leo was.

'When did he last speak?' one asked.

'Eight months ago,' Janice told him. 'He was mugged in Bristol and has been mute ever since.'

'What did he say when he spoke?'

'The Lord is my Shepherd,' said Janice, anxious

to avoid further jokes. 'The words of a Psalm, I believe.'

'That's nice,' said one of the reporters. 'Do you happen to know which Psalm it is?'

They were in the town now, marching along Magdalene Street towards the entrance to the Abbey ruins. Crowds stopped to look at this strange procession which spilt out on to the road but moved forward with a Christly determination that did not invite interference. Tim led them into the grounds, where the ruins of the Abbey stood in brown stone hunks on an immaculate lawn. The grounds were the destination for many pilgrimages during the year; in June a whole weekend was set aside for them and more than 8,000 people were there from dawn to dusk. Tim's little party attracted no attention at all and was almost lost in the grounds.

He rounded them up, determined to give value for money, and told them that St Dunstan was once Abbot here. Then he told them about the Holy Thorn which had grown when Joseph thrust his staff into the ground on Wearyall Hill, and how cuttings from it had grown in the area ever since, including one here among the ruins. He told them how Joseph was supposed to have returned to Glastonbury with the Holy Grail after the crucifixion, and he showed them the site of the wattle and daub church, subsequently preserved with a covering of wood and lead, but replaced after a fire by the Lady Chapel whose ruins they could see today.

Not wanting to over-egg the pudding, he spurned all references to King Arthur and the Round Table, who were traditionally associated with Glastonbury and the Abbey, and he steered clear of other fables and legends involving ley-lines and fertility rites with which the area was well-endowed. Some of his party were already beginning to wear benign expressions of glazed incredulity, and he didn't want to overtax them.

In the North Transept, where you could lift up wooden covers to see the remains of the mediaeval tiles on the floor, he found himself trapped by a reporter called Quinn — a short, pale young man who, despite the heat, wore not only a suit and tie but also a velvet waistcoat of deepest red.

'Anyone with two grey cells to rub together knows that this is a load of cobblers, don't they?' he asked amiably.

'Fuck off,' replied Tim, with equal charm. He could safely afford the luxury of such language as his enthralled flock had dispersed in all directions, each of them finding different relics to examine: the Lady Chapel, the vault, the Abbot's kitchen.

'Do I take that to indicate a filament of guilt?' inquired the reporter. 'Exploiting the gullible and all that?'

'Like the Archbishop of Canterbury, do you mean?' retorted Tim. The man was so afflicted with dandruff that he thought for one mad moment that it had been snowing. 'If what you're talking about is Jesus in Somerset, the evidence is there for anybody to look up.'

'The whole caboodle,' said Quinn. 'Next century

we're going to land on Mars, and now they've found a planet in another galaxy that has water and therefore probably life. Where do your pilgrims go then?'

'They'll probably still be coming here on the Jesus Trail and your horrible little rag will have been wiped out by two hundred television channels. But don't despair, because you won't be here, either.'

Ignoring this as if it had never been said, Quinn withdrew a gold pen from the inside pocket of his jacket and asked: 'How much money are you making out of this?'

The man was impervious to abuse, so Tim decided to josh him. 'Money?' he said. 'You can talk about money on a spiritual occasion like this? I'm a humble handyman, Mr Quinn, in the service of the Lord.'

'And I'm the Queen's toy boy,' said Quinn.

'You may be,' said Tim, stepping round the reporter. 'Nobody has ever admired her taste.'

He hurried away before he could be trapped into a quotation that would destroy him. His duty now was to provide free refreshments for his customers before the coaches picked them up outside. The refreshments were to be organised by Beverley and he found her pouring cups of tea at a small table near the exit. Tim took the cups and handed them round to the visitors, trying to judge from their faces what they had thought about the very first Jesus Trail. He was vastly reassured. They looked radiant, even dazed. All of them looked grateful.

Some came up to him now to tell him how thankful

they were. A lady from New Zealand said that she would come again next year and it would be an annual event in her life. The pilot from Portugal said that it was one of the high points in his life which, considering the altitudes he must routinely achieve every working day, Tim took to be praise indeed. The New Jersey businessman, who had let Jesus into his life on a trial basis, said that he thought the visit had been very valuable but he couldn't be sure until he got home and looked at the Stock Market. The dancer from Tallahassee fondled his other thigh and asked him what he was doing later, and the lecturer in practical theology said that an extraordinary day had given him a title for his book: *When Jesus Came To Somerset*.

Rowland Coaches pulled up punctually at the gate, and Tim escorted his little crowd out of the Abbey grounds. They climbed reluctantly up the vehicle's steps, and then gazed down from the windows at Tim as if he were somehow related to the man whose visit to Somerset they had come here to celebrate.

That evening, Tim, Beverley and her parents watched it all on television. They had expected it to be consigned to a regional programme that covered only that part of the West Country, but the item must have tickled somebody in London because it went out on the national news. The idea that Jesus actually came to England was a novelty too good to miss, and suddenly there was Tim on the screen talking on the hill about Jesus eating apples.

'Mind-blowing,' said Howard, drinking Scotch.

'Fantastic,' said Beverley.

Cameras followed the procession down the hill and along the street into the Abbey grounds, and cut suddenly to a Professor of Divinity in Oxford, who said in a voice that seemed to come whistling down his nose: 'The idea that Jesus came to England with Joseph of Arimathea is unsubstantiated, to say the very least.'

But the interviewer, a bright young man who seemed to have become caught up in the enthusiasm of the Jesus Trail, wasn't happy with this.

'Surely much of the life of Jesus is unsubstantiated, isn't it? You wouldn't take it to a jury at the Old Bailey, but many people believe it.'

'There is fable and legend, of course,' said the Professor, only mildly discomforted. 'But there is much that we can be reasonably certain about, and Jesus coming to England isn't part of it.'

'Nevertheless,' said a voice-over, as the cameras cut back to the ruins of Glastonbury Abbey, 'there were two hundred happy pilgrims in Somerset today.'

Tim needed a Scotch himself when he had finished watching this.

'Why are you on television, Daddy?' Chloë asked.

'I have exalted connections,' he told her.

The inquest that they now held on the day was conducted in a mood of jubilant disbelief. From the very beginning it had gone far better than they had dared to hope. The programme had unfolded without a hitch, the customers were receptive and well-behaved, and it was clear, at the end, that they were impressed and satisfied.

Howard and Doris were impressed and satisfied too, having worked out that their income had just gone up by at least six hundred pounds a week. Doris reckoned that she could double this if she was allowed to cook chips, but Tim had been firm about no food smells on the hill.

Beverley opened champagne and could not stop smiling. Tim stayed with the Scotch and dreamed of money. The following morning he bought every newspaper in the shop, and the news here, too, was good.

Journalists whose stories might otherwise have displayed an unwelcome cynicism, had been mercifully diverted by Gerry Titchmarsh's fortuitous curiosity about lavatories. It was a story that was made for them.

On its front page, the *Sun* had a white-on-black headline:

MIRACLE ON THE HILL
WHERE JESUS WALKED

Below was a large photograph of Gerry Titchmarsh wearing the strained expression of a man in urgent need of micturition.

Most of the other papers followed the line.

A man deprived of the power
of speech after a brutal

> mugging in Bristol eight
> months ago, spoke for the
> first time yesterday during
> a Christian pilgrimage in
> Somerset when he suddenly
> recited the 23rd Psalm,

said *The Times*. So interesting was the story of Gerry Titchmarsh that none of the papers had bothered to question the validity or financial background of the Jesus Trail, or raise the obvious question about whether Jesus had really visited England at all.

Only Quinn's story contained a passage that could be thought hostile:

> The venture's director Tim
> Banner denied that he was
> cashing in on the gullibility
> of thousands of people.
>   Mr Banger, 35, said: 'The
> documentation is irrefutable.
> It's just a question of
> bothering to look for it.'

'He can't even spell my name incorrectly the same way twice,' said Tim admiringly.

16

When Sam Dawson woke up on the following Monday morning it was to the bleep of his quartz alarm clock that he hadn't used for some years. It was six o'clock, and his mind rebelled at this premature conclusion to its sleep. He turned on his side and eased himself nearer to Janice's warm body. Surprisingly, the alarm hadn't woken her. He was asleep almost immediately with his arms round her waist, but five minutes later the alarm went again, bleeping repeatedly and conveying a more urgent message.

Sam rolled to the side of the bed and put his feet on the floor. It was not easy to fall asleep again with your feet on the floor. Not only tiredness made him reluctant to get up. This was the big day, and he was filled with misgivings. The number of things he had to do was beyond counting, and so was the number of possible disasters. After several moments he stood up uncertainly and looked for his dressing gown.

Taking care not to wake Janice, he went downstairs

and poured himself an orange juice. Then he opened the back door for Footprint, asleep in his basket in the kitchen. The dog, who normally bolted into the back garden when the door was opened, lay in his basket and blinked at Sam. His clock, too, told him that this was an unnatural time to start a day.

Sam's next move was to the phone where he dialled Alastair Ford's number. He had finished his orange juice before his call was answered.

'You asked me to make sure you were up,' he said.

'What's the time, for God's sake?'

'Six thirteen.'

'I'll see you at seven.'

Sam replaced the phone, stroked the dog, put the kettle on, and returned upstairs. Memories of what it felt like to have a job flooded back, all of them miserable. He shaved with his Braun, washed cursorily, and then decided to weigh himself, curious about what effect all this work was going to have on him. He was 70 kilograms or about 11 stone. In a month's time he would weigh himself again and see what the toll had been. His lanky frame needed more weight, not less.

From the wardrobe he pulled out a brown suit he hadn't worn for months and looked for a green shirt that he liked to go with it. A tie was snatched, randomly as usual, from the rack. He did not look, he thought as he studied the mirror, like a man who was going to do something remarkable today. Perhaps as the day wore on he would grow into the role.

Back downstairs he made tea and decided to boil

himself an egg. Breakfast was normally a meal that he enjoyed but this was too early for hunger. In fact, he felt sick. He turned on the radio for the current affairs programme that he usually heard only the second half of, and found encouragement in a story about a woman who had been accosted by a beggar at Waterloo Station. The demands for money had been interrupted by a mobile phone which started to ring in the beggar's pocket. He took this as a good sign: the money was moving in unexpected directions. The programme sped on to news of the latest royal romance. The fat redhead had found a new object for her lust on the tennis circuit, but Sam didn't want to know anything about the royal family and especially what they were doing with their sex organs, so he turned it off and tried to start concentrating on the day ahead.

Thirty-eight halls had been booked over an area that stretched roughly from the Mendips to the Quantocks. Each hall was expecting about one hundred pensioners to arrive at nine o'clock, and his local managers had confirmed the previous evening that the work had arrived at all of them. Tonight the same lorries would take away the work that was done and deliver more for tomorrow, although later, when the groups were established and the quality of the work had proved satisfactory, the lorries would deliver and pick up once a week.

The plan today was for Sam to visit half the halls and see how everything was working out, while Alastair called in at the other nineteen. They would each carry

£10,000 in cash – money that at present lay in a large suitcase in their office upstairs. The daily wages bill at £5 a head was £19,000, or £500 a hall.

The offer of a fiver a day, plus a hot lunch, a lot of laughs and some new company, had been warmly accepted by all the old folk who had been approached. They had, as Janice had judged, been lonely and bored at home, and obsessed with feelings of uselessness. Alastair Ford had concluded at one stage that most of them were so grateful to be given something useful to do while making new friends and getting a free lunch that they would have worked for nothing; but Sam contended that this would put Workfare in an indefensible position.

By the time that he had eaten his boiled egg, the morning newspaper had arrived, but this too was gripped by the overdrafts and infidelities of the royal family, so he tossed it to one side and made Janice a cup of tea instead.

'I feel guilty still being in bed,' she said without moving. 'What's the time?'

'Six forty.'

'Well, I don't feel *that* guilty then. It's rather a change, finding myself lying here doing nothing while you rush about like a proper husband.'

'Make the most of it,' said Sam. 'You could have a busy few hours.'

Janice had cancelled all other jobs today. She was managing the office at Workfare, taking the calls, answering the questions and relaying messages to Sam and Alastair who both now, in a final splurge of extravagance, had phones in their cars. Sam put the tea by the side of Janice's bed as the doorbell rang.

Alastair Ford stood on the step, looking faintly aggrieved. It was many years since he had left his bed this early: alcohol had seen to that.

'This is it then,' he said. 'Over the top.'

'Come in and have a cup of tea,' said Sam. 'We've got plenty of time.'

'You mean I needn't have got up this early?'

'Best to have time on your side,' said Sam.

A suitcase on the kitchen table had been opened to reveal thousands of pounds in neat packs of five-pound notes. It looked like a prop in a film about bank robbers.

'There's got to be a better way of doing this,' Alastair suggested. 'We can't drive round country lanes every morning with money like this in the car. A dishonest person with a firearm could get to hear of it.'

'There will be,' Sam promised. 'Today we're improvising.'

Half an hour later, with secret qualms and anxieties they felt it best not to discuss, they got into their cars and drove off in different directions. Alastair headed south to the Quantocks although his journey would eventually bring him as far south as Yeovil. Sam headed north to the Mendips and a succession of attractive villages that lay between the motorway in the west and Shepton Mallet in the east. Bizet's *Carmen* on the car's stereo seemed to be getting him into the right frame of mind.

He reached the first hall, the one that was far-thest away, before anyone else had arrived, but the man he had chosen to run it, a retired Army captain called Morley, appeared with the keys soon after-wards. Tables and chairs had been set up the previous evening, filling the small hall. The stage at one end was covered with boxes, containing the work that needed to be done.

'What does it cost to hire this hall?' Sam asked.

'Eight pounds a day,' said Morley. 'Ridiculously cheap, really.'

When the old people arrived, Sam's spirits soared. He had in his darkest moments pictured derelict geriatrics shambling in with their strangulated hernias and split arteries, needing help with the steps. But the people who strode in now looked ready to run a marathon, and it was hard to believe that they had reached pensionable age. People took more care of themselves these days and it was often difficult to tell whether they were forty or sixty.

He stood to one side as Morley introduced himself and took over the organisation. He invited the visitors to sit where they liked, and explained what the work was that they would be doing for the next three days. 'You'll be paid daily,' he told them, 'so if you don't feel like coming in some days it won't matter although, of course, we would prefer to see you here.'

Sam had to remind himself that although this group

of people were now known generically as pensioners, they had until recently been bank managers, prison governors, scientists, accountants, musicians, theatre producers, businessmen and teachers. The information had filtered back through his hastily-appointed local managers. There was an ex-MP at work in one of the halls, and the former conductor of a London orchestra.

'A titan of the podium!' Sam had said. 'We *are* honoured.'

And so, when lunch arrived at the hall he happened to be in at the time, and he joined the others for a steak and kidney pie, he treated them with great respect. That was the mystery of pensioners, he decided. You were never quite sure who you were talking to.

An old lady in a pink towelling tracksuit told him what a wonderful idea Workfare was and how much it meant to people of her age. A man of seventy, who had spent a lifetime in the Forces, said that it filled a gap in his life that had needed filling.

'Are you worried about the money?' Sam asked. 'Less than a pound an hour doesn't seem a lot.'

'The money is the least important part of it,' said the man. 'A fiver makes the whole thing viable. It makes it a fun thing with a good atmosphere. No pressure, see? If they paid better money we wouldn't get a look in, would we? You'd have the professionals sitting here.'

The situation couldn't have been more accurately described, Sam thought as he took his leave and drove off in the Nissan. But he worried, as he drove through Cheddar Gorge, that if the newspapers decided to write about Workfare, they might not see it quite like that.

He spent the afternoon visiting the other halls on his list. In one they were assembling portable radios, in another they were screwing up and bolting the plastic exterior of some hi-fi equipment. A third hall was painting toy soldiers with infinite care, and in another they were assembling a wooden toy, but nobody's progress was sufficiently advanced for Sam to guess what the toy was. In other halls they were stitching footballs, stuffing and sewing dolls, soldering circuit boards, making plastic flowers and putting together fan heaters. In every hall there was music and a non-stop babble of conversation, and in each hall he visited, the full complement of pensioners had turned up.

'The test is tomorrow,' he said to his local manager in one hall. 'Will they all turn up tomorrow?'

'They'll turn up,' said the man. 'They love it.'

When he got into his car the next time, Alastair came through on the phone to say that the Press, in the shape of an agency reporter and photographer, had suddenly appeared at the hall he was presently visiting in Hambridge.

'Let 'em in,' said Sam. 'A bit of publicity and we'll have a hundred halls this time next week.'

'What do I tell them about money?'

'As little as possible,' said Sam. 'How did they find out about it?'

'Well, if three or four thousand pensioners have turned up today, it's hardly a secret, is it? Then we've advertised in every newsagent's window, and there was that story Janice wrote.'

'Ah,' said Sam. 'Well, be nice to them.'

Filled by doubts that had been fed to him weeks ago by Tim Bonner, he could see headlines he didn't like (EVIL MAN WHO EXPLOITS THE OLDIES) and imagine questions in one of the more forthright tabloids that hit him on a painful spot: How much are *you* making out of it, Mr Dawson?

The truth was, of course, that he didn't know what he was going to make out of it, because he didn't know whether the workers would continue to appear in sufficient quantities, or even whether the standard of their work would be satisfactory. Today's wage bill had pushed his expenditure so far to nearly £25,000, and by the end of the week it would be nearer £100,000. Receipts so far: nil. But you had to speculate to accumulate in this world, he had always been told, and nobody could now accuse him of failing to do that. The vital ingredient in his frightening equation was the continued support of his bank manager. How big would the debt be before the first cheque arrived?

He said goodbye to Alastair and promised him a drink later. His guess was that they would both need several.

Driving east, his mind returned to the worrying subject of money. If Janice had known when she first came up with her idea that they would have to spend more than £100,000 before they saw a penny, she would have cut her tongue out. What had once seemed like a sure thing was gradually beginning to feel like an insane gamble.

But dropping down to Wells, with its beautiful mediaeval houses and a skyline that had scarcely altered in 800 years, he felt inexplicably encouraged again, and began to enumerate reasons why nothing could go wrong. If one firm asked another to provide a hundred workers in a hall, they could not pay less than £40 a person and the firm providing the workforce would want their profit on top; £5,000 a day seemed a likely figure. If the firms that Sam was dealing with paid only £1,000 he was making several hundred in profit, per hall, per day. He pulled into the side of the road and found pencil and paper, seeking to calm his nerves. If he only made £300 per hall, after paying the pensioners, the manager, the food suppliers and the hall hire, it was £11,400 a day from thirty-eight halls. Over the five-day week, this was £57,000 clear profit. And soon he would have twice as many halls.

These calculations delivered him later to The Crossed Wires in a mood of extreme contentment. He rang Janice from the pub car park to tell her where he was.

'How did it go?' she asked.

'Wonderfully. Why don't you join me for a drink?'

'I don't seem to have a car.'

'I'll buy you another one. In the meantime, we can afford taxis.'

Alastair was drinking like a man who felt he had earned it. He was in good company. The skittles team was preparing for a big game in the indoor alley at the back by consuming the five or six pints that were thought essential before action began. It was a mystery to Sam that none of the pub teams in Somerset — darts, pool, skittles — used the pub's name, but invented instead a semi-obscene title, like Sheppey Shaggers, Pheasant Pluckers or Bottom Scratchers, which were duly listed in the results section of the local papers.

Alastair said: 'Some old boiling fowl tried to pick me up. Do they get sexier as they get older?'

'You'd better hope so, kid. Let me buy you a drink.'

When they retired to a table by the window to compare notes, Alastair, famished by a thirst that never left him, revealed that he had had a hard day. Some of the local managers had ambushed him with questions that he couldn't answer, a task in one hall had seemed too difficult for some of the pensioners until it had been demonstrated to them several times, and the Press had been troublesome, showing an unpleasant curiosity about Workfare's finances, the workers' wages, and who, in the reporter's phrase, was 'skimming the cream off the top'.

'What did you tell him?' asked Sam.

'I told him to piss off,' Alastair announced proudly.

'I see,' said Sam. 'A charm offensive.'

'Only initially,' Alastair admitted. 'I deployed my usual mixture of magnetism and geniality and quite won him over. I told him that it was naturally difficult for somebody who spent their lives with the disasters and miseries of the gutter press to recognise a humanitarian gesture of startling originality, and then I introduced him to several members of the aged workforce who told him that it was the happiest day they'd had in months. It rather took the ground from beneath the poor man's feet. I think any publicity you get now will probably be favourable.'

'It's not the reporters. It's the editors and leader writers back at headquarters who will put their own spin on it. We'll just have to wait to see.' Sam drank his lager and saw Janice coming through the door.

'There are enough faxes to make a toilet roll for an elephant,' she announced. 'Gin and tonic, please.'

Sam fetched them all drinks after worming his way through the skittles team, and then sat down to listen to Janice's day. The phone had hardly stopped ringing.

'Suppliers rang to make sure their stuff had been delivered. A food firm rang to ask whether we wanted salad or hot. A couple of managers rang to let you know that the work had been satisfactorily completed, and three newspapers rang to talk to you.'

'You could have called me,' said Sam. 'That's why I bought a car phone.'

'I did call you but you must have been in a hall. The important stuff has all been faxed. It's all about what will be arriving where. It's a monumental exercise, isn't it?'

'Yes, dear,' said Sam. 'I don't know how you thought of it. I ought to talk to the papers, though. Just to put them on the right track.'

He took the names and numbers that Janice had brought and went out to the phone in his car.

A man at the *Daily Mail* asked: 'What about the trade unions?'

'What?' said Sam.

'Trade unions. It's an association of employees that has a certain reputation for defending its corner.'

'What have they got to do with it?' Sam asked. It was a long time since he had even thought about trade unions.

'They won't let them do productive work in prisons,' said the reporter. 'Well, this sounds a bit like that.'

'It's not a bit like that,' said Sam.

'Cheap labour. Undercutting the market. It's the same thing, isn't it?'

'Simple jobs that require no prior training? Not worth the attention of our great trade unions, I'd have thought.'

But the call worried him so much that he didn't bother to ring the other papers. If the trade unions took an interest, his scheme would be ruined. They'd nearly ruined the country once or twice: Workfare would be a pushover. For a start, the drivers would refuse to deliver the raw materials, and that's all it would need to kill Workfare stone dead.

He returned to the bar in sombre mood, but Alastair, now comprehensively pixilated, dismissed the threat. 'These are old ladies sewing on buttons. They're not into mechanical engineering or powder metallurgy. The unions wouldn't be bothered with it.'

'Don't tell me,' said Sam. 'I belonged to them for ten years and they were a vindictive bunch of sods.'

'Well, they're not now. They got dragged to the right. They're quite cuddly.'

Cuddly was not the word that sprang to Sam's mind when he pictured the workers' leaders he had seen hollering at factory gate meetings on television, but Alastair's consumption of Famous Grouse made further debate impracticable.

He told Janice: 'If every day goes like today, we're going to make a lot of money.'

'Trade unions permitting?'

'Exactly.'

'Well, let me know when I can give up making cakes, running playgroups, minding shops, writing columns and giving talks. I've discovered this word in the dictionary, leisure. Apparently it means a time or opportunity for ease or relaxation. I quite like the sound of it.'

He didn't want to dampen her spirits by telling her how their debt was increasing at the rate of £20,000 a day, and he tried not to think about it himself. His immediate problem was actually delivering the money, and he wondered whether he should open bank accounts all over the area. The local managers could collect the money and pay it — but could they all be trusted? He suddenly saw the answer: a security firm that would deliver the money each day.

'Talking about leisure,' said Alastair, slurring his

speech only slightly, 'what time do I have to get up tomorrow?'

'You don't,' said Sam. 'Take a day off. I'll dash round with the money myself, and by Wednesday I'm going to organise a security firm to do it. In return, I'd like you to run the office on Wednesday, answer the phone, keep an eye on things.'

'Why's that?' said Alastair. 'What are you doing on Wednesday?'

'I'm on a course.'

'Really?' said Alastair. 'What course have you got to go on?'

'A golf course,' said Sam.

He woke the following morning without the benefit of an alarm clock. He had hardly slept. The problems came, zapping him one after another, as he lay in the dark listening to Janice's relaxed breathing. And with the problems came the worries – notably today how the newspapers were going to react to the concept of Workfare. Would he be portrayed as hero or villain? Was he the man who had brought contentment and satisfaction to thousands of lonely and ignored pensioners, or was he a hard-faced racketeer who exploited the elderly?

Stirred by guilt, he had been taken in the long sleepless hours by a generous idea that he hoped would make him feel better. He would pay any pensioners who completed a five-day week a bonus of £20. This would help to produce good attendance figures and blunt the charge of exploitation. But when he sat up in bed and consulted his pocket calculator, he found that to pay 3,800 people £20 would cost him £76,000. Workfare would be running at a loss! He abandoned the idea and struggled to find another.

Downstairs, Footprint appeared no more enthusiastic for the early call than he had the previous day, but when he was shown his lead and offered a walk he cautiously vacated his basket. At the newsagents Sam bought every morning newspaper they had, but couldn't bring himself to open one. He stuffed them into a supermarket bag and walked slowly back to his house.

He fed Footprint and poured himself an orange juice. Then he put the kettle on, and it was only when he had a cup of tea in front of him that he felt bold enough to open the bag. It wasn't difficult to find the stories.

The *Daily Mirror* had a neutral account that was headed SAM PUTS THE OLDIES TO WORK.

The tone of the *Sun* was more critical, but despite its headline, PENSIONERS CLOCK ON FOR PEANUTS, it never quite managed to paint Sam as a villain:

> Businessman Sam Dawson is paying old folk just £5 a day to tackle a multitude of jobs in village halls all over the West Country.
>
> The scheme, which will undercut conventional labour, was launched yesterday — and

4000 pensioners turned up to take part.

'It gives us something to do,' said Mavis Peacock, 73, of Westonzoyland, Somerset. 'At last we feel wanted.'

But MPs were not so sure that it was a good idea.

Labour's Rod Speed talked of exploitation and asked: 'Who's making the money here?'

Sam skipped from this to the *Daily Mail*, which had evidently made a few more phone calls after talking to him.

The trade unions, which have traditionally supported the elderly in their struggle for a decent pension and adequate medical care, don't know which way to jump as they watch this incursion on their territory.

But all his fears slipped away when Sam came to *The Times*. A four-column photograph on the front page showed the smiling faces of the pensioners as they worked in neat rows in the village hall at Hambridge. And, inside, the paper had devoted one of its leaders to the project. Sam spread the paper on the table and read every word, but when he had finished, one sentence stuck in his mind: *Mr Dawson's brilliant idea has unleashed a huge untapped resource which could revolutionise British industry.*

He made his wife a cup of tea and took it up to her.

'Have you got the papers?' she asked, waking suddenly.

'Mr Dawson's brilliant idea has unleashed a huge untapped resource that could revolutionise British industry,' he told her.

'Whose brilliant idea?' Janice asked.

17

Out on the golf course, where the sun was beating down with an intensity that seemed savage even by the standards of this blistering summer, Tim Bonner had arrived in an outfit that was new to him: a pale lilac Ralph Lauren shirt in very fine cotton, purple Armani cotton trousers and a new golfer's cap with AUGUSTA blazoned across the front.

The joyful mood of truant schoolboys which infected them both was mitigated somewhat in Sam's case by these extravagant amendments to the Bonner wardrobe, with which Tim was obviously delighted.

'It's a funny old world,' he said rapturously. 'One minute there I am without a roof to my mouth, and the next I'm knee-deep in money. Beverley's talking about mink coats. Wild mink or ranch mink? That's the sort of problem we wrestle with now. Look at this.' He shot out his left arm so that Sam could inspect closely the chunky new watch which adorned his wrist. 'Baume and Mercier.'

'Good, are they?' asked Sam.

'Only the best,' said Tim. 'How's Workfare?' He placed his ball on the tee and took a few practise swings while he waited for a reply.

'Workfare is fine, but the cash flow is a bit worrying.'

Tim hit the ball and watched contentedly as it soared straight and true. 'The trouble is,' he said when he was satisfied with the ball's position, 'I get paid for the work before I do it, but you have to wait until afterwards. You've got an overdraft?'

'Just a bit.'

'You're well bitched then in today's market. Worry, uncertainty, bank charges and interest rates. You're always playing catch-up.'

Sam poked his tee in the hard ground and placed the ball on it. 'I understood that your own little venture started life overdrawn?'

'Only slightly, and not for long. The cheques pretty well poured in from Day One.'

Sam took a practise swing. 'How's it going now, anyway?' The strenuous demands of Workfare had pushed the Jesus Trail from his mind.

Tim leaned on his club and looked utterly carefree. 'Very few problems, really. Some demented cleric in Lincoln has delivered himself of the opinion that Jesus never set foot in England, but as he's currently on remand for buggering thirty-eight schoolboys nobody's disposed to listen to him.'

'Lucky for you, really.'

'Bloody lucky. Not so good for the schoolboys, of course. Hit that ball, old man.'

Sam's drive began promisingly, but veered suddenly as if he had somehow imparted some spin when he hit the ball. It vanished into the trees on the left of the fairway.

Tim hardly seemed to notice. 'There was some cor-respondence in *The Times* quoting a letter from St Augustine to Pope Gregory about the church that Jesus and Joseph built here.'

'It was so impressive you even believe the story yourself?' Sam suggested.

'I certainly believe it every Tuesday and Thursday. Drive off again. We can't spend the morning trying to find your balls.'

Feeling wrong-footed on several fronts, Sam placed another ball on the tee while Tim watched. Their game had lost some of its interest now that they weren't playing for the usual fiver. He had suggested the bet in the clubhouse, but Tim decided there was so much money about now that they would have to play for £500 to get a comparable kick out of it.

'We'll play for fun then,' said Sam, who didn't have £500.

But this wasn't fun. He had lost what golfing touch he had, and Tim's sartorial overhaul was beginning to depress him. And there was something else. Even when he embarked on a risky business venture like the Jesus Trail, Tim's life remained remarkably untroubled, while Sam was consumed by doubts about his own delicate position.

His second attempt avoided the trees and scythed through the grass, but stayed well short of Tim's ball. They picked up their bags and set off down the fairway.

'Are you finding it all rather exhausting?' Sam asked.

'Why should I?' asked Tim. 'I only work two days a week.'

Sam felt wrong-footed again. He had been tired for days, and worried constantly about the fragile empire he was constructing. Watching television, his mind wandered immediately to the problems of Workfare, and at night he lay awake and worried some more. Now on the golf course he felt guilty about stealing a day that he felt his health needed, and fretted about the phone calls and faxes that Alastair was dealing with at home.

'I've ordered a Mercedes,' said Tim when they returned to the clubhouse. 'It seemed silly driving round in a Honda.'

'My goodness,' said Sam. 'What will that cost?'

'I didn't ask. I think the one I want is about forty thousand. A deep, deep blue.'

The idea of buying something without inquiring about the cost was not a concept that Sam had encountered before, and as he got into the Honda for a lift home he felt again the ignoble stabs of envy that had distracted him during the game.

'I'm glad it's going well for you, Tim,' he said. 'The customers are queuing up, are they?'

'We're booked up now until September. We're going to take a break in December and January. The hill will be too cold, too wet, too icy or all three. Beverley wants to go on a winter cruise.'

'A cruise?' said Sam. 'That'll be nice.'

When Tim had dropped Sam off at his house he wondered whether Sam was too old to shoulder the burden that his imaginative wife had placed on him. He looked harassed beyond endurance, and the grey hair at his temples was spreading. Sam was only forty, but he was an old forty who could easily convince anybody that he was fifty or more. In addition, he was a worrier which, in Tim's view of the world, immediately doubled the size of any problem, often rendering it insoluble.

Howard and Doris were sitting at the back of the house without a care in the world. Doris was swinging gently in the hammock seat in a red one-piece swimming costume, and Howard, in white shorts, was sitting in a deck chair and drinking a supermarket bottle of sangria. It seem to Tim that they were both pretending that they were still in Spain.

'Timothy!' said Howard. 'Did you win?'

'I did,' said Tim.

'Of course you did. You murdered him,' said Howard, beaming proudly. Howard's admiration for Tim, which until very recently had been less than boundless, had lurched embarrassingly towards adulation in the wake of the Jesus Trail's success, and Tim found himself constantly struggling to keep the relationship on a level that he could handle.

Howard handed him a glass of sangria and asked: 'What do you think about Bev selling the shop?'

'I'm happy about it,' Tim said. 'The Jesus Trail needs her.'

'Trouble is, it's a lot easier in this world to buy something than to sell it. I can tell you that from a lifetime's experience.'

'Somebody will buy it. It's a nice little shop,' Tim told him. 'But there are a lot of fixtures and fittings we need to take out first.'

'Leave it to me, Timothy,' said Howard.

'A handyman, are you?'

'Give him the job and he'll finish the tools,' said Doris, chuckling in the swing hammock.

Tim wanted to ask why Howard gave his daughter a nice name like Beverley and then abbreviated it to Bev, while at the same time managing to drag Tim's name out to three syllables that overworked the tongue. But he needed to avoid any such discordant notes at the moment. The formal reason for politeness — that the couple were his guests — wasn't even the half of it. Their contribution to the Jesus Trail was too valuable to lose, and he lived in fear that they would blithely announce one morning that it was time they returned to Spain.

'I'll put a Se Vende sign up with your phone number,' said Howard, sipping his sangria.

'Better make that For Sale,' said Doris.

'My God, I keep thinking I'm in Spain, doll,' said Howard. 'It's this heat.'

Beverley emerged from the house in a white bikini, followed by Chloë in an identical garment.

'Chloë says she wants a swimming pool,' she said, joining her mother on the hammock. 'It sounds like a good idea to me.'

'It is a good idea,' said Tim. 'We'll do it.'

'What you want to do,' said Howard, 'is build it in one of the stable blocks, then you can use it all the year round.'

'That's a good idea, too,' said Tim, marvelling at the way he could calmly accept this latest expensive proposal. A new Mercedes, a mink coat, a winter cruise, a swimming pool – the world no longer seemed real.

Beverley smiled at him gratefully. She had developed a new way of looking at him now. Glances that had once suggested that he was something unpleasant clinging to the heel of her shoe, were now infused with admiration and satisfaction. Her sexual demands, perhaps hoarded during her long dormant spell, exploded nightly, hauling him into wanton and imaginative exertions he thought he would never see again. Every night, drained and debilitated, he sank into a dreamless sleep wondering whether he would recover enough strength to perform tomorrow. During the day, conscious of the challenge, he began to take extreme care of his health, even buying various pills from a health food shop, watching his alcohol consumption and sometimes doing press-ups.

If he didn't keel over, he thought, she would probably want to marry him.

*　　*　　*

In the Dawson household, where mink coats, swimming pools and winter cruises were never discussed, a phone call arrived one morning that chilled Sam's blood.

His main job now was to maintain the supply of work, a task made more urgent by the addition of a dozen new halls − and 1,200 new pensioners − to the enterprise. While Alastair Ford toured Oxford and Gloucestershire interviewing and appointing local managers and arranging the daily delivery of lunches, Sam spent ten hours a day with his phone and his fax machine, arranging a non-stop flow of suitable jobs.

The manufacturers he had started with had all stayed with him, satisfied with the standards that were being produced, but an expanding workforce was creating an appetite that not even they could satisfy. It was the third week and eventually he had to get in the Nissan and spend three days in the north soliciting work, often from firms who had turned him down on his earlier visit. Now, with the scheme a proven success and legitimised by favourable publicity in the newspapers, they were anxious to join. He returned home wearily, confident that he had enough assignments in the bag to keep any number of pensioners happily occupied for some time, and got to work on his invoices. This should have been the triumphant culmination of his labours, the blissful moment when he could begin to see his reward. But it turned out to be a wearisome chore and he was relieved to be interrupted by the phone.

It was McAllister, the bank manager. His voice sounded like stone.

'We've got to talk, Mr Dawson. Could you drop in?'

Worrying thoughts about McAllister and the bank had been hovering in Sam's head for two weeks, but he had never had the time to give them the attention they deserved.

'I'll come in now, if you like,' he said, feeling guilty.

'Do that,' said McAllister, and hung up.

Sam did not see the brusque termination of the call as being a good augury, and was further disheartened on going downstairs to be reminded that Janice was out on one of her talks and had taken the car. He rang for a taxi, reproaching himself for remaining a one-car family when he had all this money. It was only when he was sitting in the back of the taxi, recalling McAllister's icy tones, that he remembered he didn't have any.

It was this melancholy deficiency that had miraculously transformed McAllister in a matter of weeks from an ebullient banker with the scent of profit in his nostrils into a sad and broken creature who looked as if his doctor had recommended he make a will. He sat in an office of Stygian gloom beneath a terracotta bust of Queen Victoria, and said: 'Mr Dawson, this is serious. What's going on?'

'Going on?' said Sam, not entirely prepared for this frontal thrust.

'We agreed a more or less open-ended overdraft facility. We want to lend, and I was enthusiastic about your project. But you're taking money out of this bank at the rate of a hundred thousand a week. Do you know what you owe us now? More than a quarter of a million.'

He looked down at papers on his surprisingly small desk. 'In fact, more than three hundred thousand.'

'I thought it was always understood that the start-up costs would be considerable,' said Sam. 'It takes a while for the money to start coming through.' He realised with alarm that McAllister's initial enthusiasm for Workfare had already cooled to the sort of temperature that made brass monkeys justifiably pessimistic about their chances of parenthood.

'And when will this be?' he asked. 'When will this money start to come through?'

'I was doing the invoices when you rang, as a matter of fact.'

McAllister leaned forward in his chair. 'That's no good. They won't pay until the end of the following month. Those firms never do. And what will your overdraft be then? Eight hundred thousand? A million?' He was beginning to look like a man who had absent-mindedly voided his bowels, and didn't care if people noticed.

'The point is that whatever the debt, I am owed far more than that, and always will be. The figures are built into the system.'

'The concept of creditors going bust obviously hasn't occurred to you. What you don't seem to understand, Mr Dawson, is that the bank has no security to protect itself against an overdraft like this, and the debt is already too big for you to provide any such security, unless you own one of the biggest houses in Somerset, which I understand you don't.'

Sam sat back, reflecting that McAllister's face did not, in its fundamental features, differ markedly from a gnu's anus. The man's fastidious attention to figures was clouding his vision of the future, and what use was a bank manager devoid of entrepreneurial flair? About as much use as a guillemot with vertigo, he told himself.

McAllister said: 'I thought we might reach a hundred thousand. I was prepared for that, although I naturally hoped it wouldn't happen. But *this* — we're in the stratosphere!'

'I've only spent money on the project,' Sam said, feeling a need to defend himself. 'There hasn't been any personal extravagance. I haven't even got a car. I had to come here by taxi.'

'Taxis, is it? What happened to buses?'

'I rather wanted to get here today, seeing as that was what we arranged.'

McAllister leaned back in his chair and expelled air through his teeth like a punctured balloon. 'Well, it's got to stop,' he said eventually, 'and it's got to stop now.'

Sam looked at him, unsure of what he meant. When he felt reasonably sure that he did know what McAllister meant, fear and anger brought him to his feet.

'Stop? We can't stop now!' he said. 'We're heading for huge profits, man.'

McAllister stared at the sheets of paper on his desk as if they were a meal of animal excreta, laid before him by a mad chef. 'What we are heading for is a million pound overdraft, Mr Dawson. With no security. You were never a businessman, were you? I'm afraid you're not operating in the real world.'

Sam sat down again, wondering which way to approach this man. Was it charm and friendly persuasion that he needed, or was it the righteous anger of a man who was being betrayed? As he considered this it became clear that McAllister had nothing further to say, and an embarrassed silence filled the gloomy office.

'Would you like to see the invoices I'm sending out?' Sam asked. 'Would that reassure you?'

'Invoices aren't money, Mr Dawson. And, as I told you, firms go bust — with frightening regularity in the present economic climate. Many bills today are never paid, as banks know to their cost. What we are talking about here is timescale. Any money the invoices produce wouldn't arrive until the second half of next month. It's standard business practice. And by then, your overdraft . . .' He shrugged his hands as if he couldn't bear to contemplate the way his sentence should end.

Sam sat there, a poker player with no cards to play. McAllister dragged his eyes from the documents on his desk and looked as if suicide was an option he would happily embrace if the necessary accoutrements were to hand. He pulled himself together and fixed Sam with a gaze which would have demoralised a reasonably confident herd of buffalo, and said: 'I'm closing the account today.'

'Closing it?'

'Eventually, of course, we will have to take the appropriate action to get our money back.'

'You'll get your money back by not closing the account, you idiot,' Sam shouted, seeing now that he had nothing else to lose.

'I think we've already covered that ground, Mr Dawson,' McAllister said with infinite resignation.

Sam stood up, unable to continue the conversation. He walked out of the bank and stood on the pavement, too distracted to think clearly. It seemed to be hotter than ever. He noticed that he was almost opposite a taxi rank and he threaded a dazed path through hooting traffic towards it.

Twenty minutes later he was sitting at the bar of The Crossed Wires with a large whisky gripped in both hands. There was not much chance of company: Alastair was in Oxford, and Tim usually arrived at public houses only when a meeting had been arranged. So Sam sat on his own, considering the horror that his life had suddenly become. His business had collapsed with debts of more than £300,000, the pensioners couldn't be paid, bankruptcy loomed, and the future was beyond thinking about. Apart from that, the outlook was sunshine itself, he told himself grimly.

Sometimes, in his youth, when he had dreamed of the majestic success and daunting financial accomplishments that lay ahead, he had darker visions, too, that involved subsequent failure, poverty and disgrace. Now he could only wonder at his prescience, although he knew what had inspired this spectre of defeat. Men who were famously prosperous were carted off to the dungeons as often as cat burglars. A proximity to money carried mysterious risks of its own.

He ordered another large whisky and wished fervently that Janice had never had her inspired idea. The brief journey into a world where his rewards might be huge had altered his perspectives and increased his expectations. To return to the usual world where he had little, and could confidently expect less, would be cruel indeed. After a blank few minutes during which he polished off the whisky and stared hopelessly at the wall, he ordered another drink and wondered whether the alcohol would bring him an idea, as it had his wife. And for a while it did. Ostrich farms, he had heard, were on the way, and so were ostrich burgers which were non-fat and high protein. You bought a couple and let them breed (they bred for twenty-five years, apparently) and it was money ever after. All he needed to launch himself on this exciting new career was a loan from a bank.

Bank is a four-letter word, he told himself; even thinking about it made him feel unwell. The whisky made him feel unwell, too. It was not a drink that he was used to.

He should leave — but could he move? He wrote his telephone number laboriously on a piece of paper, and handed it to the landlord.

'Can you ring that?' he asked. 'Tell my wife to collect me.'

'I think I'd better,' said the landlord.

When he got back from the phone, Sam Dawson was asleep with his head in an ashtray.

Janice Dawson was sleep-walking her way through one of her talks. These days, she thought, it was a bit like being in a long-running play where you spent too much time each day saying exactly the same thing. But soon, she knew, she would be able to give it up.

Her audience today was a group of teenage girls at a local school, and she was narrating the talk she called 'Memory Lane'. Her intention was to give her audience a glimpse of what life had been like for some before the war and, in the case of girls of this age, make them more appreciative of what they had today.

'What did a poor girl do when she wanted to make up her face before going out?' she asked. She had lost count of the number of times she had asked the question. 'First, the eyebrows. They would get a piece of firewood, burned to the exact shade of brown that they wanted their eyebrows to be, take it from the fire and leave it to cool down, and then draw it on. It made a lovely shade of brown. Next, the lips. Lipstick cost four and sixpence in 1936, a quarter of a week's wages. Sorry, twenty-two and a half pence. Lipstick was a luxury, so girls used to bite their lips to make them red. For their cheeks they used to keep an old piece of red wallpaper in their dressing-table drawer. They'd spit on their fingers, rub it on the wallpaper, and when the dye came off, they'd dab it on their cheeks.'

Janice was always gratified by the distaste and horror

285

this talk produced in an audience of modern girls, and she noticed it now in the grimaces and lowered eyebrows in her audience. Today they each had dozens of shades of lipstick in their bedrooms.

'Hair was a problem,' she continued. 'They could either use tongs like these, which gave you a wonderful frizz. It split the ends of the hair, but the frizz was good. Or you could use Dinkie curlers like these, which you put in at night. They called it the iron foundry. You slept in them and it was quite painful, but girls didn't mind because in the morning they'd have lovely sausage curls with square edges where the curlers had been. But of course there was no lacquer in those days, so what did they do to keep their curls in place? They wore a hairnet. Here's a packet of Harrods nets. They cost three for five pence, three for a shilling in those days. When I got them, I wrote to Harrods to ask where they came from. Harrods told me they were made in China from human hair.'

By the time she had finished her talk, been congratu-lated by the form teacher and handed her cheque by the headmistress, Janice felt, as usual, that she had performed a useful service in administering a small jolt to some of today's pampered youngsters. But this feeling of satisfaction did not survive for long after she had reached home and opened the front door.

The phone was ringing — the family phone down-stairs, not the phones that handled Workfare's busi-ness in the bedroom. It was the headmaster at Jake's school.

'I'm sorry to say that Jake's decamped, Mrs Dawson, but I hasten to add that you shouldn't worry unduly. We don't think it's serious.' He had the unctuous voice of a whisky-drinking priest.

Janice struggled to absorb this. 'Not serious? And he's disappeared?'

'Apparently he talked to some friends about joining the hedge monkeys — er, the *soi-disant* "New Age travellers". He's been missing since before lunch.'

'Oh, my God,' said Janice, and sat down.

'As I say, you shouldn't worry unduly. He's bolted before, I understand, though never from this school. He's a big boy and can take care of himself.'

'What are you doing about it?'

'One of our staff is taking a trawl round the sites where these people live. And of course we've notified the police.'

'Thanks for ringing. I must get in touch with my husband.'

'I'll ring you with any news.'

The moment she put the phone down it rang again.

'Mrs Dawson? I think you should come to fetch your husband. He's a little bit the worse for wear.'

'Is that The Crossed Wires?' asked Janice, recognising the voice.

'No, it's The Crossed Swords,' said the landlord irritably.

'Thank you for ringing,' said Janice Dawson, a fury seizing her now at the crass ineptitude of the male side of her family. If Sam was in a drunken stupor, what blame could she attach to Jake for behaving like an idiot? What bad genes had he inherited?

She went out again and got in the Nissan, slammed it into gear and drove off down the road in a mood of seething frustration. She found Sam slumped on the counter with what looked like an earfull of cigarette ash. It was a situation that would have embarrassed most women, but Janice's various jobs had made her immune to embarrassment a long time ago.

'Get up, you lummox,' she said, kicking him on the leg.

Sam opened one eye. 'Hallo, darling. You on the piss, too?'

She put her handbag on the counter to help him up.

'No, let me get them,' said Sam. 'Put that away, you've been working.'

'Sam, we're going home,' she said, and with one hand on his elbow she pulled him to his feet. He swayed dangerously but then steadied himself with a hand on the counter.

'What d'you come in here for if you don't want a drink?' he asked. 'That's what they sell here. Drinks. Give the man some money and you'll see.'

In the car he slumped back in the front passenger seat and closed his eyes.

'Jake's bolted,' Janice told him, as she eased the car out of the car park. She knew that any information she wanted to give him had better be passed on quickly before unconsciousness intervened.

'Good for him,' said Sam, without opening his eyes. 'That's what I'm going to do when I can remember how to stand up.'

Janice took a quick look at him and asked: 'Sam, what's this about? What's happened? You never drink like this.'

'Game's up, kid. Workfare's bust. Dream's over.'

'What are you talking about, Sam?' she asked, frightened suddenly by what she was hearing. 'What's happened?'

'No more money. Bank's closed account.' He opened his eyes briefly, and looked at his wife and laughed. 'My overdraft scared them.'

'And you can't draw out any more money?'

'Bank's closed account. Game's up, kid. Workfare's bust.'

Pondering the ramifications of this, Janice discovered, allowed her husband to fall asleep, and by the time she reached home his snores filled the car. She woke him by slapping his cheeks, an exercise that she found particularly satisfying.

'Need a slister,' he said, opening his eyes.

'A what?'

'A . . . lawyer.'

'A solicitor?'

'That's what I said.'

For the second time she got him with some effort to his feet, and hauled him with his arm round her shoulders to the door. He was awake enough now to know where he wanted to go; he climbed and then crawled his way upstairs and when Janice went up he was sound asleep, fully dressed, on the bed.

She went back down again and remembered Jake. She picked up the phone and dialled 1471 to see whether the headmaster had called. A recorded message said: '*Sorry. No telephone number is stored.*' Then she sat down and had a sherry.

The idea that all the planning and all the work was going to produce nothing but debts that would impoverish them for the rest of their lives was not something that Janice could accept. Sam might have given up in a drunken tantrum, but Sam was a man. Her great idea was too important to Janice for her to let it die on the say-so of an obscure bank clerk.

But she was distracted by thoughts of Jake, and found that she couldn't concentrate in the way that she wanted to. The chances were that he was sitting in an old van in a field somewhere, drinking beer out of cans with his new unconventional friends. He could also be kidnapped, assaulted, stabbed or dead.

She rang the police who said they had the matter 'in hand'. There had been no hospital admissions, road accidents or sightings of strange incidents, and their guess was that he was with the New Age travellers whose vans, tents and caravans the police were now methodically visiting.

Confronted by two problems of equal urgency, she decided now, in a feat of will, to concentrate on the one that she could do something about. She took her sherry upstairs to the bedroom that Sam had converted into an office, and began to work her way through the assembled papers and documents that told the story of Workfare. She had largely kept away from this since Alastair had joined Sam. They had both been frantically busy and had managed to give her the impression that they didn't need any interruptions.

What she read now surprised and even shocked her. The weekly wage bill was much higher than she had imagined, although it was something that she could have worked out if she had thought about it. The descent into a debt that would frighten any bank manager was plain to see.

But the other papers, the order sheets, the contracts with farflung manufacturers and the invoices that Sam had been preparing, told a quite different story. In less than three months there would be profits of staggering proportions.

She sat at the desk for a few minutes, drinking her sherry, and then she got up and went into their bedroom. Sam lay on the bed asleep, and it was clear that the conversation she wanted to have with him would not be taking place. She went over and shifted his head so that he was lying more comfortably. She knew now how hard he had been working and how much effort he had put into Workfare. The poor man had finally cracked, but until the bank brought him to his knees he had been achieving miraculous results.

She took her sherry downstairs again and sat at the kitchen table. It was quite obvious what was needed to save Workfare: a different bank manager.

But bank managers with the courage and the vision to carry Workfare through the next two difficult months weren't easy to find, and were certainly not known to Janice. For ten minutes she wondered who they might be known to, and then she picked up the phone and rang Monica Titchmarsh.

'Monica,' she said, 'how's Gerry?'

'He's fine, Janice. As chatty as he ever was. But he's taken up going to church, which is a bit worrying. Obviously this isn't why you rang?'

'I've got a desperate situation here, Monica, and you're the only person I can think of who might be able to help. Do you know any brilliant bank managers who can see beyond the immediate debt to the huge profits round the corner?'

'Is your little enterprise running into trouble, Janice? I do hope not.'

'Its only trouble is what they call cash flow.'

'Well, the most brilliant bank manager I know is my brother-in-law. He's in Bristol.'

'Would he see me? Urgently – like tomorrow morning?'

'He will if I ask him,' said Monica Titchmarsh. 'Shall I give him a buzz?'

18

The pilgrims on Wearyall Hill wore red stick-on badges that were given to them on arrival along with a small four-page programme which told them about the Jesus Trail and places of interest that they could visit in the area during their plentiful free time. The badges had been introduced by Beverley, who realised early on that the hill was a public place and people who had paid nothing to J.T. Ltd could quite easily tag along and pose as a fully paid-up pilgrim. At first they had considered having the visitors' hands stamped with an invisible ink that could be certified at points on the Trail by an ultra-violet light, but it was decided that not only would this be too expensive, it would also show an unseemly mistrust of a group of people who were assumed, given the occasion, to be honest.

So as Tim Bonner launched himself into his now familiar introduction on the hill one morning, he was able to spot immediately that there were two people among his listeners who had not been put to the trouble of sending him a cheque. He made a mental note of it, but could not allow the discovery to interrupt his flow.

'It was a brilliantly sunny day when the small boat that carried Joseph of Arimathea and the Boy Jesus reached landfall on Wearyall Hill,' he told them. Occasionally he wanted to alter this introduction, just to maintain his own interest. 'It was coming down like stair-rods on the day that the small boat . . .' But the speech that he had chosen at the beginning produced such gratifying smiles that he didn't dare tamper with his message.

Today there were visitors from Canada, Holland, Switzerland, a large Catholic invasion from northern Spain and, surprisingly, a group from the Falkland Islands. The Jesus Trail had received news coverage in the columns of papers that Tim knew nothing about, and it was no longer necessary for him to advertise. He was told about this free publicity by his customers when they wrote to book, and Tim's gratitude to the international news agencies was deep, heartfelt and incalculable.

When the Trail came to its first stop for the purchase of food, drinks and souvenirs, and the enrichment of Howard and Doris, Tim sought out the two freeloaders he had spotted during his talk. One was a boy in his teens, dressed in a white full-length robe and attempting, Tim realised with horror, to pass himself off as a Jesus figure. He stood there, holding a cup, and looking inordinately pure, even saintly. But this aura of godliness, which was evidently captivating his fee-paying customers, was demolished instantly for Tim by the discovery that what the youth was actually doing was begging. Only a few yards into the walk, coins were rattling in his cup.

He went over to him at a discreet speed. 'What in hell do you think you're doing?' he asked. His displeasure was caused not only by this cynical exploitation of Jesus as a beggar, but also by his earnest conviction that if any money was changing hands on this hill the direction in which it had to move was towards him and his family. He had made one exception, in the case of the bookstall, because it gave the Jesus Trail a certain intellectual integrity, but there was no room for other uninvited beneficiaries.

'Nothing,' said the youth, looking guilty.

'You're begging,' said Tim, pointing at the cup. 'I'm going to have you arrested.'

'I'm not a beggar, I'm a New Age traveller,' said the youth, as if this made arrest out of the question. 'There's no need to get excited. I'll go.'

'Where are you from?'

'Pilton. They had the idea, and I volunteered to try it.'

'Well, you volunteer to get off this hill, and we'll say no more about it.'

The youth took the escape route with alacrity, and Tim looked round nervously, worried that this impolite encounter might have disturbed his customers. But they were all looking the other way, fully occupied at the various stalls and filling bags with models and postcards and boxes of earth.

When they stopped for the second time, to listen to the girls' choir — a winsome dozen who hadn't missed a day since Tim agreed to pay them a pound each — and then started to move down Fisher's Hill, Tim remembered the other interloper, a small dark-haired man in a pale blue suit. He saw him towards the back of this marching army, and knew that as he had to lead from the front he would have to postpne their little chat.

They came down into the town and walked along the street to the Abbey ruins. The conversations behind Tim were taking place in many languages, and he fell in with one of the English-speaking visitors, a Canadian from Moose Jaw who had once played ice hockey for the Montreal Canadians. He had discovered God, he said, after getting a crack on the head from a lay preacher during a match in Ottawa. This opened up the possibility for a wonderfully cynical conversation had he been in The Crossed Wires, but on the Jesus Trail it would have been quite out of place and so he shook his head in awed appreciation of this felicitous cause and effect.

The stark ruins of Glastonbury Abbey produced the usual impressed silence among his visitors, who then began to wander in different directions in search of chapels and altars and tombs. Tim immediately looked round for the man in the pale blue suit and was surprised to see that the man was approaching him.

'Mr Bonner,' he said, offering a hand. 'I'm very impressed.'

'Thank you,' said Tim, shaking hands. It was difficult, when you were shaking hands and being congratulated, to ask where the money was, but he wanted to push the conversation in that direction. 'I don't think we had you on our list,' he tried.

'Indeed not,' said the man with a smile. 'Let me introduce myself.' He pulled a wallet from his jacket and searched through it for a card that he handed to Tim. He was a pleasant-looking man in his middle thirties with sharp eyes that looked as if they could see through walls.

The card said: T.J. WERTENBAKER *Universal Tours*.

'We want to talk to you, Mr Bonner. I think you may like what we have to say.'

'We?' said Tim.

'We at Universal Tours.'

'You'll have to excuse me for a moment,' said Tim, looking at his watch. 'This particular tour isn't quite over.'

His party had dispersed and, like a sheep dog, he had to round them up. While Beverley prepared to serve tea, he gathered them as usual next to the ruins of the Lady Chapel where Joseph and Jesus had built their wattle and daub church in honour of the Virgin Mary. T.J. Wertenbaker stood on the edge of the crowd, listening to his talk on this subject with evident approval.

When the visitors had drunk their tea, expressed their gratitude and been delivered into the tender care of Rowland Coaches, Tim went back into the Abbey grounds to find Mr Wertenbaker. He was standing by a huge cross, made from oak and given by the Queen in 1965. It was inscribed with the words *A Christian sanctuary so ancient that only legend can record its origin.*

Mr Wertenbaker jabbed his thumb at this and said: 'Doesn't that make it difficult to assert what you are asserting? Allegory, fable, legend.'

'No,' said Tim briskly. 'It makes it difficult to rebut.'

'This isn't all based on what you might call a factoid of questionable provenance?'

'Like feeding the five thousand, or turning the water into wine? We're talking about faith here, Mr Wertenbaker.'

'Of course we are,' he said, smiling. 'Don't get me wrong. I'm quite happy. Well, let's talk.'

'Yes, let's,' said Tim. 'I have a very important appointment in half an hour. Who are Universal Tours?'

'Let's just take a little walk round this amazing place while I tell you all about it,' said Mr Wertenbaker, plunging both hands into his trouser pockets. They began a slow walk over the immaculate lawns, stopping occasionally so that Mr Wertenbaker could look more closely at the harsh, powerful ruins.

'Universal Tours,' he began, in the tones of a man who loves his company, 'sends people to places. We send thousands of people to hundreds of places. We send them up the Amazon and down the Nile, round the Fjords and along the Great Wall of China. We send them to Iceland and Alaska, India and Latin America. And we send them to specific events, like Bayreuth and Oberammergau. Well, as you will already have guessed, the Jesus Trail would fit perfectly into our programme. Mr Bonner, we'd like to buy you.'

'Buy me?'

'We'd probably expand it a bit, make it a little less — dare I say it?—thin. Cheddar Gorge, the Roman Baths, and over the bridge to Wales, perhaps, but that's all down the road.'

Tim stopped walking. 'Do you mean that you want to buy the Jesus Trail and run it yourself?'

'That's it,' said Mr Wertenbaker, nodding vigorously. 'Is it for sale?'

'Everything in the world is for sale, Mr Wertenbaker. It's just a question of price.'

'Exactly. Well, as to that I'd need to come to your offices and look at some figures, but I can assure you that Universal Tours is not short of money.'

'Do you own them?'

'I'm a partner. There are six of us. But I can do a deal with you without referring it to anybody else, if that's what's worrying you. Was the Jesus Trail your own idea?'

'It was,' Tim admitted.

'You deserve your reward then, and if we can come to an agreement, you're going to get it.'

Tim Bonner was no longer sure that his feet were

touching the ground. The idea of selling the Jesus Trail venture had always been at the back of his mind, but he had never been able to figure out where he could possibly find a buyer. That one should appear unsought seemed an astonishing piece of good fortune. Suddenly he could see a future with money in the bank – a future without his twice-weekly recitation on the top of Wearyall Hill which was already beginning to pall. The endless phone calls to hotels which had become the most wearing part of the exercise would be a thing of the past, the tedious pile of documents and letters and bills in the bedroom that was now an office would be committed to the bin. He would play golf.

He would never work again.

'Those people on the hill,' said Mr Wertenbaker, seemingly unaware of the elation he had caused. 'The girl taking photographs, the woman with her food stall and the old boy with his souvenirs – is that all part of your revenue or did you sell a franchise?'

'Apart from the bookstall, it's all ours. The family run it.'

'You're a clever man, Mr Bonner.'

'I'm beginning to think so,' said Tim. 'We economise all round. These offices you want to visit – it's the spare bedroom.'

'Lean and mean,' said Mr Wertenbaker. 'Thatcher would be proud of you. Well, what do you say to Universal Tours?'

Tim Bonner managed his most doubtful face. 'I must be honest. It would be a wrench, Mr Wertenbaker.

We've only just got started and the profits are enormous.'

'I'd worked that out for myself,' said Mr Wertenbaker. 'When can I see these figures?'

Tim thought for a moment. 'Why don't you come round for a drink this evening? You can go through the whole thing.'

'That would be perfect, Mr Bonner. Of course, you have to go now. You said you had a very important appointment. Not another prospective buyer, I hope?'

'As it happens,' said Tim, 'I'm picking up my new Mercedes.'

'That almost tells me all I need to know,' said Mr Wertenbaker, looking impressed.

When Sam Dawson woke that morning he thought that there had been a mistake. Death had hovered convincingly in the turmoil of his dreams, and when oblivion seemed to beckon him he fatalistically saw the logic to it. For him to have got up yet again and resume a life that was effectively over felt like a chronological error rather than a reprieve. Breakfast would be an anti-climax.

He turned in his bed to see whether Janice's expression suggested that she, too, thought that his waking up this morning was, at the very least, in poor taste. But she wasn't there.

He lay on his back examining his hangover. Five days in a darkened room with a damp towel round his head and a bucket between his knees was what he presumably needed, but he was surprised to find that the hangover barely existed. He looked at his watch. It was ten o'clock. This was as late as he had woken up in years. Perhaps the extra sleep had repaired the damage of yesterday's excesses, and he decided to see whether he could stand up.

He had just discovered that this physical feat was within his range when Janice came in with a tray. She had washed her hair and was wearing her best blue silk dress.

'I was about to wake you,' she said. 'You've had all the extra sleep you needed.'

'I didn't hear you get up,' he admitted, taking the tray. It contained orange juice, muesli and a cup of tea. 'What's happening?'

'I've been busy, Sam. Somebody's got to do the work when one of the team is incapacitated through drink. I've phoned the police and I've phoned the school. There's no news of Jake at all. I think you and I have got to tour every New Age travellers' camp for miles around.'

Sam felt ashamed. He had not in his few waking moments got as far as thinking about his missing son.

'I'm sure he's all right,' he said hopefully.

'So am I,' said Janice. 'But I'm worried about the company he's probably keeping.'

Sam reached for the orange juice. 'Why your best dress?' he asked, having woken sufficiently to notice.

'Ah, that's the other thing. We're going to have a visitor.'

But Sam's head was still too cloudy to absorb much information. 'I must phone Alastair and tell him it's all over,' he said, remembering.

'Alastair rang here,' Janice said. 'I told him you weren't well, and he should carry on as normal. He got back from Oxford late last night and is returning there now to tie up some loose ends.'

Sam looked at her angrily. 'Why did you tell him that? We've got to wrap this thing up quickly. It's costing money. The security firm has already got today's wages, so that's another twenty-five thousand down the pan.'

'Workfare isn't dead, Sam. And I'm not going to let it die. I told you, we're going to have a visitor. He's a bank manager in Bristol.'

'And he's coming here?' said Sam, perplexed. 'Usually you visit the bank manager.'

'Sometimes they like to meet you on the premises, as it were. And this one wants to see *everything* so he thought it would be easier to talk in your office.'

Sam had seen quite enough of bank managers and could not find hope in what his wife was telling him. 'What's this going to achieve, Janice? We're buggered.'

'He's going to save Workfare, or Monica Titchmarsh and I will be having words. I spoke to him on the phone this morning and he sounded very positive. Finish your breakfast and take a shower. Then you've got to spend the morning sorting out every Workfare document you've got.'

She hurried from the bedroom, and although Sam had many more questions he was glad to see her go. He had only been awake ten minutes, and things were happening too quickly for him. He ate the muesli and tried to see in his wife's hustling and bustling some indication that all was not yet lost.

When he had eaten and showered and dressed he retired to the office and went through every piece of paper concerned with Workfare. Most of it was on the computer now, but Sam's distrust of the new technology, its moods and caprices, was sufficient for him to have kept duplicates of the important financial facts in old-fashioned notebooks.

The figures that he spread out on his desk only served to increase his hatred of McAllister and his nervous short-term thinking. A man with brains and guts couldn't fail to see the potential that these documents plainly disclosed.

Janice came in and sat at Alastair's desk.

'Have you got it all there?' she asked.

'It's here.'

'Now what I want you to do is look bullish. Your normal expression of worry and woe isn't going to produce the right feelings of faith and belief that we want to see in this bank manager.'

'Who is he, anyway?' Sam asked.

'Monica's brother-in-law. His name is Wilson and he said he'd arrive soon after two.'

Mr Wilson arrived soon after two. He looked like a rugby player. His nose had been broken in some physical collision, but it gave his smiling, brown face a certain charm.

'It was kind of you to come,' Janice said, searching nervously for a confidence that she hoped would be contagious.

'When Monica tells me to do something, I find it's easier to do it,' Mr Wilson said in a deep Somerset accent. He shook hands with Sam. 'Anyway, this whole thing sounds pretty interesting, which isn't always the case with propositions that appear on my desk. I know an outfit that does something similar. It's called Homework. They farm jobs out to people in their homes and make an absolute fortune.'

'There's money in it,' said Sam, not anxious to discuss a rival outfit. 'The trouble is, as you will see, you need an awful lot of money to make any money these days.'

'I hope I can help,' said Mr Wilson.

They took him upstairs to the office. Sam plied him with papers and Janice made him tea. At one stage he asked to be left alone while he made notes in a large pad that he produced from his briefcase, and then he called them in again to ask questions about the invoices that were still unsent.

'Do you know the average wait for payment in Britain today?' he asked. 'Seventy-eight days.'

'It's disgraceful,' said Janice.

'The Government don't help. They owe £230 million because of a deliberate policy of late payment.'

'Well, that's our problem,' said Sam.

'I see it,' said Mr Wilson. 'The most interesting things here are the invoices. They seem to vary?'

'They have to,' Sam explained. 'Mechanical work pays more than stuffing teddy bears. But in every case the bill I send will show a profit on the daily cost.'

'Yes,' said Mr Wilson, studying his pad. 'The daily cost I estimate at £750 per day per hall. Five hundred in wages, which now you have fifty halls operating is £25,000 a day. And another £250 for rent, midday meals, manager and security firm delivering the wages.'

'That's right,' said Sam. 'If I only made £100 profit on each hall each day it would be £5,000 a day, £25,000 a week.'

'One point three million a year,' said Mr Wilson. 'But I see that your invoices are aimed a little higher than that.'

'A thousand a day is how they average out,' Sam said. 'At £250 profit per hall per day it's a profit of £62,500 a week and three and a quarter million a year.'

'Excellent figures,' said Mr Wilson. 'I had arrived at them myself. Now here are two questions. Can you keep the supply of work coming in?'

'There's more than we can handle.'

'And the workforce?'

'They hardly miss a day, and there are more waiting for any vacancies that crop up. We keep a list of them, but don't want more than a hundred in each hall because it would get too crowded.'

'Fine,' said Mr Wilson, putting down his papers. He

looked up and smiled. 'I'll take you on. We'll construct a one-year debt, or something. But one thing I want you to do is get all those invoices in the post. And when they haven't paid after a week, phone them. Plead poverty. Tell them you're new. Talk about cash flows. How do you get on with them?'

'Very well. They're impressed with our work which, of course, is much cheaper than they could get elsewhere.'

'They ought to be helpful then,' said Mr Wilson, putting papers in his briefcase. 'I think the two of you had better come back to the bank with me, so that we can set it up. I take it you'll require money quickly?'

Three hours later Sam and Janice Dawson reached home in a state of dazed euphoria. The only condition the bank had imposed was that Workfare hired an accountant.

'You've done it again,' said Sam. 'You're a miracle worker, Janice.'

'I do my best,' said Janice. 'All I want now is to find our errant son.'

She rang the school and the police, and was brought back to earth quickly when she was told that there was no news.

'We're going to have to spend the evening looking,' she said. 'We've wasted too much time already trying to avoid bankruptcy.'

The doorbell rang as Sam agreed to this. He looked out of the window hoping to see Jake. Instead there was a brand new deep blue Mercedes standing in the drive.

'It's Tim,' he said. 'Come to show us his new toy. How kind.' He went to the door.

'I thought you'd like to see my motor,' said Tim, indicating the new vehicle with an expansive wave of one arm.

'You mean you thought you'd like to show it to us,' said Sam, who had always been mystified by other men's obessions with cars. 'Why don't you come in and have a drink?'

'Just the one,' said Tim. 'I'm about to engage in negotiations with a man who might buy the Jesus Trail, lock, stock and crucifixes.'

'Buy it? That's tremendous news,' said Sam, feeling a now familiar pang of envy. It was obviously not the moment to tell Tim about his own fraught negotiations that afternoon.

Janice poured Tim a gin. 'We can't stop long,' she told him. 'Our son has disappeared from school and we've got to go out and hunt for him.'

'Didn't he do that before?' Tim asked.

'He has a tendency to wander. Be glad you've got a daughter.'

'I am. You don't want a ride in my new automobile then?'

'Not unless you're going to join our search party. With two cars we could cover the ground twice as quickly.'

Tim showed genuine remorse. 'I really can't. I'm sorry. This man's meeting me at my house and I can't exaggerate the importance of it.'

'I understand,' Janice said. 'Good luck. Perhaps tomorrow, if we have no luck tonight?'

'I promise,' said Tim, knocking back his drink in one gulp. 'Don't let me hold you up.' He moved to the door, and then paused at a framed photograph on the wall.

'Is that him?' he asked. 'Is that your son?'

'That's Jake,' said Sam.

'In that case,' said Tim, 'I can tell you where he is.'

Driving home to his meeting with T.J. Wertenbaker, Tim Bonner imagined dreams of opulence that would shame a sheikh. Luxury, profligacy and self-indulgence lay all round him, but mostly it was quantity rather than quality for he had never been attracted to the glossy advertisements that urged you to buy the best. Six televisions, four cars, six holidays a year was where he could see the money being usefully spent.

But as he turned his shiny new car into the wide drive he had to admit to himself that he had no idea what offer Universal Tours might make for the Jesus Trail. It didn't seem to him that there was much to sell – a few banners, a couple of speeches, a stock of pictures and souvenirs, and the advance bookings. What was that worth?

Beverley appeared immediately as he drove up to the house. She had been waiting to see the new car.

'It's wonderful, Tim,' she said, stroking the bonnet. 'I may let you take me out in it.'

'You think *that's* wonderful,' said Tim, gripping her

shoulders to focus her attention, 'then listen to this! Remember that short chap in the pale blue suit who was hanging around and wanted to see me?'

'He's just driven through our gate,' said Beverley, looking over his shoulder. 'What does he want?'

'He wants to buy J.T. Ltd!'

'Wow!' said Beverley. 'I think I'd better get some drinks ready.' She rushed into the house.

Mr Wertenbaker climbed out of a black Rover and studied Tim's Mercedes.

'That's some motor you've got yourself, Mr Bonner,' he said. 'A symbol of success, if I ever saw one.' He was carrying a Burgundy leather briefcase and looked more businesslike than when they had met earlier.

'Let's go in and talk,' said Tim. 'Will you want something to drink?'

'Perhaps afterwards,' said Mr Wertenbaker. Despite his exotic name, Tim placed his accent somewhere in the Midlands where, in Tim's experience, the men who were in business were more businesslike than anyone else. They went indoors. It dawned on Tim that when Beverley had rushed into the house to get some drinks ready, she had other things on her mind as well. Howard and Doris had been bundled into hiding in case their droll interjections jeopardised a deal, and Tim imagined them tied up somewhere, perhaps in the broom cupboard, with a gag in their mouths, if not a bin liner over their heads. Chloë was luckily away, too, playing with a little friend for a couple of hours.

'This is Beverley, my partner,' Tim said.

'Partner, photographer and tea lady,' said Mr Wertenbaker, shaking hands. 'Let the three of us adjourn to your offices.'

When they were all sitting comfortably in the small bedroom, Tim told Mr Wertenbaker how the Jesus Trail had been launched through a single advertising agency, and the remarkable results that it had achieved. Mr Wertenbaker fell on the list of bookings like a sex maniac slavering over a dirty magazine, and used both notebook and calculator to make the picture clearer for himself.

'Phenomenal,' he muttered as he studied the results. 'You've really created something here. What's the bottom line?'

Tim was about to respond to this when Beverley spoke up. 'Our bottom line needn't be your bottom line,' she said, and Tim recalled the times that he had seen her negotiating with hard-faced dealers in her shop. 'We restrict it to 400 pilgrims a week, spread over two days. You could have more. We charge them £100 each. You could charge more. We take £20 a head, with the rest going on hotels and coaches. You could probably negotiate better deals and take more. So we make £8000 a week, a notional £400,000 a year. You could make more.'

'Why notional?' asked Mr Wertenbaker. 'That's the bottomline figure I was seeking.'

'Well, we haven't done it for a year yet,' said Tim. 'And we are planning a mid-winter break when the

311

weather will make climbing hills unpleasant, so that will obviously affect the final figure.'

Mr Wertenbaker nodded and considered this. 'I take Beverley's point,' he said. 'We probably would enlarge the tour and accommodate more customers. On the other hand, our expenses are much higher. We have secretaries and switchboards. We've got computers and couriers. We even have offices.'

'Lean and mean,' said Tim. 'Have you considered running Universal Tours from a bedroom?'

'Even in the recession it hasn't been necessary to downsize our infrastructure,' said Mr Wertenbaker.

This relapse into jargon upset Tim — he could see the conversation vanishing into a black hole of addled communication where he didn't understand a word. He decided to get it back on track.

'What sort of value,' he asked, 'do you think Universal Tours would place on this? I mean, are we all wasting our time?'

'Indeed not,' said Mr Wertenbaker. 'Indeed not. I could give you a figure right now. Here's one that springs unbidden to my mind: one million pounds.'

Tim was so taken by the symmetry of this number that he was about to offer Mr Wertenbaker his hand and volunteer to fetch the drinks. But before he could move, Beverley jumped in again. 'Obviously that isn't a figure that would be acceptable to us, is it, Tim?'

Tim loyally shook his head and wondered why he was doing it. He had never turned down a million pounds before and it had a peculiar effect on his bowels.

'The valuation of any firm, as I'm sure you know, is based on its annual income, unless there's property involved,' Beverley said calmly. 'They used to multiply it by five, which would place the Jesus Trail's value at two million. But there are other factors which you mentioned yourself. With a fuller, richer tour, a different set of hotel and coach bills, and many more customers, Universal Tours would expect to make a lot more than £400,000 a year – a figure, I should remind you, that doesn't include a revenue of about £700 a week from the stalls and photographs.'

Mr Wertenbaker smiled at Tim. 'She's hard, isn't she?' he said. 'But you're right, up to a point. For a start, we have our own coach firm.'

'I thought you might have,' said Beverley with a smile. 'Come up with another figure. This is fun.'

Mr Wertenbaker's eyes, green like a cat's, widened. 'You ought to work for Universal Tours, Beverley. I bet you could explain why we should pay ten million for the Jesus Trail.'

'No, I couldn't,' said Beverley, still smiling. 'But I could work out why you should pay two and a half.'

'Two million, five hundred thousand?' said Mr Wertenbaker to himself, as if he needed to know what it sounded like. 'Would we have a deal at that price?'

'Yes.' The word jumped out of Tim's mouth before Beverley could say a thing.

'Beverley?' said Mr Wertenbaker. 'Or are you going to torture me some more?'

Beverley stood up and offered her hand. 'It's a deal, Mr Wertenbaker,' she said. 'I'll give you the name of our solicitors.'

'And I'll give you a drink,' said Tim.

Later, when Mr Wertenbaker had driven off to a local hotel to which tomorrow he would summon his own solicitors and accountants, Tim and Beverley opened several bottles of champagne, and Howard and Doris, released from purdah, could not stop laughing at the absurdity of it.

'How can a walk down a hill be worth two and a half million?' asked Howard, who was used to dealing in more substantial commodities.

'How can my daughter be a millionairess?' squealed Doris in delight.

Tim Bonner sat pale-faced in an armchair as if in shock, worrying about his bowels.

Sam and Janice Dawson abandoned the Nissan and crept down a country lane in Pilton. In a clearing at the end of it there was a camp of New Age travellers and their children. Their homes were mostly converted vans, although some used old caravans and others had tents. Their water supply was evidently contained in milk urns, and their rubbish was packed neatly in black plastic sacks.

On the steps of one of the caravans, Jake Dawson sat staring dreamily into the distance and picking his nose. Scared that he might bolt if he saw them, Sam and Janice were obliged to observe this painstaking exercise from behind a hedge. Their son was furtively accumulating between his left thumb and forefinger the detritus he was diligently excavating from his nose with his right forefinger, and this debris was being rolled around and moulded together between finger and thumb as if he was curious to see how large a ball he could make.

'I don't think I can bear to watch this any more,' said Janice. 'Don't New Age travellers have handkerchiefs?'

'Too conventional,' said Sam. 'Let's go for it.'

They came out from behind the hedge and walked quickly towards the caravan where Jake was sitting. Mothers were playing with their children in the evening sun, and men were sitting around with cans of beer, except for an industrious couple who were at work on one of the van's engines.

Jake saw them immediately and, to their surprise, gave them a big smile. 'Hi,' he said.

'Hallo, darling,' said Janice, relieved. 'What are you doing?'

'I'm exploring an alternative lifestyle,' said Jake, still smiling.

'And what do you reckon?' Sam asked.

'I'm pretty dirty and I'm bloody hungry,' said Jake. 'How did you find me?'

'A friend told us you were at Pilton,' Janice said. 'Why didn't the police find you? They've been looking everywhere.'

'They came here,' Jake said, 'but I hid.'

'I think you'd better come home,' Sam said. 'We have baths and food at home and things like that.'

A man with long hair and a woolly hat came up. 'You okay, Jake?' he asked.

'I'm okay,' said Jake.

'Let's go,' said Janice, taking his hand.

Jake still sat on the steps.

'I have steak and egg and chips,' said Janice. 'I have trifle.'

Jake stood up. 'You know my weakness, Mum.'

'I ought to,' Janice remarked, 'after nearly sixteen years.'

'The thing is,' said Jake, 'I don't want to go back to school tomorrow.'

'We'll talk about it,' said Sam. His son looked thinner, and reminded him of when he had played Fagin in a school production of *Oliver*.

They began walking up the lane towards the car.

'Who was this friend,' Jake asked, 'and how did he know that I was at Pilton?'

'He runs the Jesus Trail on Wearyall Hill.'

'That plonker,' said Jake.

'What were you doing there, anyway?' Janice asked.

'They agreed to let me stay here as long as I brought some money in. No room for any passengers, they said. That's why I've hardly eaten today.'

'I'd have thought that in a wonderful communal exercise like this it would have been share and share alike,' Sam suggested.

'It is to a certain extent,' said Jake. 'They've been

very good. But they couldn't afford to go on feeding me if I didn't contribute.'

'So much for the alternative lifestyle,' said Sam.

They climbed in the car and reversed back on to the road.

'Steak, egg and chips,' said Jake.

'And trifle,' said Janice.

'And a bath,' said Sam.

19

A sparkling barbecue, prepared by Doris and financed by Howard, was held on Saturday evening to mark the successful sale of J.T. Ltd. Under the influence of the emigrants, the cuisine was conspicuously Spanish, with plenty of chicken and prawns; but the red wine of Rioja was largely ignored in favour of the more certain pleasures of champagne.

The people who arrived for this celebration — the Dawsons, Monica and Gerry Titchmarsh, Gemma Swan and Alastair Ford, Laura Morton and Beverley's assistant Melissa — listened in awe to the story of Tim and Beverley's financial coup and found that it enabled them to consume huge quantities of champagne without the compunction which often inhibited polite guests.

Sam Dawson, wearing a flowery yellow shirt he thought appropriate to the occasion, offered congratulations that weren't entirely free from envy. His persistent feeling of being beaten by Tim Bonner wasn't alleviated by this latest news. The fact that

Tim was younger and more relaxed and nearly always won at golf had, after this extraordinary summer, receded somewhat as a source of resentment. But that his venture was a commercial success from day one, that he had survived with none of the financial dramas that had left Sam haggard, and that he had finally sold the whole thing for two and a half million pounds without even trying, made it hard for Sam to wear the correct expression of delight and admiration that was supposed to accompany the offer of congratulations.

'It's Beverley you should be congratulating,' Tim told him. 'I'd have sold it for a million, but she just stood there and yanked the price up.'

His elevation to the status of millionaire seemed to Sam to have aged him a little, and produced a more serious personality. The young man with a taste for jokes had disappeared, and Sam found himself looking at a solemn middle-aged man who threatened to discuss his shares portfolio and his pension plan.

Beverley, no longer concerned on a Saturday evening with the numbers that won the lottery, arrived to hear this. She refilled their glasses with a bottle of champagne that she was carrying around with her.

'He was going to give it away, Sam,' she said, 'but luckily I was there to straighten him out. Why don't you sell Workfare?'

'Love to,' said Sam. 'Particularly for two million.'

'That's the way to do it,' said Beverley. 'Think it up, set it up, and flog it. You have the money, and they have the worry.'

Janice was talking to Howard and Doris who were cooking food.

'When we're at a party in Spain and I want to go home, I start talking about euthanasia,' said Howard. 'People leave you alone then, and you can slip away.'

'Ingenious,' said Janice. 'And do you get invited to lots of parties?'

'Hardly any,' said Doris.

Monica Titchmarsh was discussing her husband's recovery with Gemma Swan.

'He seems to be developing a kind of religious mania,' she said. 'He thinks Jesus restored his power of speech, and he goes to church twice on Sundays.'

'Be patient with him,' counselled Gemma Swan.

'Patient? I want to shake him by the ankles until his teeth fall out.'

'He's certainly drinking religiously,' said Gemma Swan. 'But then he's fallen under the evil influence of Alastair.'

A few yards away, oblivious to the gastronomic treats in store, Alastair Ford and Gerry Titchmarsh were drinking as if they had never encountered alcohol before and were fascinated by its power and flavour. They were pouring, admiring and demolishing drinks with the clinical precision of participants in a laboratory experiment.

'Christ turned water into this stuff,' said Gerry

Titchmarsh. 'My God, you can hold your drink, Alastair.'

'Oh, I can hold it all right, but it makes me horizontal,' Alastair admitted.

Melissa, a single mother, was contemplating the loss of her part-time job which would follow the sale of Beverley's shop. Potential buyers had been coming in for days, measuring and visualising and trying to judge whether the tiny premises could be converted to accommodate the new purpose they had in mind. For Melissa, a shop sale would result in a loss of income she could barely afford, and she was worrying now about how she was going to make up the deficiency in her pay.

Laura Morton, in a bright pink trouser suit, had arrived during a break from filming, and was entertaining Beverley with an account of the story-line of her new series which involved a wedding of homosexuals conducted by a heroic black vicar, and a drug-dealing Old Etonian who was persistently beaten to a pulp by his 16-stone wife.

'You have to have all those things in it these days, darling,' she said. 'It's called political correctness.'

'You should never have left The Lunch Club,' said Beverley. 'That's where the real world is.'

Tim was showing Sam the plans for a swimming pool in one of the stable blocks.

'I must say a fat cheque has worked wonders on Beverley's depression,' said Sam.

'Oh, that's all behind us,' said Tim. 'The sexual

demands she makes on me would put an Olympic champion in a Zimmer frame. That's why I need this pool – to get fit.'

'And I always thought the bedroom was a haven of rest,' said Sam, feeling old.

'Not our bedroom,' said Tim. 'I try to rest during the day now, to prepare for it. My God, I was upside down in the shower last night. I can't even remember what we were trying to achieve.'

'An orgasm, I imagine,' said Sam. 'Haven't you heard about this exciting new concept, the missionary position?'

'Those *were* the days,' said Tim.

Howard summoned them now to the large oak table where he and Doris had laid out an impressive display of food: chicken breasts, prawns, sardines, sausages and steaks. Tomatoes, courgettes, onions and lettuce filled bowls around the main food. Guests loaded their plates and retreated to one of many small tables that had been put on the lawn in the evening sunshine.

Alastair Ford spurned the food but joined Sam at a table, bringing with him his own bottle of champagne. 'How's it going, boss?' he asked, releasing a belch which sounded like a dog barking.

'It's going very well, Alastair,' said Sam, forking a piece of chicken. 'Quite soon, with any luck, I'll actually be able to pay you.'

'You're not planning to jeopardise my amateur status?' Alastair said. 'I told you, I don't want any money.'

'You're going to have to accept it for the sake of my conscience. If I make a lot, and you make nothing, how will I feel?'

'Pretty damn clever, I should think.'

'Guilty, Alastair. Greedy. Mean.'

'Now I've got to accept your money to stop you feeling bad? The demands you make on me, Sam.'

Melissa was discussing the shop with Howard.

'If you're going to lose out, kid, why don't you run the shop yourself?' said Howard. 'Find an assistant so you still only work part-time.'

'Would you let me do that?' Melissa asked.

'Sure,' said Howard. 'I wanted to keep it open. I like it. I might want to come back to it one day myself.'

'He misses it, you see,' said Doris. 'It was his life.'

'I'd love to keep it open for you,' said Melissa. 'What will Beverley say?'

'Bev's got other things to think about now, like how to spend all that money.'

Janice joined Sam and ate prawns at a table on the lawn. Recent events had sapped her energy and she felt unusually tired. The speaking engagements and the newspaper columns and the playgroup and the cake-making and the shop she could handle without slowing up, but worry had always drained her; her vanishing son and the financial affairs of her husband had produced enough worry over the last few days to make her crave for rest. She had never been interested in holidays but could imagine herself now in a good hotel where somebody else cleaned the rooms and bought the food and cooked it and brought it to your table, and all you had to do was eat it. It sounded like bliss.

Her reverie was interrupted by Sam who said: 'It's nice to have millionaires among your friends, isn't it? It gives you a feeling of security.'

Janice glanced over to where Tim and Beverley were standing with their arms round each other, drinking some toast that was being proposed laughingly by Howard. The sun glinting on Tim's blond hair seemed to give him a halo. Perhaps he is being rewarded from above, she thought, for the tremendous public relations campaign he had run on Wearyall Hill.

Beverley, at thirty-two only six years younger than Janice, and yet so slim and fit compared with her own untidy proportions, looked as if sudden success had bestowed a special aura on her too. She glided across the lawn, refilling glasses, like a Celtic goddess, and even these guests who knew her well looked up at her with a new respect.

'I don't see why someone else's money should give you a feeling of security,' Janice said.

'It's nice to be near it,' said Sam. 'It's nice to hear it sloshing around.'

Janice didn't see it like that at all. She was happy to observe the transformation and liberation in Beverley who at the time she launched The Lunch Club seemed to be bitter and withdrawn, but it was not something that Janice could derive personal comfort from. She had always been aware of her own boundaries, and didn't invade other people's. She drank her champagne, looked at the glittering occasion that this seemed suddenly to be, and thought: this is how it is when the money is limitless and the problems which plague everybody else have been triumphantly dispelled.

'There's no future in delighting in the riches of others, Sam,' she said. 'In this world you've got to concentrate on looking after yourself.'

And witnessing the apotheosis of Tim Bonner she knew that, tired or not, there was one more job that she had to do.

The pleasure that Howard and Doris felt two days later at being driven to the airport in a new Mercedes was diminished a little by their suspicion that all the exciting things were happening here.

'Why are we flying back to the sun?' asked Doris. 'They have sun here now.'

'Only temporarily,' said Beverley, who having been presented with a house that she loved could foresee the awful possibility of having to hand it back if her parents gave up their Spanish exile.

'We're making the money last longer,' said Howard, who in shorts and a floppy hat was already prepared for the heat that would hit him in a couple of hours.

'We don't need to worry about these economies now,' Doris protested. 'Bev's rich.'

'That's Bev's money,' said Howard. 'Don't be embarrassing, doll.'

'You're welcome to some,' said Beverley. 'I thought you were loaded.'

'I am loaded,' said Howard. 'Comparatively.'

Tim Bonner didn't feel entitled to participate in these family discussions. He wasn't even the son-in-law. He had thought that Beverley might give her parents a big cheque to help with their living costs in Spain, but he had no idea how much money Howard had stashed away in his high-interest, tax-free Gibraltar account.

They reached the airport early and went for a drink.

'It's been a wonderful holiday,' said Doris when Tim had bought her a gin.

'Holiday? You've been working,' Tim said. 'I'm very grateful to you.'

'It was lovely,' said Doris. 'I've never served Coca-Cola before.'

'They were such nice people,' said Howard. 'I suppose religion makes you peaceful.'

'Beer makes *you* peaceful,' said Doris. 'In fact, it makes you unconscious.'

'She's a one, isn't she?' said Howard.

Beverley's impression now was that her mother would have to be dragged to the plane, and she tried to make the departure easier.

'You never invite us out to see you,' she said. 'We could fly out any time now.'

'It's a two-bedroom apartment, Bev,' said Howard. 'It's not big enough for guests.'

'Okay,' said Beverley, 'but there must be a hundred hotels within five miles.'

'Lovely ones,' said Doris. 'You can have your own spa bath. Why don't you come?'

'We will, won't we, Tim?' said Beverley. 'Chloë would love it.'

'That would be nice,' Tim said. He had nearly had enough of the sun now and was looking forward to the red leaves of autumn. A blistering summer had persuaded him that there was something after all to be said for the British climate. He looked at his watch. 'You ought to be going through,' he said.

While Beverley gave her father a hug and several kisses, Tim was left to ponder the perennial airport mystery of why the women in Departures were so pretty, and the women in Arrivals so plain. This line of thought brought him naturally to another: what unbridled sexual extravaganzas did Beverley have lined up for him now that her parents would no longer be in the vicinity? And was he strong enough?

He resolved to meet her expectations, even if it meant joining a gymnasium. After all, he had nothing else to do. He delivered a chaste kiss to Doris's cheek and told her to look after Howard. Howard shook his hand and said how pleased he was with the change in Beverley, who had seemed so depressed when they arrived.

'Perhaps you two will get married now?' he suggested, taking Tim by surprise.

'You'll be the first to know,' Tim assured him.

Driving south, through the sheep country of the Mendip Hills and past the remains of mines and mills, Beverley asked: 'What did my dad say to you?'

'He said perhaps we'll get married now.'

'Well,' said Beverley, 'I suppose we could.'

Watching her husband's exertions now, Janice began to fear for his health. The work burden with which he was saddled was unlike anything she had ever seen, and he handled it obsessively, skipping meals and sleep. Quietly furious at how close he had come to losing everything, Sam Dawson threw himself into the job with a passion and an intensity that nothing else in his life had ever engendered.

The rescue by a second bank, so far from providing him with relief, had brought home to him the size of his debt – starkly visible now that Mr Wilson had paid off the first bank's overdraft.

No sooner were his invoices in the post than he was on the phone asking where his cheques were. He feigned an agitated tone, evoking pictures of unpaid pensioners, suicidal bank managers and financial oblivion, and sought to produce in the listener a distress at least as traumatic as the anguish he was claiming for himself.

These tactics, he worked out later, produced a sixty per cent success rate, because the recipients of these emotional phone calls knew that Workfare was unlike any other enterprise that they dealt with, and was probably less capable of surviving the cash-flow problems that attended the birth of a business. Most of all, however, they were not anxious to see Workfare fail – this strange little outfit was producing the goods at half the price.

Soon five-figure cheques were finding their way to Sam's doormat, and these he took proudly to Mr Wilson's bank, like a dog retrieving a stick. Mr Wilson, emerging personally from his inner sanctum to inspect the size and quantity of these cheques, was less ecstatic than Sam had hoped, and he would drive home thoughtfully, reminding himself that there was still a long way to go.

In this post-crisis phase of hyperactivity, Janice found that she could help best by keeping out of Sam's way, and her attention turned to her other problem, the future of Jake. Jake had made it clear that he wasn't going back to school or, if he was, it wouldn't be for long, and Janice, who would happily have beaten him with a leather strap, could not see where coercion would get her. The boy would disappear again, and it might not be so easy to find him next time. The answer emerged one afternoon as they sat in deck chairs on the lawn drinking tea. This wasn't something that Janice usually had time for, but she knew that the only answer to the problem of Jake was to talk to him − endlessly, if necessary − and find out what was going on in his head.

Eventually Jake got around to talking about the plays that he had been in at school, and the possible attractions of an acting career. Within an hour Janice was talking on the phone to a drama school in London. She went up to tell Sam.

He was on the phone to Alastair, who spent his days now touring the village halls and checking that everything was running smoothly.

'I think I've solved the problem of Jake,' she said when the call finished.

'Jake?'

'Your son.'

'Ah yes. What's the solution?'

'Just stop looking at that screen for a moment, dear, and I'll tell you. I've spoken to a drama school in London. They're going to send us some forms, and will probably give him an audition.'

'Brilliant, darling,' said Sam. 'Listen, I've got to go to Birmingham tomorrow. There are two large firms there that want to use us.'

'Brilliant, darling,' said Janice.

She left the room feeling torn between the demands of her family. Neither male seemed interested in the troubles of the other and she, as usual, was in the middle. She sat down to write her column for *The Clarion*. It didn't get any easier, and this was one of the jobs that she was going to drop when Workfare gave her the confidence to do so.

Without a moment's hesitation she began to write about the disconcerting problems that arose if you had a wayward and wilful teenage son who was difficult if not delinquent. What sanctions did you have? It was too late for the iron rule of strict discipline: teenage sons just walked away. Punishment was yesterday's weapon, and all you had were instruction and persuasion, which no boy of that age would listen to.

She was left with the sad conviction that this was one of her failures; the groundwork needed to have been done many years earlier when the boy was vulnerable and amenable to reason. But she had always been too busy for him then. She was too busy for him now.

'I like it,' said Leo, from behind a pall of cigarette smoke. 'It'll resonate in many homes.' Today's ensemble included a new red waistcoat and a multi-coloured bow tie. Janice could see that there was an entertaining column to be written on the subject of the editor's wardrobe, but doubted that he would publish it.

'You look tired, Janice,' he said, studying her face.

'I am tired,' she agreed. 'Perhaps I do too much.'

'I suppose if your husband's venture is successful you'll give up the column?'

'It's crossed my mind, Leo.'

'I'll pay you more money.'

'If I give it up, Leo, it will be because I don't need the money.'

And Leo ruefully acknowledged the truth of this with a death-defying drag on his Gauloise.

When Sam left for Birmingham the following morning, Janice at last found the space and time to think. It was only recently that she had realised that for most of her life she had spent most of her time with her head too filled with jobs that needed to be done, or little problems that needed to be solved, to think in any depth at all. But today she could, and when she sat in an armchair and immersed herself in the subject of Workfare it soon became quite glaringly obvious not only what she had to do, but precisely how she could do it.

The precious moments of peace and tranquillity did

not last long. The postman arrived with a form from the drama school. One glance showed that filling it in was going to be a major exercise — they even wanted to know the colour of Jake's eyes. She put it on one side — another little job, awaiting her attention — and went upstairs to Sam's office. Here she laid out on his desk the most up-to-date figures referring to the bills going out and the cheques coming in, and then she sat there for some time, gathering her thoughts. She decided to phone Directory Inquiries, but then she thought for a while longer and rang instead Mr Wilson's bank. Inevitably he was busy, and his secretary promised that he would call back, and quite soon — perhaps because of the Monica Titchmarsh connection which had given Janice a special status in Mr Wilson's mind — he did.

'What can I do for you, Mrs Dawson?' he asked, and Janice felt greatly encouraged by his tone which seemed to suggest that, contrary to all the evidence, he certainly had not done enough so far.

'When you came round to our house you mentioned a firm called Homework who farm jobs out to people in their homes,' she said, hoping that he would remember.

'That's right. I did,' said Mr Wilson.

'You said they make an absolute fortune.'

'I said that, too,' said Mr Wilson.

'Did you say that you knew them?'

'Yes, I was able to help at their launch.'

'Well,' said Janice, 'do you think they'd buy Workfare?'

A pause came silently down the line and Janice held her breath. It was the most important question she had asked in her life.

'It's an interesting idea, Mrs Dawson. Is it yours?'

'Yes, I'm doing the thinking here today. Sam's chasing up some business in Birmingham.'

'It would make a lot of sense for them to buy you. Do I gather you want to get out?'

'Take the money and run,' said Janice.

'I have to advise you frankly that you would get a lot less money now than you would if you hang on for a year or two. All the signs for Workfare are highly encouraging.'

'I realise that, Mr Wilson, and of course it would depend on what they offered now, assuming they wanted to buy it. But it's an awful treadmill for us — for Sam. I had no idea how big it would be when I first suggested it.'

'Workfare was your idea?'

'I'm afraid it was.'

'Don't be afraid, Mrs Dawson. It's a brilliant concept. Well, what do you want me to do?'

'I'd like you to give me their address and a name so that I can contact them.'

'I'll do better than that, Mrs Dawson, seeing as how I admire you so much. I'll ring them for you myself. I think it would be better if the call came from me. They know me, and I have all the figures. I can give them . . . reassurance.'

A smile that was rare these days appeared on Janice's

face. 'That would be terribly kind of you, Mr Wilson. Would you mind doing that?'

'I'm here to help,' said Mr Wilson. 'I'll call you back when I've spoken to them.'

Janice replaced the phone and went downstairs with her fingers crossed. A strident din which her son had assured her was music emanated from his bedroom. She tried to shut her mind to it, and sat down in the kitchen to fill in the drama school's form. An hour later, when she was looking out a photograph of Jake which had to accompany it, the downstairs phone rang.

'Good news,' said Mr Wilson. 'They're very interested. They read about Workfare in the papers when you started up and wondered how you were doing. I told them marvellously. So they're sending their two top men down here in the morning. Stand by for visitors!'

'Fan-bloody-tastic,' Janice shouted, and calmed down enough to say: 'What would we do without you?'

'I'll see you in the morning,' said Mr Wilson. 'I'll bring them round.'

Janice did a little pirouette across the kitchen, tripped over the dog and sat on the floor laughing with relief.

'Come on, Footprint,' she said. 'I'll take you for a walk.'

20

S am Dawson's long drive home from Birmingham
on the following afternoon was packed with all
the stress ingredients the highway could hold: jack-
knifed lorries, motorway tailbacks, lobotomised motor-
ists, homicidal motorcyclists, temporary traffic lights
and mysterious and unwelcome diversions. He reached
the house in a bemused state and dragged himself
through the door, soaked in sweat. With infinite
concentration, he managed the last ten yards of his
nightmare journey and slumped on the sofa demanding
liquid that had been either fermented or brewed.

Janice looked at his lined and weary face, and hurried
to fetch a can of lager from the fridge.

'Now then,' she said, sitting down beside him and
patting his arm, 'do you want the good news or the
bad news?'

Sam looked as if he would be quite happy to forego
news of any kind, and recover from his travels in the
peace and quiet of the sofa.

'Give me the bad news,' he said. 'I'm used to it.'

'You're out of work again.'

He looked at her curiously. 'And what's the good news?'

'You're a multi-millionaire.'

The men had arrived that morning after an exploratory session with Mr Wilson at the bank. One, a tall man with large hands and staring eyes, had all the imagined characteristics of a paroled rapist; the other, small and dapper, with greased-back hair and a small lovingly-tended moustache, looked like the sort of man you avoided at parties if you were a woman, and probably with even greater urgency if you were a man. Janice greeted them both with warm enthusiasm.

Mr Wilson, who had escorted them to this crucial tryst with the urbane demeanour of a Government minister, urged an immediate withdrawal to the offices upstairs to study the impressive list of manufacturers who were now using Workfare.

'I'm sorry my husband's not here,' said Janice, when the two men were seated comfortably and surrounded by papers.

'But you are able to speak on his behalf?' asked the small, dapper man who turned out to be called Hatcher.

'It's been known,' said Janice.

'It's an extraordinary business,' said Mr Hatcher, after studying the paperwork for a few minutes. 'Why on earth do you want to sell it?'

It was a question that seemed to have a trap built into it, but she found the right answer. 'It's growing too quickly,' she told him. 'It's too big for us already and, as you can see, we're trying to run it from a bedroom.'

'Quite so,' said Mr Hatcher. 'Well, we'd like to buy it and take it under our wing. I make no bones about it. It fits into our operation perfectly.' He looked up from the papers and stared at her challengingly. 'It's just a question of price.'

Janice looked at Mr Wilson, hoping that he might have something to offer on this subject. It wasn't entirely clear to her which side he was representing in any discussions that took place. It was a problem that Mr Wilson, responding to Janice's look, addressed immediately.

'I'm in the middle here,' he said, 'so I may be able to help all of you reach a reasonable settlement.'

The man who looked like a rapist, whose name Janice never caught, said: 'Put a value on it, Mr Wilson.'

'We're dealing with projected profits rather than real ones, which doesn't help,' said Mr Wilson. 'But they are projected profits of around three million a year.'

'That might be over-optimistic,' said Mr Hatcher. 'I might knock thirty per cent off that.'

'There are start-up debts with your own bank that we would have to cover,' said the other man. 'Don't leave them out of the equation.'

'The debts are getting settled bit by bit as the

customers pay their bills,' said Mr Wilson. 'And don't let's regard this as a static entity. It's growing every week. By the end of the year, properly run, it should cover the country, and what would the profits be then? If fifty halls produce this profit, what would a thousand halls stretching the length of the country produce?'

'About sixty million,' said Janice, who worked out quickly that if fifty halls produced three million, five hundred would produce thirty million.

'Quite,' said Mr Wilson. 'The potential has to be taken into account.'

'So,' said Mr Hatcher, 'what figure are we talking about?'

Mr Wilson stared at the wall and frowned in concentration. The others watched while his banker's brain juggled complex figures. 'Five million?' he asked.

'Four,' said Mr Hatcher instantly.

It was obvious to Janice that Mr Hatcher, who lived in a wheeling and dealing world, would have knocked a lump off whatever had been suggested, as a matter of personal pride. If Mr Wilson had said twenty million, he would have said nineteen or eighteen or seventeen. But she had no desire to damage Mr Hatcher's self-esteem. She swallowed hard and spoke up as clearly as she could.

'My husband would be happy to accept four million,' she said in a voice which began in her throat but ended up with the shrill timbre of a tin whistle.

'When will he appear?' asked Mr Hatcher, politely ignoring this.

She cleared her throat. 'He'll be home this after-noon.'

'In that case, could we meet at the bank at about five and do the deal? I can get our lawyers to produce documents by then.'

'Certainly,' said Mr Wilson. 'Let's all meet in my office.'

The two men seemed to be in a hurry to get away, which surprised Janice who had expected a long session of bargaining, with contradictory figures being tossed across the room. She led all three downstairs, barely able to speak, and showed them to the door.

In the vacuum left by their departure, she subsided into the sofa like a life-size blow-up doll that had developed a serious leak. Then she started to shake. Worried, she pulled herself up and went looking for a glass of sherry – for medicinal purposes, she told herself. The events of the morning began to assume a dream-like quality and seemed, in retrospect, to be unreal. Quite soon she was able to torture herself with the idea that none of it had really happened.

As she finished her sherry, the phone rang. It was Mr Wilson.

'We can talk now,' he said. 'They've gone. What did you think about it all? Are you happy?'

'I've been sitting here with a glass of sherry won-dering whether I imagined the whole thing.'

'Do I take that to mean that you're satisfied?'

'Very satisfied, Mr Wilson. I'm amazed that they're paying so much.'

'It's a snip for them at four million, Mrs Dawson. They'll make more than that in their first year with their know-how. But there were the debts to consider, plus the element of uncertainty with a new business that has barely begun.'

'They're happy, too, then?'

'They're delirious,' said Mr Wilson. 'Which is why, incidentally, they left so quickly and asked to close the deal tonight. They don't want to give you time for second thoughts. You're not having any, I suppose?'

'I never have second thoughts, Mr Wilson. I'm not that sort of person. I don't worry what it all might be worth in a year's time. We all might be dead in a year's time. I don't even care about the way the chap with a moustache knocked the price down. If you're as poor as we are, what on earth is the difference between five million and four million? Even after tax, we'll never spend it all.'

'You're a very sensible woman, Mrs Dawson,' said Mr Wilson admiringly. 'I'll see you at five o'clock with your husband. Please tell him to bring his solicitor and the accountant. How do you think he'll react to the news?'

'He'll probably faint,' said Janice, feeling faint.

'What do you mean, I'm a multi-millionaire?' asked Sam. 'Have you been at the sherry?'

'I have, actually,' said Janice. 'I started to shake.'

'My God, delirium tremens,' said Sam. 'I'm married to a secret toper.'

'The shaking was before I drank the sherry, dear. I had a rather tense morning with some hard-faced businessmen on your behalf, and during the course of it I sold them Workfare. I could see it was a strain for you, and I thought; which would he prefer? All that hassle, or four million pounds?'

'Four million pounds?'

'That's what you're getting, Sam. You can stop using my car now and buy your own. How about a blue Mercedes?'

But Sam was staring at her, looking dazed, as if the information was arriving too quickly for him to grasp.

'Listen,' he said eventually, 'you'd better tell me what's been going on.'

'We're going to the bank at five o'clock to sign some documents. After that you will no longer have Workfare, but you will have four million quid. Okay? Take a shower and find your best suit. You also need to brief that accountant you hired and bring your solicitor.'

'Listen,' he repeated. 'How firm is this?'

Twenty minutes later when Jake came in from a bird-watching expedition on the Somerset Levels, he was astonished to see his normally sedate parents shouting and dancing round the room.

Having decided that The Lunch Club deserved a final meeting to celebrate its successes, Beverley selected a more comfortable venue than the cheap hotel where they had gathered before. The surviving quartet drove to a magnificent hotel in the country, a sixteenth-century mansion furnished with seventeenth-century tapestries and eighteenth-century ceramics. Outside were gazebos, orangeries and archery lawns.

They ate quail eggs with caviar and cold fillet of beef, and Beverley paid.

'It's a pity we're closing down now that we've reached a standard of cuisine and accommodation that we can all appreciate,' said Monica Titchmarsh, gazing contentedly round the ornate dining room.

'We're victims of our own success,' Beverley told her. 'We've done the job. We've turned two idle drinkers into millionaires. What more could we achieve?'

'Alastair is still an idle drinker,' said Gemma Swan, looking sour. 'For a moment, you had him working there, but now he's sliding back into his old ways.'

'Alastair has got a big cheque coming,' Janice promised. 'He's a brilliant worker when he's motivated. Get him to start up his own thing with the money he's going to get.'

'You're the ideas lady, Janice,' said Gemma.

'I'll see what I can come up with,' Janice told her. 'I have plenty of time to think now. I've given up playgroups and talks and writing columns. I've taken up reading holiday brochures.'

On her way to the lunch she had stopped briefly at the cramped offices of *The Clarion* to announce the end of her career as a columnist, and was touched by the disconsolate reaction of Leo, who pronounced her weekly scribblings 'the throbbing heart of the newspaper'.

Janice could not resist saying that it seemed curious that so vital a function produced so flimsy a cheque, and Leo said that times were not good and, anyway, she had never asked for a pay increase.

'I suppose you are going to be working for Sam now?' he asked.

Janice nodded guiltily. The truth would have given Leo the best front-page story he had had in months, but she was determined that the sale of Workfare would stay a secret, and that money would not be allowed to change people's attitudes to her and Sam.

'I shall miss your column,' Monica Titchmarsh said. 'It was the authentic voice of the housewife.'

'And, like the housewife, it was sadly underpaid,' said Janice, hearing praise now the column was dead that nobody had thought to offer when it was alive. 'I could never write, anyway. I just gabbled on paper.'

'To great effect,' said Gemma Swan. 'And you, Beverley? Are you selling your shop?'

'Not exactly,' said Beverley, 'although I hope never to be seen in the place again. Melissa, the girl who helped me run it, is taking it over. I have other plans for myself.'

'Are we going to be allowed to know them?' asked Monica Titchmarsh. 'I must say that when I saw Tim trailing clouds of glory on Wearyall Hill it never occurred to me that anything as sordid as money was going to enter into it.'

'Luckily it did,' said Beverley, 'or the plans I have for myself would not be taking place.'

'Beverley's got another money-spinner,' said Monica Titchmarsh, winking at Janice. 'What is it this time, dear? King Arthur and the Round Table?'

'Nothing like that,' said Beverley. 'I'm going to marry Tim.'

'You're going to *what* him?' cried Gemma, seizing her arm.

'Marry him,' said Beverley. 'I hope you'll all be there?'

'I think we should put this to the vote,' said Gemma, sweeping the table with a disapproving gaze. 'For the lady who launched The Lunch Club to be contemplating marriage seems a kind of betrayal.'

Beverley shrugged and laughed. 'It'll please Chloë, it'll please my parents and it'll please Tim. When was the last time you pleased four people in one go?'

'Sod them,' said Gemma. 'It's you we're thinking about. I'm addressing you from the wreckage of two and a half marriages. I know what I'm talking about. I thought The Lunch Club was founded to put men in their place, to analyse their failings and, if possible, administer a few wounds — not to marry the bastards.'

'Gemma, Gemma,' said Monica Titchmarsh. 'You can't do anything about it. Human nature pays no attention to trendy abstractions.'

'Anyway, you're missing the point, Gemma,' said Janice, who liked the idea of the marriage, and thought that it was just what Beverley needed. 'When we started The Lunch Club, the idea of marrying Tim was out of the question. But we've changed him. We've made him marriageable. Why shouldn't Beverley enjoy the fruits of her own handiwork?'

'Men don't change,' Gemma scoffed. 'That's one of the great feminine illusions.'

'Well, Tim's changed,' said Beverley calmly. 'He used to be irresponsible and frivolous. Now he's mature and serious. He's kinder. He's not a boy any more. If you don't want to come to the wedding you don't have to, Gemma. It's not compulsory.'

'Of course I'll come,' said Gemma. 'I love weddings. It's men I can't stand.'

Mute waiters appeared now as a team, removing plates, cleaning table cloths and replacing champagne. Huge bowls of strawberries, previously ordered, appeared from nowhere, and suddenly the waiters had vanished.

'What is absolutely certain,' said Monica Titchmarsh when she had disposed of her strawberries at a speed which surprised them, 'is that if you are going to marry one it's best to do it when he's financially successful.'

'The great irony there,' said Beverley, 'is that we were responsible for the men's success, but they think *they* were. They are strutting around now, proud as peacocks, convinced that their genius has made them rich. They haven't noticed that it was all the work of the women.'

'It's true,' said Janice, laughing. 'I'm sure Sam sees

himself as a self-made tycoon. He's even taken to correcting some of the expert opinions on the financial pages as if he is in possession of information that these pundits have missed.'

'It's best to leave it that way, dear,' said Monica Titchmarsh. 'Men have such fragile egos, they tend to unravel when confronted with the truth of their own inadequacy. I see it in the Council Chamber every month. I always let them take the credit. I can't bear to see a grown man cry.'

Gemma Swan glowered with exasperation at this charitable proposition. 'I don't see why men can't be made to face up to their own deficiencies,' she said. 'Are they to be treated like children?'

'Yes,' said Monica Titchmarsh, with great firmness. In the more belligerent surroundings of the Council Chamber, she thought, she would have gone on to say that with two disastrous marriages behind her, and a third which evidently stopped some way short of connubial bliss, Gemma should be listening and learning on this particular subject, and not talking. 'You treat them like children because children is basically what they are,' she said. 'And then sometimes, like children, they surprise and delight you.'

'I must say it's a long time since Alastair surprised or delighted me,' said Gemma, with an expression that reeked of disappointment.

'That's because you treat him as if he were a proper person,' said Beverley merrily. 'You expect too much, Gemma. They're only men.'

'Let's drink a toast to them,' said Janice. 'They're quite useful sometimes.'

'For simple tasks,' said Gemma, 'like getting rid of spiders or putting out the dustbins or answering the phone when you're in the loo.'

'Only men,' said Janice, raising her glass.

'Only men,' said the others, lifting glasses that were newly filled.

'Where are these self-made successes, anyway?' asked Monica Titchmarsh when they had drunk their toast. 'What are they doing these days with all this leisure?'

'Playing golf,' said Beverley. 'It's something they can handle.'

On the golf course Tim Bonner said: 'I've given up smoking.'

'You want to live for ever now,' Sam suggested.

'Well, I can certainly afford to live longer,' said Tim. He was wearing new trousers of dazzling whiteness and a rubiginous shirt with a foppish collar.

'It's a laugh,' said Sam. 'You achieve your heart's desire, you make the elusive million, and what's the first thing you do? You start eliminating pleasures from your life.'

'It's all right for you. You don't smoke. You haven't heard that death rattle in your chest. Anyway, having money makes you take life more seriously, don't you find? I've had an invite already to a seminar on invest-ment strategy and inheritance tax mitigation.'

'What's that?'

'How do I know? I haven't been to the seminar yet.'

'You're not going, are you?'

'Beverley thought it would be a good idea. You know, for Chloë's sake. Fancy coming?'

Sam shook his head. 'The money men aren't going to get their claws into me. They'll find it easier to get blood out of a billiard ball.'

'Nevertheless I see you've lashed out on a car. A Jaguar XJ6, isn't it?'

'I needed a car,' said Sam. 'I didn't have one. Whose turn is it here?'

They had reached the third tee, but there was something lackadaisical about their game today, as if neither man could bring sufficient concentration to the contest. Tim drove off and watched the ball curve into the trees.

'A Jaguar is a wonderful car,' he said, not wanting to discuss his shot.

'It's a comfortable device for getting from A to B,' said Sam. 'Beyond that, cars don't interest me.' He drove off and found for once that the ball flew straight down the fairway. 'You could always pay for golf lessons, Tim,' he said, 'or is this another activity that will get the chop in your new lifestyle?'

'I suppose you're too old for money to change you, old man?'

'Absolutely,' Sam agreed gladly. 'It's still me, only richer. But you've already changed. You've become more serious. You behave as if oppressive responsibilities rest on your shoulders at the precise moment when you've shed most of them.'

Tim gave him a solemn look. 'I'm taking on new ones,' he said. 'I'm getting married.'

Sam tried to conceal his surprise at this and behave as if Tim had expressed an intention to visit the cinema. 'Why are you going to do that?' he asked.

'Oh, I've always wanted to marry her, now more than ever.'

'Better get hitched before she bonks you to death, you mean? Where's this taking place?'

'Don't worry, you'll be invited. The venue hasn't been decided yet and I'm not fussy. I don't care whether it's canon law or secular law or done on a bloody ice rink as long as we marry. Apart from anything else, Chloë needs it.'

They found their respective balls and drove on towards the green. When they met up again, Tim said: 'You should have got more money for Workfare with the profits you were expecting.'

'Probably. Janice sold it when I wasn't there, but we're delighted with the figure. There were big debts that would have taken me months to settle.'

Tim chipped his ball neatly on to the green. 'It's funny about the women, isn't it? It was Beverley who made me do the Jesus Trail, and it was she who got the price doubled when we sold it. Workfare was Janice's idea, and she made the millions for you when you weren't even there. And they both behave as if we are two clever little sods who became millionaires.'

'It's humiliating really,' said Sam. 'But luckily nobody else knows. I'm not going to tell them, are you?'

'I'm bloody not,' said Tim. 'It could make us look pathetic and feeble. People wouldn't respect us.'

'Christ,' said Sam, 'we couldn't have that.'

They arrived on the green laughing, three-putted and decided to abandon the game.

'Let's go and have a drink,' said Tim. 'It's difficult to concentrate today.'

'When I think of all that money I wonder if I'll ever be able to concentrate again,' Sam said. 'My bank manager calls me "sir" now.'

'What did he call you before?'

'Janice Dawson's husband.'

They ordered champagne which caused a stir among the prosperous businessmen and disreputable dealers who, they imagined, avoided the public's gaze by using the exclusive facilities of this club — along with disgraced accountants and struck-off solicitors, men with middle-class tastes who had suddenly found time on their hands. Tim and Sam, having avoided all summer the ever-present danger of a conversation with these people, felt no obligation now to explain the champagne which they carried off to a table of their own.

Sam filled their glasses and said: 'Has it crossed what passes for your mind that people don't actually get married any more? It's passé, it's outmoded.'

'What's that got to do with me?' asked Tim. 'If I did what everybody else does I'd be working in some godforsaken office now for twenty grand a year, wouldn't I?'

In recent years Sam had attended more funerals than weddings, and had thought that his numerous appearances at friends' marriage ceremonies were all in the past. But it was clear that nothing less than a wedding was going to satisfy Tim.

'She wouldn't marry me before and I was always rather hurt,' he explained with disarming honesty. 'After all, I was the father of her daughter. Of course, the fact that I was poor, out of work and frequently plastered didn't help to enthuse her.'

'I can see how that might be a bit of a damp-ener,' Sam conceded. 'But now, here you are at thirty-five getting married for the first time. It's quite moving really. Did you ever want to marry anyone else?'

Tim stared into his champagne, recalling the past.

'There was a girl once in the dim and distant days of the Crown and Anchor,' he said, smiling. 'Short dark hair, bright eyes, a vivacious smile. I thought I couldn't live without her. She was a trainee journalist called Bianca — which I've always thought since is a lovely name.'

'What went wrong? Why didn't you marry her? What stopped this great passion from ending up at the altar?'

Tim pursed his lips and shook his head. 'I never really knew. I suppose it didn't gel. I think she thought I was a bit of a wanker, to be honest.'

Sam laughed, while at the same time managing to register a dutiful shock.

'In the Crown and Anchor a girl named Bianca thought you a wanker? Pity she didn't come from Sri Lanka. You could have written a ballad about it.'

'Christ, you're so bright now you've made a few bob,' said Tim, irritably.

'Do you hanker after Bianca, or feel only rancour?'

'Give it a rest, Sam. I'm not in the mood for your linguistic columbines.'

'Is that what they are?' said Sam, pouring them more champagne. 'I think money and this stuff are liberating my brain cells. I've never felt better. I'll tell you what – why don't I show you my new car, seeing as you were kind enough to come round and show me yours?'

'I'd like to see it.'

And when they had finished the champagne they strolled across to the club's tree-lined car park where Sam's new black Jaguar was parked next to Tim's new blue Mercedes. It was necessary for Tim to get into the Jaguar and sit for some time in the driving seat to fully savour the experience.

When he climbed out, he said, 'Wonderful. How come you made a million and a half more than me, you bastard?'

'It's like this, young man,' said Sam, putting a hand on his shoulder. 'I'm older than you are.'

Tim Bonner lit a Silk Cut on the pavement outside the register office and peered down the road in search of the hired Bentley that would bring his bride to this momentous appointment. Seeing no car, he looked round at the run down shops and offices in the immediate vicinity, hoping that one of them had the necessary licences to sell strong drink, but here, too, he was disappointed.

'I thought you didn't smoke?' said Sam, who was sweating uncomfortably in his best suit and tie.

'I don't,' said Tim.

'You are,' said Sam, indicating the cigarette between his fingers. 'That thing you're holding is a fag.'

'I've made an exception for today,' Tim explained. 'There's a lot of tension in getting married.' He was wearing a new pale grey suit with a white shirt and a royal blue tie. Pinned to his lapel was a white rose, and Sam had been prevailed upon to sport a similar adornment on his own suit.

'I don't know why you couldn't arrive together,' said Sam. 'It's not as though it was in church.'

'Beverley wanted it this way,' said Tim. 'She wants to arrive with her parents.'

'Howard and Doris? Are they here?'

'They couldn't wait to get back.'

Eventually, driven by the heat, they retreated into a side room in the register office where other guests, including Janice and Chloë, had already gathered. Business here was conducted on the conveyor belt principle, and another couple were already getting married in the main hall. They appeared looking sheepish and posed for pictures at the door. To Tim's relief they had gone before the Bentley pulled up at the kerb.

Beverley disembarked in virginal white, carrying a bouquet of cream roses, lilies and freesias. Behind her, like pageboys, were Howard and Doris. Beverley and Doris couldn't stop smiling, but Howard, in a smart dark suit, looked as if something serious was going on here.

'Is everything in order?' he asked Sam anxiously.

Sam's role at this ceremony was as Tim's witness, but he wasn't sure what duties it carried. 'I think so,' he said. 'We've got a bride and a groom. What more do we need?'

'It's got to be right,' said Howard. 'It's Bev's big day.'

'Are they going on honeymoon?' Sam asked. 'Tim's being rather evasive about it.'

'They're going, but the destination's a secret,' said Howard.

'Why? Where are they going?'

'Antigua. We've got to stay here and look after Chloë. Doris is delighted. I think she's getting tired of Spain.'

They were summoned into the hall now, and filed in to face the registrar. Beverley, with Melissa, and Tim, with Sam, sat in the front row at a table behind which the registrar stood with books and forms. He smiled at them all in a sinister fashion, as if he possessed some awful secret that was quite unknown to the rest of them.

Outside, a photographer was waiting with two

cameras and a lot of ideas, and for ten minutes he organised different poses, angles and groupings until they were all more than ready to go. They escaped in a succession of cars which delivered them twenty minutes later to the hotel where the last meeting of The Lunch Club had been held. To Janice, Beverley admitted that she had brought The Lunch Club here because she wanted to see whether the place was suitable for her wedding reception.

Inside, a buffet of lavish extravagance was spread out before them. The canapés included tartlets filled with salmon mousse, tiny crêpes containing crab, shrimps on German black bread and red cherry tomatoes stuffed with cream cheese. There were several whole salmon, ham carved on the bone, big bowls filled with giant prawns and ice cubes, and fillet of beef. New baby potatoes and a dozen kinds of salad and pasta were on hand to accompany this, and after that, for those who were still hungry, there were bowls of strawberries and raspberries, lime syllabub served in fluted glasses, passion fruit soufflé, and various cheeses, grapes and biscuits. There was far more than anyone could eat. The bar was in a corner where a liveried barman stood waiting to produce whatever obscure drink was demanded.

Sam, feeling called upon to do something, helped dispense food until all the guests were eating, and then headed for the bar. There were no telegrams and there were to be no speeches. This welcome proscription had been imposed by Beverley, who wanted to keep the occasion as informal as possible, by which she meant, according to Tim, unlike all the other weddings she had ever attended. Having lived together for five years, and with a three-year-old daughter among the guests, they had agreed that this wedding should have a feeling and a mood that was quite different from the more conventional ceremonies of younger participants where, even if virginity had been mislaid during the courtship or before, the loving couple still managed to exude a chaste and innocent glow when they reached the altar.

When everybody had eaten they stood up and went in search of drinks.

His duty done, Sam settled into a heavily upholstered chair and studied the scene. Beverley Bonner, as she now was, had changed into a short-sleeve linen suit that was suitable for a long journey, and was working the room like a politician in search of votes. At this moment she was chatting to Monica Titchmarsh who wore a startling blue hat into which had been plunged a nine-inch feather. From a distance it looked as if the Indians had got her. Tim was talking to Howard and Doris between hefty gulps of champagne, Melissa was telling Janice about her plans for the shop, and Gemma Swan was valiantly trying to restrain the youngest guest, Chloë, who obviously believed that attending your parents' wedding was an intrinsic part of growing up. She was wearing a beautiful blue silk dress and running round the room telling everybody: 'I'm not a bastard any more.'

There were other guests whom Sam didn't know, friends and relatives of the bride and groom who had come to see for themselves an event that they had given up all reasonable hope of ever attending. Foremost among these was a maiden aunt of Beverley's from Hastings, torn between a lingering affection for her niece and a palpable embarrassment at the rude discovery that the newlyweds already had a child of three. Not present was Tim's car-selling brother, an absence Sam noticed but decided not to ask about.

He spotted the drinkers, furtively tucking it away in a corner of the room, and went over to them. Gerry Titchmarsh and Alastair Ford, partners in alcohol, didn't bother to conceal their delight at discovering another hoard of free liquor, and seemed to be engaged in a competition to see who could drink the most. Sam led Alastair to one side, and handed him an envelope.

'Your pay-off, kid,' he said.

'What is it?' Alastair asked.

'A banker's draft for fifty grand.'

'My God, Sam,' said Alastair. 'That's too much.'

'Well, I got too much. And without your timely appearance I wouldn't have made anything at all.'

The truth of this seemed to impress Alastair and he showed no inclination to argue.

'What's wrong with cheques?' he asked.

'You pay tax on cheques,' Sam told him. 'We tycoons know about things like that. Bung that into a bank in Jersey and you'll get great interest rates without the Inland Revenue relieving you of a penny.'

Alastair looked as if this was a blinding revelation to him. 'Perhaps Gemma and I will go and have a little holiday there,' he murmured.

'Do that, Alastair. She looks tired.'

Sam wandered back across the room in search of today's star. Tim stood alone in the middle of the room with a satisfied smile on his face and a champagne glass in his hand. 'It all went rather well, didn't it?' he said, looking relieved. 'Pain-free.'

'What were you expecting? The rack?'

'I didn't know what to expect. I've never got married before.'

'I hope you're not going to make a habit of it. Have a good time in Antigua, by the way.'

'How did you know about that?'

'It's confidential information. You mustn't tell anyone.'

Across the room the former members of The Lunch Club were gathered round the bride.

'Well, you've done it now, Beverley Bonner,' said Gemma Swan.

'I believe I have,' said Beverley. 'It feels rather good.'

'If it doesn't work out, you could always resurrect The Lunch Club,' said Monica Titchmarsh.

'Of course it will work out,' said Janice. 'They'll make a fine couple.'

'We make a fine trio already,' said Beverley, hoisting Chloë into the air.

Tim floated across the room, all smiles now, and wrapped his arms round both of them.

'Photo call,' he said. 'I'm ready for my close up, Mr de Mille.'

And the guests who had brought their own cameras obediently came forward to record this unexpected moment.

Expensive garden furniture – loungers, sunbeds and hammocks – had replaced the ripped deck chairs in the Dawsons' modest back garden, and the novelty of this comparative luxury had gripped the family.

Janice swung gently in the hammock, trying not to spill a fruit drink she had brought out from the kitchen; Sam, in new white shorts, was sprawled in a lounger, hoping to catch some of the sun which over the last four weeks had given everybody else a deep tan; and Jake was lying on the sunbed in bathing trunks with a Sony Walkman clamped to his ears. They were in celebratory mood.

After an audition in London, Jake had been offered a place at one of the country's best drama schools. He would start in September. The long agonising battle to accommodate their son had been won.

Looking across at the prostrate men in her family, Janice thought how pleasant it was to see them at peace. The boredom that she had feared might engulf her when she dropped all her jobs had not materialised, and she felt at peace, too.

'Did you realise,' she called to her husband, 'that Beverley is pregnant?'

'The way they've been behaving, it would be a

361

miracle if she wasn't,' said Sam, without moving. 'How do you know?'

'Oh, I guessed at the wedding and she admitted it.'

Sam recalled Tim's reference to 'new responsibilities' and presumed that this was what he had in mind. He lay in the sun, imagining the two of them lying on the clean white sand of an endless Antiguan beach, and was conscious suddenly of the proximity of the low hedges which bordered the small garden.

'You know something,' he said, pulling himself up from his recumbent position, 'this garden's too small. This house is too small.'

'It's not big,' Janice agreed.

'We've got to move,' said Sam, sitting up. The idea filled him with pleasure. 'What I fancy is a Tudor mansion in the Home Counties. Swimming pool, tennis court, triple garage. We'd be close to Jake and could keep an eye on him. We'd be able to reach London in half an hour. We'd be handily placed for the airports now that you've taken to studying holiday brochures. We would cover the south coast and could shoot down there for the day at any time. What do you think?'

Janice, delighted, looked at him and shrugged. It was an expansive gesture that required both shoulders, both arms and both hands.

'It's up to you to decide, Sam,' she said, smiling faintly. 'You're the man.'